ENSURE THAT THIS BOOK

# Exploring Public Sector Strategy

**Pearson Education**

We work with leading authors to develop the strongest educational materials in strategy, bringing cutting-edge thinking and best learning practice to a global market.

Under a range of well-known imprints, including Financial Times Prentice Hall, we craft high quality print and electronic publications which help readers to understand and apply their content, whether studying or at work.

To find out more about the complete range of our publishing please visit us on the World Wide Web at: www.pearsoned.co.uk

# Exploring Public Sector Strategy

*Edited by Gerry Johnson
and Kevan Scholes*

FINANCIAL TIMES
Prentice Hall

*An imprint of* **Pearson Education**

Harlow, England · London · New York · Reading, Massachusetts · San Francisco · Toronto · Don Mills, Ontario · Sydney
Tokyo · Singapore · Hong Kong · Seoul · Taipei · Cape Town · Madrid · Mexico City · Amsterdam · Munich · Paris · Milan

**Pearson Education Ltd**
Edinburgh Gate
Harlow
Essex CM20 2JE
England

and Associated Companies throughout the world

*Visit us on the World Wide Web at:*
www.pearsoned.co.uk

**First edition 2001**

© Pearson Education Limited 2001

ISBN-13: 978-0-273-64687-7

*British Library Cataloguing-in-Publication Data*
A catalogue record for this book can be obtained from the British Library

*Library of Congress Cataloging-in-Publication Data*

Exploring public sector strategy/edited by Gerry Johnson and Kevan Scholes.
    p. cm.
  Includes bibliographical references and index.
  ISBN 0-273-64687-7
  1. Public administration. 2. Strategic planning. I. Johnson, Gerry II. Scholes, Kevan.
JF1351. E96 2000
352.3'4–dc21

                                  00-064367

10 9 8
07

Typeset in 10pt New Century School Book by 3
Printed in Great Britain by Henry Ling Limited, at The Dorset Press, Dorchester, DT1 1HD.

# Contents

## 3 Global influences on the public sector 38

*Jan Eppink and Steven de Waal*

## 4 Trust and distrust in regulation and enforcement 57

*Les Prince and Ray Puffitt*

## 5 Measuring up to the best: A manager's guide to benchmarking 84

*Mik Wisniewski*

# *Preface*

*Exploring Corporate Strategy* by Gerry Johnson and Kevan Scholes is now established as the leading text in its field in Europe and beyond, with world-wide sales exceeding 400,000. It is a text for students and practising managers which aims to develop their conceptual understanding of why and how organisations of many different types develop and change their strategies. It does so within a practical context while drawing on best strategic management practice, as researchers, writers and practitioners understand it. With so many managers and students now familiar with *Exploring Corporate Strategy*, we have responded to the requests for material which takes the themes and concepts of strategic management further, in a way that is not possible within the confines of a broad textbook on the subject. The publishers agreed to publish a series of short practical books that build on the basic framework of *Exploring Corporate Strategy*. This book, on *Exploring Public Sector Strategy*, is the fourth book in this series. The others are *Strategic Financial Management* by Tony Grundy, *Exploring Techniques of Analysis and Evaluation in Strategic Management* edited by Véronique Ambrosini and *Exploring Strategic Change* by Julia Balogun and Veronica Hope Hailey. All the books are developed under the editorial guidance of Gerry Johnson and Kevan Scholes and have the following aims:

- to provide further depth on aspects of strategic management which should already be familiar to readers of *Exploring Corporate Strategy*;
- to do this in a practical and applied way (for example by relating to a particular sector) while drawing on best practice from researchers, writers and practitioners.

For this particular book in the series, Gerry Johnson and Kevan Scholes have brought together or commissioned a series of 17 chapters which provide readers with material on a range of important strategic issues of particular relevance to the public sector. The chapters cover most of the major strategic themes from *Exploring Corporate Strategy* and the chapter sequence reflects the structure of that book:

- The first two chapters set the broad scene about the *content and processes* of strategy making in the public sector – with some private sector comparisons.

- There are two chapters about important issues in the *'business'
  environment* of the public sector – global influences and regulation.
- These are followed by four chapters about the *strategic capability* of
  public sector organisations and their ability to provide best value services. This includes benchmarking, the Best Value Initiative, clinical
  governance and portfolio analysis.
- Issues of *ownership and accountability* are covered in two chapters
  on stakeholder mapping and commercial freedom in the public
  sector.
- *Partnerships* have been a theme of growing importance and there are
  two chapters that between them cover the various types of partnership
  between public sector organisations and with the voluntary and private sectors.
- *Structure and management control* are issues of continuing debate in
  the public sector reflecting concerns about accountability, managing a
  professional workforce and the IT revolution. There are four chapters
  devoted to this theme.
- The book concludes with a chapter about culture and *cultural change*
  as an issue of critical importance when managing change in the public
  sector.

This book has been designed to illustrate strategic issues in public
sector organisations. However, if readers are to gain most benefit from
this book it is recommended that they should have a rounded view of
strategic management concepts in general. The appropriate sections in
*Exploring Corporate Strategy* provide this and the brief editors' introduction to each chapter of this book provides some guidance on these
connections.

This book can be valuable to students, tutors and managers as
follows:

- Students can find here a practical supplement to their textbook,
  *Exploring Corporate Strategy* – to learn how strategic issues apply to
  the public sector.
- Tutors, who may require support with the practical aspects of strategic management in the public sector, may use *Exploring Public
  Sector Strategy* in parallel with the textbook, and this should allow
  them to show students how strategy is 'played out' in the public
  sector.
- *Exploring Public Sector Strategy* is an invaluable companion for public
  sector managers dealing with strategic management issues.

Finally, we would like to thank all the authors – John Alford, Nardine
Collier, Frank Fishwick, Jan Eppink, Steven de Waal, Ray Puffitt, Les
Prince, Mik Wisniewski, Simon Speller, David Herbert, Eleanor Doyle,
Richard Butler, Jaz Gill, Sandra Hill, John McAuley, Barbara

Harrington, Kevin McLoughlin, Duncan Riddell and Tom Forbes. We would also like to take this opportunity to thank those who have helped us in the preparation and completion of this book. We are also grateful to many of our colleagues who have commented on drafts of our own chapters.

Gerry Johnson
Kevan Scholes
*January 2001*

## Publisher acknowledgements

Exhibit 3.3 © OECD, *Facing the future*, 1979.

Exhibits 13.2, 13.3 and 13.4 from *Corporate-Level Strategy: creating value in the multi-business company*, Goold et al., © 1994 Wiley. Reprinted by permission of John Wiley & Sons, Inc.

Exhibits 8.1, 9.1, 9.2, 9.3, 9.6, 12.4, 12.6, 12.8, and 16.1 first appeared in Johnson, G. and Scholes, K., 1999, Exploring Corporate Strategy, 5th edn, Prentice Hall Europe.

Chapter 5 is based on the Accounts Commission for Scotland's publication Measuring up to the best which was distributed to all Scottish councils to support their benchmarking activities as part of Best Value. We are grateful to the Commission for allowing us to adapt the publication for use in this text.

Chapter 9 is adapted from Chapter 10 of Ambrosini, V., with Johnson, G. and Scholes, K., 1998, Exploring Techniques of Analysis and Evaluation in Strategic Management, Prentice Hall.

Chapter 11 is reproduced from *Public and Private Sector Partnerships: Furthering Development*, Sheffield Hallam University Press, ISBN 0-86339-865-0, edited by L. Montanheiro *et al.*, pp69–78, 1999.

Chapter 15 first published in *New Technology, Work and Employment*, vol 13, 41–50, © Blackwell Publishers Ltd/Brian Towers 1998.

Chapter 16 is adapted from Chapter 9 of Ambrosini, V., with Johnson, G. and Scholes, K., 1998, Exploring Techniques of Analysis and Evaluation in Strategic Management, Prentice Hall.

# The authors

**John Alford** is Associate Professor of Public Sector Management at the Melbourne Business School, University of Melbourne, Victoria, Australia.

His book *The Contract State: Public Management and the Kennett Government* (co-edited with Deirdre O'Neill in 1994) is a text widely cited in Australia on the contractual approach to governance. He won the Richardson Award of the Institute of Public Administration of Australia for 'the most important or most influential article' published in the *Australian Journal of Public Administration*: 'Towards a New Public Management Model: Beyond "Managerialism" and Its Critics' (**52** (2), 1993).

John's MBA and PhD are from the University of Melbourne. His doctoral research looked at clients as co-producers of public services. His research and publications are in the fields of strategic management in the public sector, performance monitoring in public organisations, governing through contractual methods and client–organisation relationships. He has also developed over 40 case studies of management strategies and practices in a variety of public sector organisations.

John joined the Business School in 1988 from the Victorian Public Service, where he had held managerial positions in industrial relations policy and change management. In 1990, he was appointed by the Premier to the Committee of Review of Public Service Personnel Management in Victoria, and was lead author of its *Report*. He lectures on public sector strategy, contracting and privatisation, resource management and regulation to MBA students at the School, and also runs short courses for public sector managers from all over Australia.

**Richard Butler** is Research Director at the University of Bradford Management Centre.

His main research interests concern organisational design and decision making. Major publications from this research include: *Top Decisions* (with D.J. Hickson, D. Cray, G. Mallory and D. Wilson: Jossey Bass, 1986); *Strategic Investment Decisions: Theory, Practice and Process* (with L. Davies, R. Pike and J. Sharp: Routledge, 1993); *Designing Organizations: A Decision Making Perspective* (Routledge, 1991); *Managing Voluntary and Non-Profit Organizations* (with D.C. Wilson: Routledge, 1990). More recent research has involved an investigation of partnerships and strategic alliances which is still being written up.

From 1996 to 1999 he was chair of the University of Bradford's Graduate School.

**Nardine Collier** graduated in 1998 with first class honours in business administration from De Montfort University. After working a year with a public relations consultancy, providing contact with several corporate clients, she was appointed to Research Assistant at Cranfield School of Management in the Strategic Management Group and has contributed to a variety of projects.

**Steven de Waal** (1955) received his degree (cum laude) in adult educational theory, specialising in organisational science, from the universities of Utrecht and Leiden in 1979. Subsequently he was active as co-ordinator of welfare planning for the city of Helmond from 1979 to 1982, the period in which the welfare sector faced the first cut-backs. He then transferred to the Ministry of the Interior, where, as management consultant in the interdepartmental network, he was involved in 'the major operations'.

In 1985 he joined Boer & Croon Management Consultants in Amsterdam. BCMC is an independent consultancy firm, specialising in issues of determining strategy, that currently employs 40 senior consultants. For the most part their activities are carried out in trade and industry. This firm is part of the Boer & Croon Group, a leading European enterprise for high-quality management services, of which BCG Interim-management, among others, is also a part.

Steven de Waal is a partner in and presently chairs the Boer & Croon Group. Since 1989 he has headed the consulting practice in the public sector in particular. Change processes in complex administrative and strategic circumstances, such as non-profit concerns, the transformation of political–official performance, directors–management relations and branch organisations in the social centrefield, are his speciality. He frequently writes about these subjects, in contributions to conferences, columns, articles and books, which include *Handboek Maatschappelijk Ondernemerschap* (1994) (Handbook of Civic Entrepreneurship) and *Besturen op leven en dood* (1997) (Life-and-Death Administration). The concept of 'Civic Entrepreneurship', a registered trademark, has been developed from this consulting practice since 1990 and has been adopted by nearly all public sectors in the Netherlands.

He is a member of various professional organisations, including the Academy of Management, International Society for Third Sector Research and the Orde van Organisatie-adviseurs. He is also the initiator of *Openbaar Bestuur Magazine* (a news magazine on public administration) and member of the editorial board of *Besturen en*

*Innovatie* (Administration and Innovation). He is the founder and director of Public SPACE, the international research and consultancy centre of the Boer & Croon Strategy and Management Group, active in the field of Strategies for Public and Civic Entrepreneurs.

**Eleanor Doyle** is College Lecturer in Economics at University College Cork in Ireland. She has experience of lecturing, consultancy and executive development within the public sector as well as writing in the areas of business and international economics. Her current lecturing duties include courses in the Economics of Firm Strategy and the Macroeconomics of Business, which she teaches to postgraduate students on the MBS in Business Economics. She contributed to the development of this popular MBS and has been Co-ordinator of the programme since its inception in 1996. She has also contributed to MBA workshops on organisational culture and Economic Value Added and has recently developed a course on Organisational Resources and Competitive Advantage.

Recent developments in Irish competition policy – largely prompted by EU directives – coupled with government attempts to improve public sector efficiency create an interesting environment in which the investigation of strategic issues facing public sector firms becomes particularly pertinent. These issues provide a rich source of material for both lectures and workshops that Eleanor gives and directs. She has direct experience of the public sector working environment, having worked in the Finance Department of Cork's City Hall prior to working in the education sector. This experience has proved valuable in her study of the implications of deregulation of the Irish gas market on the government-owned Irish Gas Company, published in *Exploring Corporate Strategy* (5th edition, Prentice Hall, 1999).

**Jan Eppink** is Professor of Management and Organisation at the Faculty of Economic Sciences and Econometrics, Vrije Universiteit Amsterdam. He is also an adviser to Boer & Croon Management Consultants in Amsterdam. He has lectured and published on the topic of strategic management, for both managerial and academic audiences in the Netherlands and abroad (Europe, Asia, South America, USA). He is author of the best-selling Dutch management textbook *Management en Organisatie* (with Doede Keuning), of which the seventh revised edition appeared in early 2000.

Jan has a special interest in strategic management in the private and the public sector, and in the role and structure of the corporate centre in large companies. He has acted as consultant for the Minister of Justice, the Department of Economic Affairs, healthcare organisations, a large telecom company, an international brewer, a large bank, an airline company, etc.

He is vice-chairman of the supervisory board of 'ROI Foundation', a privatised organisation that provides education for government officials, and member of the advisory board of the European Contract Manufacturing Company. He is a director of the Japan Strategic Management Society and serves on the editorial boards of *Strategic Management Journal* and *Nyenrode Management Review*. He has been non-executive director of several companies in the Netherlands, vice-president of VSB (Dutch Strategic Management Society) and of the European Planning Federation, and member of the editorial advisory board of *Long Range Planning Journal*.

**Frank Fishwick** retired from the position of Reader in Managerial Economics at Cranfield in 1997. He graduated in economics from Manchester University, having previously worked in the textile industry. After University he worked for a short time in the embryonic computer industry before spending five years in town and country planning with Lancashire County Council.

The rest of his working life has been spent in Business Schools, first at the University of Aston and then at Cranfield University. His research specialism for the past 15 years has been mainly in the economics of competition policy, the subject of his PhD and of a series of research studies for the European Commission.

**Tom Forbes** is a lecturer in the Department of Management and Organisation at the University of Stirling. Tom initially trained and then worked as a radiographer in the UK National Health Service (NHS) for five years before taking a BA (Hons) in Public Administration and Management at Glasgow Caledonian University and then a PhD in Strategic Management at the University of Glasgow. His teaching areas are Strategic and Change Management at undergraduate, postgraduate and post-experience level. Current research focuses on three areas: the development of professionals as managers, NHS reforms, and organisational communications.

**Jaz Gill** is a Research Fellow in Organisational Analysis at the Bradford Management Centre, where he has been undertaking research on the processes underlying the formation and evolution of joint ventures in the UK and South East Asia. His major interests are in partnerships, innovation and development. He is co-author (with Peter Swann) of *Corporate Vision and Rapid Technological Change*.

**Barbara Harrington** has carried out research on healthcare evaluation and change management in the public sector. She is currently a Research Fellow in the Social Welfare Research Unit at the University of Northumbria at Newcastle.

**David Herbert** is a teaching fellow in the Management and Organisation Department of the University of Stirling. He held quality manager/director posts for 20 years in the electronics and instrumentation sectors before becoming an academic in 1992. His experience was originally in design and manufacturing but over the past few years he has developed an interest in the use of quality techniques in service design, particularly quality function deployment. For five years to 1999 he was a local councillor in Fife in Scotland, an experience which has left him with trenchant views on the operation of the public sector.

In the University he co-ordinates the undergraduate courses in quality management and participates in the delivery of postgraduate quality management education. He is also involved in a teaching and consultancy role in the work of the University's Scottish Quality Management Centre. His main research interests now lie in the local government and health sectors in activities associated with Best Value, clinical governance and partnership arrangements.

**Sandra Hill** is a senior lecturer at Glasgow Caledonian University. She is the Programme Director for the MBA and teaches strategic management. Her specialist interests are in the areas of health service management development and Leadership Development. She has published a number of journal articles in these areas and has contributed case studies in Johnson and Scholes's text *Exploring Corporate Strategy*.

Before entering education Sandra worked for 15 years in the public sector, firstly as an occupational therapist and then in a range of general management posts. She is currently involved in a number of consultancy and development projects, including Clinical Leadership Development for a number of NHS Trusts and Management Competency Profiling for the Strategic Change Unit of the National Health Service in Scotland.

**Gerry Johnson** is Professor of Strategic Management at the University of Strathclyde Graduate School of Business. After graduating from University College, London, he worked for several years in management positions in Unilever and Reed International before becoming a management consultant. He taught at Aston University Management Centre, where he obtained his PhD, and Manchester Business School before joining Cranfield School of Management in 1988, where he remained until taking up his current appointment in 2000.

Professor Johnson is co-author of Europe's best-selling strategic management textbook *Exploring Corporate Strategy* (Prentice Hall, 5th edition, 1999) and co-editor of a book series which develops themes in that text. He is also author of *Strategic Change and the*

*Management Process*, editor of *Business Strategy and Retailing, The Challenge of Strategic Management* and *Strategic Thinking*, author of numerous papers on Strategic Management and a member of the editorial board of the *Strategic Management Journal*. His research work is primarily concerned with processes of strategy development and change in organisations. He also works extensively as a consultant at a senior level on issues of strategy development and strategic change with UK and international firms and public sector organisations.

**John McAuley** is Professor of Organisation Development and Management at Sheffield Business School. He has taught on a very wide variety of programmes, mainly in the postgraduate area. He was, for a time, Head of the Division of Organisation Behaviour and Human Resource Management. This position gave him considerable experience in developing Human Resource Strategies in a period of major change. He has also been Head of Postgraduate Programmes within the Business School. This position gave him a keen awareness of some of the key issues in the management of change in professional organisations. He has worked as consultant for a wide variety of organisations, including a major project for a Probation Service. He has published in journals such as *Human Relations, the International Journal of Human Resource Management*. His particular research interest (for which he, with others, was awarded an ESRC grant) is in the area of the ways in which research scientists have responded to the managerialist agenda. A number of co-authored articles have appeared in journals such as *Human Relations*, *Organisation* and *R&D Management* which reflect this research work. He is currently Acting Head of Research Strategy within the Business School.

**Kevin McLoughlin** is a Senior Lecturer in the Division of Sociology and a Director of the Cyber Society Research Unit at the University of Northumbria. He has conducted research on the impact of information and communications technologies on management roles and change management in the public sector. He is currently involved in researching organisational change in the delivery of primary care in the UK health service.

**Les Prince** is a social psychologist working in the School of Public Policy at Birmingham University. He originally trained in graphic design at Loughborough College of Art and Design, and spent several years in the print, design, advertising and publishing industries, holding several management positions, including studio manager for several advertising agencies and a national supermarket chain. During this period he also held posts as a branch official in SLADE&PW, one of the printing trade unions. He gave up his design career to study psychology and philosophy at the University of Warwick, and completed a PhD in Small Group Dynamics and Leadership at Aston University in 1988. The same year he achieved Chartered Psychologist status and was elected Associate Fellow of the British Psychological Society.

He has been involved for many years in management training and development, teaching, *inter alia*, on MBA courses at Warwick Business School, Aston Business School and INLOGOV, as well as long-term management development courses at Birmingham University and within various British Local Authorities, specialising in Organisation Theory. He also contributes regularly to courses in Science Communication at the Wellcome Trust, the Imperial Cancer Research Fund and Oxford University.

His research interests include leadership, communication, dissent and mutiny, small group dynamics and categorisation for the real world.

**Ray Puffitt** is a Senior Lecturer in Public Policy at the Institute of Local Government Studies, The University of Birmingham. He has long and extensive experience working with and for local authorities and other public service agencies at both a practical and an academic level as an analyst, teacher and consultant on public service problems.

**Duncan Riddell** is Information Systems Strategy Planning Manager for the National Insurance Contributions Office (formerly the Contributions Agency) of the Inland Revenue. He was closely involved with the development of the research partnership between the Contributions Agency and the University of Northumbria which led to the research on which the chapter here draws.

**Kevan Scholes** is Principal Partner of Scholes Associates – specialising in management development in strategic management. He is also Visiting Professor of Strategic Management and formerly Director of the Sheffield Business School, UK. He has considerable experience of lecturing, consultancy and writing in strategic management for both the public and private sectors both in the UK and overseas. He is author of Europe's best-selling text *Exploring Corporate Strategy* (with Gerry Johnson) with over 400,000 sales world-wide.

Kevan has a special interest in strategic management in public service organisations stemming from his 15 years' personal experience as a senior manager in the public sector. He has an extensive client list from many parts of the public sector, including *criminal justice* (police, home office, magistrates courts, probation service), *healthcare* (hospital trusts, Fincare, British Association of Medical Managers), *local government* (several authorities, Scottish Social Services, SOLACE), *Education, Inland Revenue, Audit Commission*. He also runs open programmes for public sector managers in the UK, New Zealand and Australia. He has been an adviser on management development to a number of national bodies. He is a Companion of The Institute of Management and a past Chairman and President of the Sheffield and Chesterfield branch of the Institute.

**Simon Speller** is the MBA Programme Leader at Middlesex University Business School, London. He is also Director of the Middlesex Centre for Public Management Practice. He teaches, researches and consults in public sector quality management and best value areas. Simon was the winner of the EFQM Award for his masters thesis on public sector quality in 1992. His working experience as an officer in UK local government for over 20 years included economic development, corporate planning and strategic management. He is now on the other side of the fence as an elected member at Stevenage Borough Council, where he is Executive Councillor for the Environment. He was Labour Party Parliamentary Candidate for Hertford and Stortford in the UK 1997 General Election.

**Mik Wisniewski.** In addition to a background of almost 25 years' experience of management training and development, Mik has considerable expertise in the areas of strategy, business planning and performance improvement in both the public and private sectors. He has worked with British Energy, British Gas, Babcock Rosyth, Coopers & Lybrand, General Accident, PricewaterhouseCoopers, Scottish Nuclear Ltd, Shell UK Exploration, ScottishPower, Weir Pumps and Yarrow Shipbuilders. He has also worked extensively with a variety of public sector organisations, including a number of local authorities, the Inland Revenue, the NHS and the Scottish Police.

He is the author and co-author of a number of texts in the areas of economics and business decision making. He has published a number of articles in business journals on management development, strategic customer service and quality measurement and presented papers at a variety of international conferences.

He has been involved in a number of MBA programmes, including the MBA in Retail Studies, the MBA in Health Care Management for medical clinicians and the Public Service MBA at the University of Stirling, the MBA programme at Warsaw Business School, Poland, the Consortium MBA at Heriot-Watt University and the International MBA programme at Kuopio University, Finland.

Mik works on a freelance basis in the areas of training and development and management consultancy. He is a Senior Research Fellow at the University of Stirling and also Senior Manager with Audit Scotland, where he is involved in a number of public sector performance improvement initiatives.

# 1

# The implications of 'publicness' for strategic management theory

## By John Alford

### Editor's introduction

As the purpose of this book is to illustrate how strategic management theory is applicable to public sector organisations and, in reverse, what theory has to learn from public sector practice, John Alford's chapter sets the scene for what is to follow. His arguments connect to the issues raised in Chapters 1 and 2 of *Exploring Corporate Strategy* about both the content and process of strategic management and how they need to be interpreted and applied differently by sector. The major theme of this chapter is that managers should not regard the public/private contexts as a dichotomy but rather as a continuum from 'pure private' to 'pure public'. So it is the degree of publicness that matters in customising strategic management ideas – of both content and practice – to the specific circumstances that an organisation faces.

## 1.1 Introduction

Given that most of the tools and concepts of strategic management were developed in the private sector, is it valid to apply them to public sector organisations?

Certainly, governmental reformers around the world over the past three decades have thought so. Their efforts to introduce more business-like management and market discipline into the public sector have included the fostering of strategic management techniques. The 1970s and early 1980s saw the adoption of devices such as corporate planning and objective-setting, program budgeting and management by results, for example in the Financial Management Initiative (FMI) in the UK, and similar initiatives elsewhere (Pollitt, 1990; Boston et al., 1991; Alford, 1998b). A further wave in the 1990s saw efforts to create intra-governmental arm's-length relationships between purchasers and service-delivery agencies, subjecting the latter to the discipline of 'quasi-markets' (Lowery, 1998), and enabling them to adopt longer-term strategic outlooks, and focus on their missions. This was the logic of the 'Next Steps' Initiative in the UK and of the *Reinventing Government* movement in the US and elsewhere (which called for 'mission-driven government' and 'separating steering from rowing') (Osborne and Gaebler, 1992; Alford and O'Neill, 1994; Jordan and O'Toole, 1995).

However, some scholars and practitioners of the public sector have questioned the validity of corporate management approaches in a governmental context, arguing that the two sectors are different, and therefore call for different management approaches (Pollitt, 1990; Hood, 1991; Frederickson, 1997). Echoing an extensive literature (Rainey et al., 1976; Allison, 1980; Gunn, 1987; Perry and Rainey, 1988), they point to the distinctive political, ethical and organisational dimensions of public administration, and question whether concepts useful for business are also valid in government.

In reality, as many of the debate's protagonists would acknowledge, the public and private sectors are not two distinct and internally homogeneous domains. Very few organisations are purely public or purely private – most sit somewhere on a continuum between these two extremes. Indeed, the governmental reforms have been designed to install private sector mechanisms into agencies precisely in order to mitigate their public service orientations.

Moreover, only one particular type of strategic management has typically been at issue in this debate: rational planning towards clearly defined coherent goals. This is largely what has informed the government reformers in their official prescriptions and enabling legislation (although many public sector organisations tried more diverse approaches). It has formed an obvious target for its critics, beginning with Lindblom's (1959) famous articulation of 'the science of muddling through'.

In fact, there are many strands of strategic management theory (for a survey, see Johnson and Scholes, 1999, Ch. 1). Some of them, primarily prescriptive in nature, are about the *content* of strategy, and are concerned with what an organisation is to do. They include: the idea of strategy as 'setting long-term direction'; strategy as 'positioning' or 'scope'; strategy as securing a 'fit' or alignment between the environment, organisational capabilities and value or purposes; and strategy as stretching the organisation's distinctive competences to deliver better value and anticipate environmental demands. Others are concerned with enhancing our understanding of the strategy *process*, that is, with how strategies are formulated and implemented. The rational planning model cited above is one of these, but others include 'logical incrementalism', chaos theory, institutional theory and population ecology – to be discussed further below.

All these strands are constructed from particular conceptions of or assumptions about one or more of three elements:

- the value produced or purposes pursued by the organisation; and/or
- the environment in which the organisation operates; and/or
- the resources and capabilities with which value is created or purposes are pursued.

The theoretical strands vary according to how they comprehend the nature or dynamics of these elements, or the relative significance they attach to them, or the relationships among them. Because they deal with one or more aspects of what an organisation is to do, 'content' theories have something to say about value/purposes and/or environment and/or resources/capabilities. For example, strategy as 'setting long-term direction' is clearly concerned with framing organisational purposes, whereas 'positioning' and 'scope' are primarily to do with defining the value to be produced. 'Strategic fit' embraces all three elements, as does the notion of strategic 'stretch'. 'Process' theories vary, *inter alia*, in their conception of how amenable to managerial action these elements are. At one end of the scale, rational planning assumes that the organisation and the value it produces are susceptible to management choice or control, whereas at the other, population ecologists see organisational cultures as immutable, with their survival dependent on whether they suit their environments (Hannan and Freeman, 1989). In between are: 'logical incrementalism', which envisages management as adapting its path towards a defined purpose in response to changing circumstances (Quinn, 1980); complexity and chaos theory, in which managers are intuitively sensitive to changing patterns in their complex worlds; and institutional theory, in which strategy development is constrained by institutionalised ways of doing things (Scott, 1995). All of these models entail specific conceptions of purposes, environments or capabilities.

This chapter argues that these elements (value, environment, etc.) have particular attributes in more 'public' organisations, which require modification of the different strands of strategic management, or alter their relevance. The chapter identifies those attributes, then explores their implications for those strands.

## 1.2  *The private sector model*

Although, as acknowledged above, organisations sit on a public-to-private continuum, we can identify the notional characteristics of the ideal-types at each end of that continuum – the 'purely public' and 'purely private' organisation – recognising that their actual incidence will vary in each specific case.

Public and private sector management are analogous in that they both entail producing *value* for actors in their *environments*, utilising *resources* and *capabilities*. But they differ in the nature of that value, and of those resources, capabilities and environments, in ways which have implications for the making and implementation of strategy. Let us start with an ideal-type of private sector management. It can be conceptualised as in Exhibit 1.1, in which the manager's functions are:

1   to use organisational capabilities (e.g. staff, buildings, equipment) to produce particular goods and services;
2   to sell these goods and services to those in the organisation's environment who desire them, namely, customers; and
3   to obtain resources (i.e. money) from these customers (and from other funds-providers, i.e. investors) in order to maintain or acquire organisational capabilities.

In this pure private sector model, the manager's task is to perform these functions as effectively as possible, by: (1) producing the kinds of goods and services desired by customers (i.e. the most useful, the best quality, etc.); (2) producing as much of them as desired; and/or (3) doing so at minimal cost and hence at the lowest price to customers.

This model assumes that competition in the marketplace acts as a constant incentive for managers to maximise their performance in these respects. Resources will only flow to the organisation if it is producing what the customers want at the prices they are willing to pay. In other words, the measure of value of the goods and services produced is *exchange-value* in markets.

At the strategic level, therefore, the private sector executive seeks to position or 'define the business' (i.e. decide to produce particular products for particular markets) in a way which aligns with the environment, in that it maximises the flow of resources from cus-

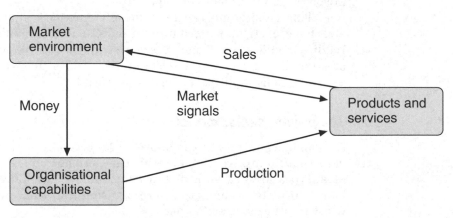

Exhibit 1.1   *Management in the private sector*

tomers (i.e. from the excess of sales revenue over expenditure) and from investors, who perceive that this positioning is one that will earn them a good return on their investment. Thus, the money the manager obtains from customers and investors is not only a resource with which to purchase productive capabilities, but also a signal that he or she is producing the right kind and amount of value. If customers do not get what they regard as 'value for money' they take their money elsewhere. Alternatively, the manager may seek to enhance the organisation's capabilities to produce more or better value.

## 1.3 How public sector management differs

How do the circumstances of (ideal-typical) public sector management compare? In a word, they can be seen as similar in form but more diverse in content. They are similar in that the public sector manager is also engaged in a process of converting resources into tangible or intangible things of value. But they are more diverse in that each part of the process embraces a wider array of possible elements than in the private sector: in the range of values produced, the productive capabilities deployed, the resources called upon, the composition of the environment in which they occur, and the nature of their interactions with that environment.[1] Each public manager faces a different mix of these elements, but they include inescapably public features, to a greater or lesser extent.

Firstly, the public sector manager is responsible for ensuring the production of not only private but also *public* value – that is, value which is consumed by the public collectively (Moore, 1995; Stewart and Ranson, 1988). Of course, there is much debate about what public value is and should be. But the mainstream political consensus is that it includes:

- the provision of the legal framework which underpins law and order as well as providing the preconditions for the operation of the market, such as reinforcing property rights and contracts: this is the core of the free-market libertarians' 'minimal state' (Nozick, 1974);
- remedying various kinds of market failure, through the provision of public goods, and intervening to counter negative externalities, to minimise transactions costs, or to curb excessive market power (Stokey and Zeckhauser, 1978, Ch. 14);
- the promotion of equity: there is much disagreement about what equity means and how it can best be advanced, but broad consensus that it is important and needs to be facilitated (Stone, 1988).

Public value often tends to be perceived in different terms to private value. The latter usually takes the form of *outputs*, that is, of products and services, whereas the former usually registers in the public mind in the form of *outcomes*, that is, in terms of impacts on social groups or conditions. For example, the public is more likely to be concerned about the incidence of crime (an outcome) than about the number of police patrol-days (an output). Not surprisingly, public value is often harder to define and measure, and the focus of contending views about what it means – a problem aggravated by the non-comparability of values (e.g. AIDS treatment vs. preventing breast cancer).

This leads to the second difference: public managers produce this value for a more complex cast of actors in their environments. Public value is 'consumed' by the *citizenry* rather than by paying customers, who consume private value. The citizenry expresses its needs and wants through the complex deliberations of the political process, which is subject to the influences of a diverse array of stakeholders, who convey their preferences by the mechanism of voice rather than exit (Hirschman, 1970). Thus, the public manager faces an *authorising* environment rather than a market one, which is often turbulent (Lax and Sebenius, 1986; Moore, 1995). Moreover, this authorising environment is relatively short-term in nature, most notably because of the electoral cycle that is an inevitable feature of a democratic polity.

Moreover, some of the consumers of *private* value are not paying customers, but rather either beneficiaries (who receive private value but don't pay for it, e.g. welfare recipients) or obligatees (who have consumer-like interactions with the agency but in the process are being subjected to legal obligations, backed by the coercive power of the state, e.g. prisoners). These consumers violate the normally understood parameters of customer transactions (Flynn, 1990; Walsh, 1991; Patterson, 1998).

Of course, the public manager has an overriding responsibility to the citizenry. But in any provision of value to the public as a whole, other people are somehow affected or involved, as customers, beneficiaries or obligatees. Every alternative deployment of productive capabilities means a different distribution of values among the public and the other consumers, with differing impacts on their interests. This is important, because often the consumers are organised as stakeholder groups having disproportionate effects on the political signals legitimising the organisation's definition of its 'business'. One important consequence of this is that even where a manager has an apparently clear mandate from an elected political master, this may be at odds with the needs or wishes of other stakeholders, who may succeed in undermining or overturning that mandate, sometimes precipitately.

Thirdly, public sector managers use more diverse resources. In the pure private sector model, resources are unambiguously *economic,* that is, money provided as revenue or investments. Aside from its function as a signal, this money provides the means of acquiring or renewing labour, equipment and raw materials. In the public production process, however, not only is public money a resource, but so too is *public power*. Public managers use the legitimate authority of the state, as well as money, in order to carry out their tasks (Lasswell and Kaplan, 1950; see also Moore, 1995; Hood, 1983; Heymann, 1987). They are empowered by citizens through the political process to deploy the force of the state in pursuit of governmental objectives.

At first glance, it may seem strange to think of public power as a resource, but less so if resources are regarded as 'available means' (see Pfeffer and Salancik, 1978; Pfeffer, 1992). This is most obvious in the archetypal regulatory function, the police force. Moore and Trojanowicz (1988) cite an official study of policing in a US city:

> *The police are entrusted with important public resources. The most obvious is money. ... Far more important, the public grants the police another resource – the use of force and authority. These are deployed when a citizen is arrested or handcuffed, when an officer fires his weapon at a citizen, or even when an officer claims exclusive use of the streets with his siren.*

This resource is used not only by regulatory agencies, such as in corporate affairs, environmental protection and consumer affairs, but also in a wide variety of other governmental functions. Just as significantly, it underpins the use of public money, in that public power is used to compel the collection of taxes.

There is another important consideration here as well: each of these resources has a cost as well as a potential beneficial effect (Moore, 1995). In the case of public money, this cost is measurable in dollar terms. In the case of public power, however, the costs have to do with how that power is used. They include misuse or abuse of power, waste, and unintended side-effects of government intervention (Bardach and Kagan, 1982; Wolf, 1988). The task of the public manager, therefore, is to maximise benefits for the public while minimising resource costs – not only dollar costs but also the costs of using public power. Thus, creating value can be seen as a calculus embracing both economic and non-economic values, including procedural ones.

Finally, public sector managers typically utilise a more diverse range of productive capabilities. Private sector managers utilise *organisational* capabilities (labour, equipment, buildings, raw materials, etc.): they are controlled by owners or managers, or can be purchased by them with money. They are at the manager's disposal, to be deployed in a variety of ways to optimise production.

Public management, however, often entails tapping a wider range of productive capabilities – not only the capabilities available within the organisation but also those available from outside it.

Accomplishing the objectives of a government programme can often call for some of the work to be done by people or organisations other than the producing unit, such as the target group being regulated, or the programme's clients, or other public sector agencies, or citizens generally. This is called *co-production* (Brudney and England, 1983; Osborne and Gaebler, 1992; Alford, 1998b).[2]

Take a simple example: a fire brigade. One way of looking at its work is to see it as engaged in putting out fires, using fire fighters, engines and stations as productive capabilities. Thus, good management is about ensuring the maximum crew readiness, quickest response time and most effective fire-dousing with minimum financial resources. Another perspective, however, is to see it as seeking to minimise human risk and property damage from fire. This calls for some additional capabilities to be deployed: fire safety and prevention work by building owners and occupiers. This work can be induced by: educational, advisory and promotional activities on the part of fire officers; subsidies or tax incentives to property owners; or regulatory power, backed up by inspections and prosecutions.

Thus the value for the public – reducing the negative externalities of fires – can be created through the use of any of several resources. One is public money: fewer or more quickly controlled fires would constitute 'value for money'. Another is public power: thus the fire reduction could be seen as 'value for public power'. Still another is the voluntary effort of the building owners in response to education and persuasion. In this context, good management is about ensuring the minimum fire damage using the most economical and effective mix of money, power and persuasion.

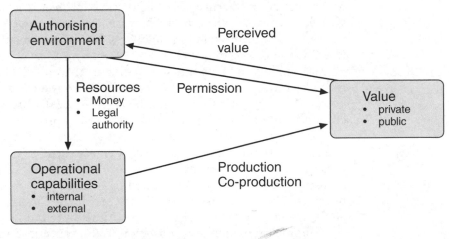

*Exhibit 1.2    Management in the public sector*

These characteristics of ideal-typical public management are brought together in Exhibit 1.2. Each element is more complex than in the purely private management process. The government organisation produces not only private but also public value; it faces not only a market environment but also a political one; its key resource is not only money but also public power; and it harnesses not only organisational but also external capabilities. In the real world, as already noted, public sector organisations will exhibit different permutations of environments, resources, capabilities and values, depending on where they are located on the continuum between 'pure private' and 'pure public'.

## 1.4   Implications for 'content' theories of strategic management

These differences have important implications for the key concepts of strategic management. Firstly, they call for adaptation of the 'content' models, to take account of the more complex textures of value, environment, resources and/or competences present in public sector management:

- *Strategy as setting long-term direction*. The more the organisation is subject to the vagaries of the authorising environment, the more problematic it is to establish and hold to a long-term direction, especially in the context of the electoral cycle. Thus, a core department of state will be less able to maintain a long-term direction, whereas a relatively autonomous nationalised enterprise, producing clearly identifiable products or services, will be more able to do so.
- *Strategy as positioning or scope*. The more purely public the organisation, the less it is positioned in terms of the outputs (products) it produces and the markets it serves. Rather the value it produces will be conceived in terms of outcomes, defined by contrast with alternative outcomes it could have pursued, and its 'market' will be the authorising environment in which it operates. Indeed, core government enterprises will more likely need to look to the political environment to signal the appropriate positioning. This positioning may be more or less abstract, depending on the nature of the value and the environment. Similar points can be made about scope.
- *Strategic fit* is conceived not as whether the product-market strategy fits the opportunities and threats of the market environment and the strengths and weaknesses of the organisation, but rather as whether the organisation's purposes attract permission and resources from the authorising environment and can be achieved by the internal and external capabilities of the organisation. At the strategic level, the public manager seeks to define the organisation's mission in terms that maximise value to citizens and stakeholders while still attracting sufficient consent to provide both permission and resources for that

mission. In more purely public organisations this will sometimes involve difficult trade-offs between what is valuable for the public and what is acceptable to those who have predominant influence in the political environment, since the two are not necessarily synonymous in a world of unequally distributed wealth and power. Public managers therefore have a special role to play in imagining value-creating purposes which are both politically acceptable and operationally feasible.

- *Strategy as stretching distinctive competences.* To the extent that an organisation relies on either the commitment of its employees or the 'co-productive' contribution of clients, volunteers or other organisations, stretching distinctive competences entails tapping their consent, and the application of indirect influence, rather than simply the purchasing and commanding of productive capabilities. Put another way, public managers may need to enhance the contribution of not only internal producers but also external co-producers in order to 'stretch' operational capabilities, and this will entail attracting support from them, which in turn will mean that the purposes pursued by the organisation must be attractive to those external contributors.

## 1.5    *Implications for 'process' theories*

Second, the incidence of these 'purely public' characteristics qualifies the relative applicability of the different 'process' models in the public sector. Most importantly, the more public the organisation, the less relevant is the very model which has featured most prominently in the prescriptions of government reformers: the rational planning model. A 'purely public' organisation is less likely to have a clearly defined, unitary goal, its political mandate is more likely to be contested and changeable, it is more likely to be subject to argument about the use of resources (especially legal authority), and it is less likely to have direct control over the productive capabilities it needs to perform its work – all of which are at odds with the requisite conditions for employing the rational planning model. Thus, the model may be relevant for an autonomous agency delivering outputs within a settled mandate, but less so for a core policy department responsible for outcomes. That, of course, is why the reformers seek to shift more 'public' activities along the continuum towards the more private end, for example by creating separate service-delivery agencies. But it may be that in some of these cases, 'publicness' is inherent in the organisation's activities, and cannot be reorganised out of existence.[3]

How then should we characterise strategic processes in more 'public' agencies? In terms of description (or 'positive' theory), any of the other process models may have some validity, depending on the circumstances, although they may need to be modified to take account of 'publicness'. For example, it is true that at certain junctures, as population ecologists aver, particular government organisations no longer suit the demands of their environments, and become defunct. When this occurs in private sector organisations, the result is usually that the firm simply disappears along with the market demand for its products. This sometimes happens in the public sector, but more often the government organisation transmutes rather than disappears, for example through privatisation, contracting out or corporatisation. The reason is that the underlying value it provides is inescapably necessary, and the citizenry expects it to be delivered, precisely because the market fails to provide it.

It is also true that, as institutional theorists argue, organisations in the public sector seek to enhance their legitimacy by conforming to social prescriptions derived from the institutional context, and that these may be similar to those in comparable organisations. However, this 'institutional isomorphism' (Meyer and Rowan, 1977) is manifested in different ways in government.

Some prescriptions are transmitted into public agencies via mechanisms similar to those operating in the private sector (DiMaggio and Powell, 1983). Government organizations are themselves subject to regulation – by central bodies such as the Prime Minister's Department or the Treasury – which has a significant impact on practices, exemplified most notably by the waves of system-wide management reforms imposed by governments since the 1970s, amplified by mimetic processes across and between governments (see Boston, 1996). Because they employ many professionals, ranging from foresters to doctors to social workers, public bodies are also subject to occupational norms deriving from professional socialisation. Some of these normative influences are sector-specific: the values of public service, such as avoidance of partisan politics, the duty of care, and the form of briefing notes. These values sometimes lend weight to the popular stereotype of an embedded, procedurally oriented public service culture, artfully embodied by Sir Humphrey in *Yes, Minister*. Other normative influences cross-cut the sector. For instance, a public works body employing engineers may have more in common with private construction companies than with other government agencies.

But there is another type of legitimacy which is mostly specific to the public sector, namely, that deriving from interest groups in the authorising environment. These entities do not transmit social prescriptions through coercive, normative or mimetic processes (DiMaggio and Powell, 1983). Rather they do so by the mechanism of *voice* (e.g. letters to editors and MPs, public meetings, campaigns), through which stakeholder concerns are raised, but also through which underlying social prescriptions can be transmitted – for example, the relative weight to be given to achieving results vs. observing procedural probity. What makes this complex is that different stakeholders often have conflicting demands, which can change significantly within relatively short time horizons, as can their relative influence. There is therefore a less clear-cut and more fluid set of prescriptions than might emerge from regulation or professional norms, and securing legitimacy is more complex.

Thus institutional theory makes sense of some public sector circumstances but not of others. This perhaps explains why some government organisations are examples of hidebound bureaucracy, but others exemplify significant positive change – and in some cases radical transformation – which is demonstrably attributable to managerial 'thinking outside the loop' and consequent action (for examples, see: Barzelay, 1992; Moore, 1995; Cooper and Wright, 1992; Kelman, 1992).

Logical incrementalism also has much to offer, in terms not only of description but also of prescription. It suits the ambiguity, uncertainty and changeability of purely public situations. If purposes or value are not clearly defined, at least in the short term, then part of the manager's job is to help discover what should be those purposes, through a process of putting forward interim goals and gauging reactions to them. If there is uncertainty as to how those purposes might be achieved, the manager can usefully engage in trial and error, or what Behn (1988) terms 'management by groping along'. If the political environment's expectations or the available capabilities change, the manager needs to change tack to accommodate this change. All of these managerial behaviours can be sensibly understood as those implicit in logical incrementalism. None of this is to suggest that managers do not have some picture of where the organisation is heading. Rather it is to suggest that such pictures are tentative, more like working drafts than tablets of stone.

Complexity theory is also useful descriptively, but less so in prescriptive terms. It acknowledges that many public sector issues are 'wicked' (rather than 'tame') problems (Rittel and Webber, 1973), in that not only is the solution hard to identify, but also the very nature of the problem. Income inequality, long-term unemployment, global warming and the drug problem are examples. However, in some cases, there is more that managers can do than simply be sensitive to deviations from the normal patterns prevailing in their chaotic contexts and respond to them. One of the ways in which problems are complex is that they are beyond the capacity of any one manager's mind to comprehend. Rather, the knowledge and capacity to generate insights into these problems is distributed across those who have some stake in it, including those the manager leads. In such circumstances, the task of the manager is not so much to name the problem, find the solution and present it for implementation, as to lead others in identifying and deliberating about it. Heifetz (1994) calls this managerial task 'mobilising adaptive work'. It entails challenging others to confront uncomfortable realities, framing issues, and providing an environment within which deliberation can occur, and if necessary orchestrating but containing conflict.

This, of course, throws up an image of the public manager quite different from the traditional stereotype of the obedient, faceless civil servant, who faithfully implements policy instructions handed down by political masters. Rather it suggests that managers in more 'purely public' contexts play a role in facilitating the process whereby the polity defines what is valuable. As Robert Reich (1988: 5–6) puts it:

> *The core responsibility of those who deal in public policy – elected officials, administrators, policy analysts – is not simply to discover as objectively as possible what people want for themselves and then to determine and implement the best means of satisfying these wants. It is also to provide the public with alternative visions of what is desirable and possible, to stimulate deliberation about them, provoke a re-examination of premises and values, and thus to broaden the range of potential responses and deepen society's understanding of itself.*

## 1.6   Conclusion

Strategic management theory largely evolved in the corporate sector, and in the business schools which trained that sector's managers. Organisations vary in the extent to which they approximate private corporations, and as a consequence the applicability to them of the various strands of strategic management theory also varies. In the case of 'content' theories, greater 'publicness' of an organisation calls not so much for their abandonment as their modification. Notions such as 'long-term direction', 'positioning', 'fit' and 'stretch' still have use in managing more public organisations, but their content needs to be adapted to take account of the specific types of values, environments and capabilities those organisations entail.

In the case of 'process' theories, the complexity and turbulence facing more public organisations tends to vitiate the relevance of rational planning. Instead, strategy making tends to be more open-ended and less subject to managerial control. As a result, being strategic means imagining alternative visions and attracting support for them internally and externally, or on occasion mobilising others to deliberate about what those visions should be.

## References

Alford, J. (1998a) 'A public management road less travelled: clients as co-producers of public services', *Australian Journal of Public Administration*, **57** (4), December, 128–137.

Alford, J. (1998b) 'Corporate management', in J. Shafritz (ed.), *International Encyclopedia of Public Policy and Administration*, vol. 1, Boulder, CO: Westview Press.

Alford, J.L. and O'Neill, D. (eds) (1994) *The Contract State: Public Management and the Kennett Government*, Geelong: Deakin University Press.

Allison, G. (1980) 'Public and private management: are they fundamentally alike in all unimportant respects?', in R. Stillman (ed.), *Public Administration: Concepts and Cases*, 4th edn, Boston: Houghton Mifflin.

Bardach, E. and Kagan, R. (1982) *Going by the Book: The Problem of Regulatory Unreasonableness*, Philadelphia: Temple University Press.

Barker, A. (1998) 'Political responsibility for UK prison security: Ministers escape again', *Public Administration*, **76** (1).

Barzelay, M. (1992) *Breaking Through Bureaucracy: A New Vision for Managing in Government*, Berkeley: University of California Press.

Behn, R. (1988) 'Managing by groping along', *Journal of Policy Analysis and Management*, **7** (4), 643–663.

Boston, J. (1996) 'Origins and destinations: New Zealand's model of public management and the international transfer of ideas', in P. Weller and G. Davis (eds), *New Ideas, Better Government*, Australian Fulbright Series, St Leonards, NSW: Allen and Unwin.

Boston, J. et al. (1991) *Reshaping the State: New Zealand's Bureaucratic Revolution*, Auckland: Oxford.

Brudney, J. and England, R. (1983) 'Toward a definition of the co-production concept', *Public Administration Review*, **43** (1), 59–65.

Cooper, T. and Wright, N. (eds) (1992) *Exemplary Public Administrators: Character and Leadership in Government*, San Francisco: Jossey-Bass.

DiMaggio, P. and Powell, W. (1983) 'The iron cage revisited: institutional isomorphism and collective rationality in organizational fields', *American Sociological Review*, **48**, 147–160.

Flynn, N. (1990) *Public Sector Management*, Hemel Hempstead: Harvester Wheatsheaf.

Frederickson, H.G. (1997) *The Spirit of Public Administration*, San Francisco: Jossey-Bass.

Gunn, L. (1987) 'Perspectives on public management', in J. Kooiman and K. Eliassen (eds), *Managing Public Organizations: Lessons from Contemporary European Experience*, London: Sage.

Hannan, M. and Freeman, J. (1989) *Organizational Ecology*, Cambridge, MA: Harvard University Press.

Heifetz, R. (1994) *Leadership Without Easy Answers*, Cambridge, MA: Belknap Press.

Heymann, P. (1987) *The Politics of Public Management*, New Haven, CT: Yale University Press.

Hirschman, A. (1970) *Exit, Voice and Loyalty: Responses to Decline in*

*Firms, Organizations, and States*, Cambridge, MA: Harvard University Press.

Hood, C. (1983) *The Tools of Government*, London: Macmillan.

Hood, C. (1991) 'A public management for all seasons?', *Public Administration*, **69**, Spring, 3–19.

Johnson, G. and Scholes, K. (1999) *Exploring Corporate Strategy*, 5th edn, London: Prentice Hall.

Jordan, G. and O'Toole, B. (1995) 'The next steps: origins and destinations', in B. O'Toole and G. Jordan (eds), *Next Steps: Improving Management in Government?*, Aldershot: Dartmouth Publishing.

Kelman, S. (1992) 'Managing student aid in Sweden', Case No. C16–92–1161.0, Case Program, Kennedy School of Government, Harvard University, Cambridge, MA.

Lasswell, H. and Kaplan, A. (1950) *Power and Society: A Framework for Political Inquiry*, New Haven, CT: Yale University Press.

Lax, D. and Sebenius, J. (1986) *The Manager as Negotiator*, New York: Free Press.

Lindblom, C. (1959) 'The science of "muddling through"', *Public Administration Review*, **19** (2), 79–88.

Lowery, D. (1998) 'Consumer sovereignty and quasi-market failure', *Journal of Public Administration Research and Theory*, **8** (2), April, 137–172.

Meyer, J. and Rowan, B. (1977) 'Institutionalized organizations: formal structure as myth and ceremony', *American Journal of Sociology*, **83**, 340–363.

Moore, M. (1995) *Creating Public Value: Strategic Management in Government*, Cambridge, MA: Harvard University Press.

Moore, M. and Trojanowicz, R. (1988) 'Corporate strategies for policing', *Perspectives on Policing*, No. 6, National Institute for Justice and Harvard University, Cambridge, MA.

Nozick, R. (1974) *Anarchy, State and Utopia*, Oxford: Blackwell.

Osborne, D. and Gaebler, T. (1992) *Reinventing Government: How the Entrepreneurial Spirit is Transforming the Public Sector*, New York: Plume.

Patterson, P. (1998) 'Market metaphors and political vocabularies', *Public Productivity and Management Review*, **22** (2), December, 220–231.

Perry, J. and Rainey, H. (1988) 'The public–private distinction in organization theory: a critique and research strategy', *Academy of Management Review*, **13** (2), 182–201.

Pfeffer, J. (1992) *Managing with Power: Politics and Influence in Organizations*, Cambridge, MA: HBS Press.

Pfeffer, J. and Salancik, G. (1978) *The External Control of Organizations: A Resource Dependence Perspective*, New York: Harper and Row.

Pollitt, C. (1990) *Managerialism and the Public Services: The Anglo-American Experience*, Oxford: Basil Blackwell.

Quinn, J. (1980) *Strategies for Change: Logical Incrementalism*, Homewood, IL: Irwin.

Rainey, H., Backoff, R. and Levine, C. (1976) 'Comparing public and private organizations', *Public Administration Review*, **36** (2).

Reich, R. (ed.) (1988) *The Power of Public Ideas*, Cambridge, MA: Ballinger.

Rittel, H. and Webber, M. (1973) 'Dilemmas in a general theory of planning', *Policy Sciences*, **4** (June).

Scott, R. (1995) *Institutions and Organizations*, Thousand Oaks, CA: Sage.

Stewart, J. and Ranson, S. (1988) 'Management in the public domain', *Public Money and Management*, Spring/Summer, 13–19.

Stokey, E. and Zeckhauser, R. (1978) *A Primer for Policy Analysis*, New York: Norton.

Stone, D. (1988) *Policy Paradox and Political Reason*, Glenview, IL: Scott Foresman.

Walsh, K. (1991) 'Citizens and consumers: marketing and public sector management', *Public Money and Management*, Summer, 9–16.

Wolf, C. (1988) *Markets or Governments*, Cambridge, MA: MIT Press.

## *Notes*

1   To talk of it as a 'production process' is not to conceive of public sector management in terms of Taylorist assembly-lines. Production simply means any conversion of resources into what is valued.

2   Some private sector organisations also make use of co-production (e.g. supermarkets, self-service petrol stations) but its incidence in private business is not as extensive or as varied as in government. This is not surprising, given that much of government is in the business of intervening in social processes for collectively agreed purposes.

3   This seems to have been the case, for example, with the 1995 dispute between the UK Home Secretary and the head of the Prison Service – a separate 'executive agency'. The latter was blamed for two serious prison escapes and dismissed. He subsequently sued the government successfully for full compensation and costs, arguing that the ministerial policy framework was partly responsible for the escapes. This framework included prisoners' rights and prisoner allocation policy, which embodied different values to the performance criterion of effective containment under which he was dismissed. See Barker (1998).

# 2

# The processes of strategy development in the public sector

*By Nardine Collier, Frank Fishwick and Gerry Johnson[1]*

### Editor's introduction

Chapter 2 of *Exploring Corporate Strategy* is concerned with the way in which organisations formulate and implement strategy – the strategic management process. This ranges from planning through cultural influence to 'command'. The research described in this chapter applied the categorisation of processes used in *Exploring Corporate Strategy* to the public sector context to answer two important questions: First, whether there is a significant difference in the 'weight' of these different processes between the public and private sectors. For example, is planning more commonly used in one or other sectors? Second, within the public sector, are there any significant differences in the weight of processes between the different types of public sector organisation and their degree of publicness referred to in John Alford's chapter?

## 2.1 Introduction

The context and influences impinging on strategy in the public sector differ from those in the private sector. These include less exposure to market pressures (at least in the past), a greater need to conform to statutory and other formal regulations, responsibility of managers to different stakeholders, greater emphasis on net public welfare and in some cases different core objectives. Alford's chapter in this book considers the differences between the public and private sector. He noted that there were specific differences with regard to the environment and context within which the organisations operated; the managerial performance; and access to and use of resources. Other authors have also highlighted the differences which exist in these areas between the two sectors (Clarkson, 1980; Ring and Perry, 1985; Perry and Rainey, 1988). This chapter explores whether these differences are reflected in the processes of strategy development, and, if so, in what respects.

The chapter addresses these questions by analysis of responses to a questionnaire completed by 6,280 managers in public and private sector organisations. The questionnaire is designed to identify the processes of strategy development, as perceived by managers.

An analysis of the data comprised three sets of comparisons:

- comparison of perceptions of strategy development among 1,017 managers from all public sector organisations with 4,263 managers in all other organisations;
- a closer focus on the difference between public sector organisations and organisations in 'archetypal' private sector activities where market pressures are likely to be greatest;
- an analysis of perceived strategy development in different sub-sectors within the public domain, with differing degrees of market-type pressures.

These comparisons demonstrate highly significant differences between public and private sector organisations, and suggest clearly that exposure to the different pressures public sector organisations face have an important influence on strategy development processes.

## 2.2   A framework for the strategy development process

The strategy development process has many interacting dimensions. Six of these have been used as the basis of the strategy development questionnaire. The definitions of these dimensions are not mutually exclusive, since an organisation could have varying degrees of each trait.

Each of the dimensions is related to one of three overarching frameworks: strategy as managerial intent; strategy as the outcome of organisational processes; and strategy as imposed by external forces.

## 2.3   Strategy as managerial intent

Managerial intent regards the development of strategies as a deliberate managerial process. In the questionnaire this is represented by two dimensions.

### 2.3.1   The planning dimension

The planning dimension is, perhaps, the approach traditionally associated with how strategies develop. It is characterised as a sequence of analytical, logical and rational procedures, followed precisely to formulate an intended strategy. Goals and strategic objectives are set, often by specialised strategic planning departments, after a detailed exploration of the opportunities and threats in the business environment, which are matched to the strengths and weaknesses of the organisation. After a systematic analysis and evaluation of the potential options compared to the objectives, the chosen strategy is then detailed as precise plans for implementation, throughout the organisation.

### 2.3.2   The command dimension

The command dimension represents a situation in which an individual has a high degree of control and direction over the strategy development process. The organisation's strategy is associated with this individual, who may be the chief executive, owner or other powerful person in the organisation. This role may also be performed by a small group of top executives. The senior figure's vision of the future can become the strategy or determine the strategic direction of the organisation. The strategy can become so intrinsically linked with the senior figure that he or she is often perceived as the embodiment of the strategy. This can occur to such a degree that internal and external observers attribute responsibility for the success or failure of the strategy to the key individual. Furthermore, this widespread belief that one person creates strategy reinforces the individual's own perception that it is solely his or her responsibility.

## 2.4   *Strategy as the outcome of organisational processes*

Strategies can also develop as the outcome of the organisation's cultural and political processes. The culture and politics of an organisation may encourage emergent strategies, or may stifle innovative strategy development.

### 2.4.1   The political dimension

All organisations are political entities and susceptible to internal and external influences from various groups or stakeholders which guide or constrain strategies. Strategies are developed as a process of bargaining and negotiation between the stakeholders involved in the development of the strategy who have conflicting concerns and expectations. As the outcome of such bargaining, strategies represent the wishes of the most powerful groups, or compromises to accommodate conflicting interests, rather than the fulfilment of pre-planned objectives and careful analysis and evaluation.

### 2.4.2   The cultural dimension

This dimension represents the taken-for-granted assumptions and beliefs (or paradigm) that are shared by members of an organisation about that organisation, its purpose and role. Such assumptions and beliefs can be specific to an organisation or common to an industry or sector. Strategy does not develop as a result of the use of analytical tools so much as drawing upon experience and attitudes, values and perceptions and taken-for-granted ways of doing things that are referred to as 'culture'. The linked and reinforcing assumptions, routines, systems and symbols of an organisation's culture are described and explained in Section 2.8.1 of *Exploring Corporate Strategy* in terms of the cultural web.

Strategy development proceeds in accordance with, and within the confines of, this organisation's culture and its dominant paradigm. Innovative, new or change strategies outside of the frame of reference are therefore likely to be resisted, so strategies reflect a future and direction which tend to perpetuate the organisation's history and routine ways of doing things.

### 2.4.3   The incremental dimension

Studies of strategy development in organisations show that, typically, strategies change incrementally, that is, in relatively small-scale steps. Over time, of course, such small-scale changes could build to produce much more significant change; but this is likely to be gradual. Explanations of such incremental change take two forms which bridge both explanations based on managerial intent and the outcome of organisational processes.

The first view is that of 'logical incrementalism'. According to this, managers have a view of where they want their organisation to be and attempt to move towards this in a step-by-step way (Quinn, 1980). Strategy formulation is, then, purposeful and intentional. However, because of the complexity of the environment the process of strategy development is adaptive; managers attempt to be sensitive to that environment and gradually adapt to it as it changes. Strategic changes will thus be relatively small scale and commitment to strategy likely to be tentative. Implementation may proceed slowly and in stages so as to gauge its success and to refine the strategic direction of the organisation. Such environmental sensing takes place throughout the organisation, not just at the top, and by people who have operational responsibility, not just strategic responsibility. So strategy development is not, here, seen as the sole responsibility of top management but as a process in which organisational members engage more generally. Since there is more widespread involvement in strategy development and strategic change is gradual, it is also likely that there will be greater commitment to strategy that has been developed in such a way.

However, there is an alternative explanation for the observed phenomenon of incrementalism (Johnson, 1988). This builds on the previous explanations of cultural and political processes. Here the argument is that, if strategy is the outcome of the taken-for-granted assumptions and ways of doing things in the organisation, and of bargaining and negotiation between powerful groupings, it will tend to take the form of adaptation to the status quo. It is unlikely in such circumstances that there will be major divergences or changes in strategic direction, so incremental strategic change will be observed. Proponents of this view argue that such incremental strategy development may be post rationalised as a logical process, but is in fact the outcome of cultural and political processes.

There is of course an overlap between these two arguments. Both suggest that strategy development is likely to build on current strategy in an adaptive way and involve people throughout the organisation in its refinement and development.

## 2.5 Imposed strategy: the enforced choice dimension

The enforced choice dimension is characterised by the external environment operating to limit strategic direction. Strategies could be instigated externally, the government may dictate a particular course of action to follow or insist on regulatory control, particularly so within the public sector, or an operating business within a multi-divisional organisation may have strategies imposed on it from corporate head-office. Furthermore, market circumstances may exist where choice is delimited, for example in a commodity market or in an oligopoly where a dominant player will establish the strategic norms.

Powerful stakeholders such as customers, suppliers or professional bodies may also impose strategies on the organisation, thereby constraining managerial choice, by encouraging or determining the adoption of organisational structures and activities.

### 2.5.1 Integrating views of strategy development

The dimensions explained above are not mutually exclusive; each explains some aspects of the strategy development process. In fact we find that in almost all organisations it is a mix of these dimensions that explains how strategies develop. The different combinations of these dimensions appear to relate to the types of organisation being studied and the nature of the environment they face in particular. Illustrations of this are given in Appendix 2.9 of Chapter 2 of *Exploring Corporate Strategy*. Here, we are concerned with the nature of strategy development in the public sector; and since there are differences in organisational form and context in the public sector, we would also expect to see differences in the dimensions of strategy development within the public sector. In the rest of this chapter, we explore what these differences are and why they might exist.

## 2.6　*The strategy development questionnaire*

The questionnaire (see Appendix 2.1) was derived after extensive research. A review of research on strategy development processes was undertaken and questions developed from this which represented the characteristics that were uniquely attributable to each of the underlying dimensions. To ensure validity an expert panel evaluated each item's characteristicness using a Likert scale. Items were included if they had been endorsed by 70% of the panel and if they scored above the mean score on the Likert scale. These items were then analysed by managers to gauge their relevance to strategy development in a practical working environment. This produced 39 items which were transferred into a self-report questionnaire. Over 6,300 managers, from over 1,000 organisations, have completed the questionnaire since it was first used in 1992.

There are two parts to the self-report questionnaire. Part A comprises 49 statements, including a small number of 'dummy questions', related to strategy development (see Appendix 2.1). For each of these an individual manager is asked to indicate the degree to which the statements are characteristic of their organisation, according to a seven-point Likert scale, ranging from 1 = strongly disagree to 7 = strongly agree. Part B is designed to collect additional information about the manager's organisation.

Within the total of 6,280 managers completing the questionnaire, 1,017 classified their organisation to 'the public sector', though these included some organisations which were subsequently transferred to private ownership. The sample of 1,017 was large enough for a comparison of the perceptions of public sector managers with those of managers in other types of organisation. For an overview of how processes of strategy development in organisations can be gained by using the strategy development questionnaire see Bailey and Avery (1998).

## 2.7　*Analysis and results*

### 2.7.1　*Comparison of public sector organisations with the rest of the sample[2]*

As shown in Exhibit 2.1, the outstanding feature of strategy development in the public sector is the importance of the enforced choice dimension. On average, public sector managers gave this the highest score of all six dimensions. In contrast, managers from other organisations rated it the lowest. It is important to recall that the analysis

Exhibit 2.1   *Rank-adjusted mean scores for public sector and all other organisations*

| Dimension | Public sector | Other organisations | Significance of difference |
|---|---|---|---|
| Planning | 3.92 | 4.01 | 5% |
| Command | 3.97 | 4.19 | 0.1% |
| Incremental | 4.34 | 4.38 | Not significant |
| Political | 4.14 | 3.99 | 0.1% |
| Cultural | 4.26 | 4.20 | Not significant |
| Enforced choice | 4.76 | 3.81 | 0.1% |

Note: The probability that the observed difference could be due to chance (random sampling) is less than the percentage displayed, the 'significance' of the difference.

described here is based on managers' perceptions of how strategy is developed within their organisations. In recent years, much has been said and written about the constraints placed by public ownership or control on enterprise and managerial freedom. This research finding demonstrates that this view is shared by managers from the public sector themselves.

The second most important feature of the strategy development process in the public sector is the incremental dimension, which is also the single most important dimension in the rest of the sample. Indeed, there is no significant difference between the public sector and the other organisations in this respect. Managers in both sectors therefore stress the way in which their organisation is continually changing strategy in response to its changing environment. If the one component statement referring explicitly to changes in the marketplace is omitted from the computation of the score on the incremental dimension, the means for public sector participants and the rest of the sample become equal at 4.34.

Public sector managers accord less importance than those from other organisations to the command dimension statements, although this difference from the rest of the sample is less pronounced than that observed in the case of enforced choice. In part, these two differences are reciprocal. Where strategy is largely imposed or constrained by external pressures, managers see senior executives as less able to 'determine our strategic direction' or to implement their 'vision of the future'. (Both statements are components of the command dimension.)

The strategy development process in public sector organisations is also perceived to be more political, though this difference ranks only third in order of magnitude. It is probably consistent with the two other main differences. When strategy is largely driven by external influences, such as government, with reduced scope for the direction of strategy internally by a powerful figure, then bargaining and nego-tiation are inevitable. In public sector organisations this often takes the form of explicit bargaining by senior executives with external agen-cies, such as government, for resources or to influence the direction of the organisation; but it also is likely to include bargaining and nego-tiation for scarce resources internally between departments or with local political influences, for example in the form of the elected repre-sentatives in local government. Indeed, the art of political negotiation in such a context may not only be essential to develop strategies, but a basis upon which executives develop their managerial careers.

Exhibit 2.1 also shows that a lower emphasis on planning is of only a marginal statistical significance and that there is no significant difference between the public sector and the rest of the sample on the cultural dimension. However, with regard to culture, it is interesting to note that, when the public sector is compared with a commercial subset of other organisations characterised by their competitive environments, a highly significant difference is found. The significance of this finding is discussed in the next section.

### 2.7.2    Comparison of public sector organisations with those in archetypal commercial private sectors

A subset of economic activities within the private sector was chosen to represent those commercial activities conventionally regarded as the domain of private enterprise. In total, 1,186 managers within the sample classified their organisations to these activities. These were:

- manufacturing;
- retailing;
- wholesaling;
- pharmaceuticals.

These economic activities were chosen because they all have readily identifiable customers, are characterised by commercial objectives con-cerned with the interests of shareholders and operate mainly within competitive markets. In contrast to the public sector, and some other highly regulated activities, there is less explicit concern with general social benefit, and less direct control by government.

For this reason it was expected that the differences between this 'archetypal private sector' and the public sector would be similar to, but greater than, those between public and all non-public organis-ations. This expectation was fulfilled in the case of five of the six dimensions and in the sixth case the difference between the private enterprise subset and the rest of non-public organisations was of no statistical significance (see Exhibit 2.2).

*Exhibit 2.2*   *Hierarchy-adjusted mean scores: public sector vs. private sector subset*

| Dimension | Public | Private subset | Significance level of difference |
|---|---|---|---|
| Planning | 3.92 | 3.94 | Not significant |
| Command | 3.97 | 4.17 | 0.1% |
| Incremental | 4.34 | 4.39 | Not significant |
| Political | 4.14 | 3.82 | 0.1% |
| Cultural | 4.26 | 4.09 | 0.1% |
| Enforced choice | 4.76 | 3.64 | 0.1% |

A difference in composition by seniority had again to be accommodated in the analysis and averages were computed on the assumption that the distribution by hierarchy in each of the two groups was identical to that of the total population of all managers.

Comparison with Exhibit 2.1 shows that organisations in what were identified as archetypal private enterprise activities do indeed show stronger differences from public sector organisations than the residue of organisations outside the public sector. This is particularly true of the cultural and political dimensions. The differences between the public sector and the private sector subset can be seen very clearly on profile diagrams such as that shown in Exhibit 2.3.

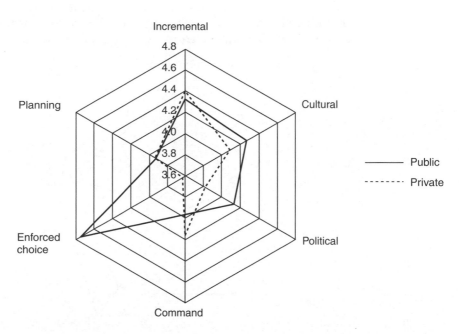

*Exhibit 2.3*   *Public vs. private sector: mean dimension scores (a six-dimension profile)*

The difference in the enforced choice dimension is so great that it overwhelms the differences in the other five dimensions. These can be more clearly identified when this dimension is omitted as in Exhibit 2.4, highlighting higher scores in the public sector on the cultural and political dimensions.

Perhaps the higher scores on the political dimension are to be expected given the public sector context discussed earlier. The higher scores on the cultural dimension are found when comparing the public sector with the archetypal private sector organisations. These organisations were specifically selected to represent private sector businesses in competitive markets. Arguably such market pressures may pose – or be seen by managers to pose – continual challenges to taken-for-granted assumptions and established ways of doing things. In public sector organisations, on the other hand, managers may perceive a greater need for continuity of service provision and therefore a greater adherence to core assumptions associated with such services and ways of providing them.

On the command dimension the subset score is slightly less than that for the non-public organisations in total, and this is also true of the planning dimension. However, these differences are not statistically significant and could be due to sampling. It is, however, interesting to note that on the planning dimension the effect is to make insignificant the contrast between the private sector subset and the public sector. There could of course be differences at work here. If planning is viewed as a means by which management justifies itself to external stakeholders, then it is not surprising, perhaps, that planning

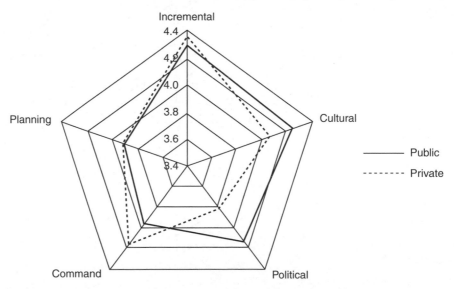

*Exhibit 2.4    Public vs. private sector: mean dimension scores (a five-dimension profile)*

is seen as just as significant in the public sector as it is across most non-public sector organisations. However, the role of planning is perceived to diminish the higher the influence of competition. The findings seem to bear out, then, the notion that planning is more to do with legitimisation to stakeholders than it is to do with the forging of competitive strategies.

The fact that the distinctive features of strategy formation in the public sector become more pronounced when this is compared with archetypal private sector activities reinforces the conclusion that these features are associated with different strategic objectives. Rather than meeting commercial objectives (profits, sales growth, long-term survival) within a competitive environment, many parts of the public sector are concerned with fulfilling statutory requirements and regulations with the objective of providing social benefit and value for money.

### 2.7.3   Differences within the public sector

For several years governments have attempted to introduce market-type forces into the public sector, with the implication that this improves efficiency and effectiveness in terms of 'best value'. In order to identify the effects of diverse pressures within different parts of the public sector five categories of organisations were examined separately:

- Market organisations, which sell a product to consumers commercially. These include public utilities and other organisations that were within the public sector at the time the questionnaire was completed, but have subsequently been privatised. They also include the Post Office and Royal Mail. The BBC was added to this category, because it was regarded as competing for customers with other television and radio companies, whose output is supplied free of charge at the point of delivery. (179 respondents)
- National Health Service (NHS), including health authorities and hospital trusts. Government has attempted to introduce market forces into the NHS, but there is no explicit commercial competition. (141 respondents)
- Local government, where competitive tendering, subcontracting to the private sector and value for money systems have also introduced some quasi-commercial pressures, but where competition for the final product remains very limited. (187 respondents)
- Police and the Prison Service, where subcontracting to the private sector has been more limited, and commercial pressures are mainly restricted to cost-benefit analysis and related economies. (132 respondents)
- Probation Service, to which similar comments apply, but where activity is more homogeneous, a difference which may affect the strategy development process. (205 respondents)

In examining whether there were significant differences between the mean scores of these subsets on each of the six dimensions of strategy development process, it was again necessary to make adjustment for differences in the hierarchical composition of the five subsets. For example, just over 50% of respondents from the NHS were chief executives or at one level below; among the respondents from the market organisations the corresponding proportion was 27%; among those from the police and Prison Service it was 23%.

Smaller numbers and marked under-representation of some hierarchical levels within specific sub-sectors make it impossible to compute seniority-adjusted means to compare dimension scores. Without adjustment for hierarchical differences, the sub-sector averages are meaningless. In Exhibit 2.5, the results of a multiple regression calculation have been used to determine whether there is a significant difference between the score of each sub-sector on each of the six dimensions and the score of the public sector as a whole. Where there is a significant difference, the entry states whether the score in the sub-sector is (on average) more or less than that in the total public sector and shows the level of significance (the probability that the difference could be due to chance is less than the percentage stated).

The activities defined here as 'market' (mainly those where the customer chooses to buy at the point of delivery) show a very significant positive difference from the rest of the public sector on the command dimension. This suggests that the more 'commercial' the organisation, the more managers at lower levels believe that strategic decisions are taken by those at the top. In such organisations, the lesser emphasis on the cultural dimension may well be due to change in the 'market-oriented' activities, since most were preparing for full or part privatisation. This finding is consistent with the observation in the previous section that the cultural dimension is significantly weaker in those private sector activities characterised by commercial objectives. The pressure of rapid change, led by senior executives, may

**Exhibit 2.5**    *Significant differences between sub-sectors and the public sector as a whole*

|  | Planning | Command | Incremental | Political | Cultural | Enforced choice |
|---|---|---|---|---|---|---|
| Market | Less** | More*** | Less** | – | Less** | – |
| NHS | Less* | – | – | More*** | – | – |
| Local gov. | – | Less** | More*** | – | More** | More** |
| Police etc. | More*** | – | – | Less** | Less* | – |
| Probation | – | Less** | Less* | Less*** | – | – |

* Significant at 5% ** Significant at 1% *** Significant at 0.1% – Not significant

also explain the lesser emphasis in the 'market' organisations on the planning and incremental dimensions.

In the NHS the most outstanding feature is the greater importance of the political dimension. This may reflect the participation in strategy formation in the NHS of a large number of active stakeholders (managers, clinicians, nurses, public funding bodies, trade unions). This is a characteristic that differentiates the NHS from other public sector bodies such as the police or Probation Service, where the political dimension gets a much lower score than in the rest of the public sector. It may be noted that the Probation Service, which is characterised by a more singular vocational objective, also has a significantly lower score on the command dimension.

In some ways local government may be considered the archetype of the public sector, which is reflected in the significantly greater score on the enforced choice dimension. The restriction of choice comes not only from imposition by elected bodies, but also from limits placed by central government. The very high score on the incremental dimension may be due to the absence, indeed some executives would say the impossibility, of a long-term strategy, given the frequency of changes in externally imposed policies. The structure of local government, with elected representatives determining policy, helps explain the low emphasis on command. However, it should also be remembered that many local government services are run by executives with their roots in professions such as the social services, education, library services, and so on. It is a structure for the provision of services which tends to emphasise departmental responsibility rather than overall central executive direction. Further, the emphasis on professional norms and standards might help account for the high cultural emphasis on strategy development.

The other main finding from the study of different activities within the public sector is the significantly greater score on the planning dimension recorded by managers from police forces. This may be a reflection of the high levels of operational planning required for the police. In this respect management generally in the police force is dependent on planning and is likely to 'spill over' to the strategic level. The lesser emphasis on the political dimension may be accounted for by the clear hierarchy of command within the police force; and the perceived lesser emphasis on the cultural dimension, the result of explicit pressures for change in policing taking place in the UK in the 1990s.

## 2.8   Conclusions and implications

This analysis of information from a large database shows that the distinct factors influencing strategy in the public sector are reflected in managers' perceptions of how strategy is determined. Taken as a whole, public sector managers place much more emphasis than those from all other organisations on the enforced choice dimension of strategy development, the result of a requirement to comply with statutory and other formal regulations together with guidelines handed down by political masters at national level. Less pronounced, but still considerable, is the lower emphasis placed in the public sector on the importance of the contribution to strategy development of senior individuals. This may partly reflect the less frequent identification of the organisation with the individual or small group at the top. However, the breakdown of the results for different categories within the public sector shows that the closer the activity comes to the commercial sector, the greater becomes the importance of this 'command' dimension, suggesting that commercial pressures impose a need for stronger leadership and direction.

Political processes are regarded as more significant within the public sector. As explained above, this is likely to be the result of a number of characteristics of public sector organisations. There is explicit bargaining between executives in the public sector and central government in order to obtain resources. For some public sector organisations, such as local government, there is similar bargaining occurring at the local level. In others there will be bargaining between departments for the allocation of resources too. In other public sector organisations such as the NHS, there are multiple influence groups on strategy development.

To answer the questions posed in the introduction, there are substantial differences in the process of strategy development between the public sector and other types of organisation. These differences become even more pronounced when the comparison is between the public sector and those private sector activities most closely associated with profit seeking in a competitive environment. However, the public sector is not homogeneous in terms of the factors which determine strategy, and our analyses have shown ways in which this is so. What then are the implications for executives in managing strategy in the public sector?

The overriding observation would be that managers should recognise the reality of strategy development. Not only in the public sector, but in many private sector organisations, there have been traditions of equating strategy development and strategic planning. However, it needs to be recognised that formal planning mechanisms are not necessarily the only way – perhaps not the most effective way – in which strategies develop (Mintzberg et al., 1998). Strategic management is concerned with managing the long-term development of the organisation to meet the pressure of the changing environment and the needs and expectations of stakeholders. Our analysis suggests that managers seek to undertake this in different ways according to their different organisational objectives and their different contexts. Planning may, indeed, provide a useful means of developing strategy; but there are other means too. It is clear that within public sector organisations an overarching consideration is the strong influence of agencies such as government and pressures to provide for the social good. In such a context, it would be surprising if political bargaining and negotiation did not play an important role. Indeed it may be that there needs to be a more explicit recognition of the importance of political processes in the management of public sector organisations.

However, it is certainly the case that public sector organisations are being made more accountable for achieving 'best value' performance and, often, within a more market-focused arena. In such circumstances we have seen that there may be a greater role for strategic direction by senior executives – the command role. It is also likely that in such circumstances these individuals will have to face the challenge of managing strategic change within their organisations; and hence the need to understand and cope with culture change. In other chapters in this book the political dimension of public sector management is explicitly addressed (see Chapter 9), as is the challenge of culture change (see Chapter 16).

## *References*

Bailey, A. and Avery, C. (1988) 'Discovering and defining the process of strategy development', in V. Ambrosini with G. Johnson and K. Scholes (eds), *Exploring Techniques of Analysis and Evaluation in Strategic Management*, London: Prentice Hall.

Clarkson, K.W. (1980) 'Managerial behaviour in non-proprietary organisations', in  K.W. Clarkson and D.L. Martin (eds), *The Economy of Non-proprietary Organisations*, Greenwich, CT: JAI Press.

Johnson, G. (1988) 'Re-thinking incrementalism', *Strategic Management Journal*, **9**, 75–91.

Mintzberg, H., Ahlstrand, B. and Lampel, J. (1998) *Strategy Safari: A Guided Tour Through the Wilds of Strategic Management*, London: Prentice Hall.

Perry, J. and Rainey, H. (1988) 'The public–private distinction in organisation theory: a critique and research strategy', *Academy of Management Review*, **13** (2), 182–201.

Quinn, J.B. (1980) *Strategies for Change – Logical Incrementalism*, Georgetown, Ontario: Irwin.

Ring, P. and Perry, J. (1985) 'Strategic management in public and private organisations: implications of distinctive contexts and constraints, *Academy of Management Review*, **10** (2), 276–286.

## *Notes*

1    Acknowledgements: The original work on the Strategy Development Questionnaire was sponsored by ESRC grant no. R000235100, and was developed by Andy Bailey and Gerry Johnson at Cranfield School of Management.

2    It was not possible to perform a simple comparison between the public sector and the rest of the sample because of the difference in the two groups regarding hierarchical level; see Appendix 2.2 for an explanation of how this problem was overcome.

# Appendix 2.1 The strategy questionnaire

### Planning

We have definite and precise strategic objectives
When we formulate a strategy it is planned in detail
We evaluate potential strategic options against explicit strategic objectives
We meticulously assess many alternatives before deciding on a strategy
We have precise procedures for achieving strategic objectives
We have well-defined planning procedures to search for solutions to strategic problems
We make strategic decisions based on a systematic analysis of our business environment
Our strategy is made explicit in the form of precise plans

### Command

The strategy we follow is directed by a vision of the future associated with the chief executive (or another senior figure)
Our strategy is closely associated with a particular individual
A senior figure's vision is our strategy
Our chief executive tends to impose strategic decisions (rather than consulting the top management team)
The chief executive determines our strategic direction

### Incremental

To keep in line with our business environment we make continual small-scale changes to strategy
We keep early commitment to a strategy tentative and subject to review
Our strategy develops through a process of ongoing adjustment
We tend to develop strategy by experimenting and trying new approaches in the marketplace
Our strategy is continually adjusted as changes occur in the marketplace
Our strategies emerge gradually as we respond to the need to change

### Cultural

Our strategy is based on past experience

There is a way of doing things in this organisation which has developed over the years

Our organisation's history directs our search for solutions to strategic issues

The strategy we follow is dictated by our culture

The strategies we follow develop from 'the day-to-day way we do things around here'

The attitudes, behaviours, rituals and stories of this organisation reflect its strategic direction

There is a resistance to any strategic change which does not sit well with our culture

### Political

The information on which our strategy is developed often reflects the interests of certain groups within this organisation

The vested interests of particular internal groups colour our strategy

Our strategy develops through a process of bargaining and negotiation between groups or individuals

Our strategy is a compromise which accommodates the conflicting interests of powerful groups and individuals

The decision to adopt a strategy is influenced by the power of the group sponsoring it

Our strategies often have to be changed because certain groups block their implementation

### Enforced choice

We are severely limited in our ability to influence the business environment in which we operate

We have strategy imposed on us by those external to this organisation, for example the government

Our freedom of strategic choice is severely restricted by our external business environment

We are not able to influence our business environment; we can only buffer ourselves from it

Many of the strategic changes which have taken place have been forced on us by those outside this organisation

Barriers exist in our business environment which significantly restrict the strategies we can follow

Forces outside this organisation determine our strategic direction

## Dummy questions

The influence a group or individual can exert over the strategy we follow is enhanced by their control of critical resources

We deal with strategic issues as and when they arise

Our strategy is driven by a vision of the future

As a subsidiary (or division) our strategy is set by the parent company

There is a commonly shared belief in this organisation about the strategic direction we should pursue

Our strategic direction is determined by powerful individuals or groups

There is a clear vision of our future which we pursue

Our strategic direction is driven by commonly shared values

A vision of what this organisation will be like in the future guides what we do strategically

When strategy develops in this organisation I am actively involved

# Appendix 2.2 Hierarchy and comparison between public and private sectors

It became evident at an early stage of the analysis that a straight comparison between public sector organisations and the rest of the sample might be distorted by a significant difference in the composition of the two groups in terms of hierarchy. Of public sector managers within the sample 45% were at chief executive level or one below, compared with 34% of all other managers. On most of the dimensions there is a significant relationship between the hierarchical position of the manager completing the questionnaire, measured as level below the chief executive (0 to 5+), and his or her score. To overcome this problem weighted averages were calculated for each of the two groups (public sector and the rest), with the weights based on the composition by rank of the two groups combined.

A second approach was the application of multiple regression, which gave very similar results. The problem created by the different hierarchical composition of the public and private sector groups is demonstrated by the pattern of scores on the command dimension.

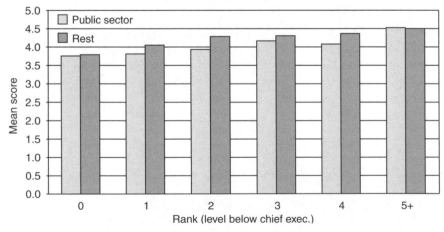

*A 2.2    Scores on the command dimension by hierarchical rank*

Two procedures were used to eliminate the distortion resulting from the different mix of seniority: regression analysis and rank-adjusted means. The regression equations related the scores of managers on each of the six dimensions to (1) their hierarchical level below chief executive and (2) whether or not they came from the public sector. The results revealed very significant differences (after compensation for rank) between the public sector and other organisations on three of the six dimensions (in diminishing order: enforced choice, command and political). A smaller difference of more marginal statistical significance was indicated on the planning dimension. On the incremental and cultural dimensions, there was no significant difference. These results match almost exactly those derived by use of rank-weighted means.

# Global influences on the public sector

## By Jan Eppink and Steven de Waal

### Editor's introduction

Chapter 3 of *Exploring Corporate Strategy* is concerned with how managers might analyse the business environment and its impact on the organisation's strategies. One important theme is the growing importance of global influences. In this chapter Jan Eppink and Steven de Waal illustrate how a selection of the analytical techniques from *Exploring Corporate Strategy* can be used to build a picture of how global forces are increasingly likely to shape the environment of the public sector organisation. This is particularly important given that many public sector managers will have worked for most of their careers in organisations whose outlook (geographically) tended to be confined to the community (local or national) they were serving – and global forces seemed of little relevance to the public sector.

### 3.1  Introduction

For a long time people working in the public sector have thought of their 'business' as intrinsically good, or unquestionably necessary and a public duty. Moreover, the outside world should keep its hands off. In the past, society has accepted these views without too many questions. In the past decade, however, developments have shown that this is no longer the case (e.g. Ryan, 1999). Society is becoming more critical of the public sector, while more external influences are making themselves felt. This makes it necessary for organisations in the public sector to think more explicitly about what is happening on a more global scale and develop plans for the future. Earlier, organisations got away with defensive actions, but this will no longer prove to be a lasting solution. A successful new strategy will be based on intimate knowledge of what goes on outside one's own organisation, own sector, and own country. Often one hears managers, in both the private and public sectors, talk about unexpected discontinuities: in many cases the idea of discontinuity is more a perception than a fact. The more one looks for information about the future, the more one will pick up bits of information that are pertinent to survival. There will always be true discontinuities, but many rapid developments are symptoms of fundamental trends. As an example, take the explosion in the computing power of PCs. This is a very rapid and, in the eyes of many, turbulent development indeed, but behind it lies Moore's law stating that the computing power of microprocessors will double every 18 months. This law has proved to be remarkably correct over the past decade.

Research has suggested that, in general, many organisations emerging from stable environments have underdeveloped planning capabilities (Brews and Hunt, 1999). In this chapter we will therefore alert managers in the formerly more or less stable public sector to developments they may not yet recognise as important for the future of their organisations. We will also show how some of the techniques discussed in Chapter 3 of *Exploring Corporate Strategy* may be used to better prepare public sector organisations for the fast-changing global environment.

We will first give a broad outline of some of the major environmental influences on the public sector using a PEST analysis (see *Exploring Corporate Strategy*, Section 3.3.1). This will provide the background for the following sections showing how other analytical techniques might be used. In that context we will describe two scenarios developed in the public sector and illustrate the decisions that were based on them (*Exploring Corporate Strategy*, Section 3.3.3). Then we will show how Porter's five forces analysis (see *Exploring Corporate Strategy*, Section 3.4) could be used to pinpoint strategic issues in the healthcare sector, and finally how strategic group analysis (*Exploring Corporate Strategy*, Section 3.5.1) can help organisations in higher education.

## 3.2   PEST analysis

The aim of a PEST analysis is to identify the forces that impact on the organisation by classifying them as Political, Economic, Social or Technological influences. An interesting question is if and how such an analysis, first developed for use in the private sector, can be applied in the public sector also. In his chapter on the implications of 'publicness' for strategic management theory, Alford has suggested that there is a public-to-private continuum, ranging from 'purely private' to 'purely public' organisations. 'Purely private' organisations are faced with environmental developments over which they may have no influence at all or where it is considered to be unethical to try to influence them. On the other hand it is acceptable or even seen as a task of a 'purely public' organisation to think about developing policies about an issue, for example policies to lower birth rates in certain countries. It is considered as forward looking if the United Nations or governments start programmes with that aim, whereas it would be deemed unacceptable if a private organisation tried to do the same. Some forces in a PEST analysis are more open to influence by public organisations than by private organisations. Another difference is that the public sector is more layered than the private. Some issues are dealt with at a global level (e.g. free trade) and others at a national, county/province or municipal level. Each higher level sets the degrees of freedom for the lower level(s). In the private sector such a 'hierarchical' structure is either not found or expressly forbidden (cartels).

Not all influences can be discussed in detail here, but the following global trends are of particular importance to the future strategy of public sector organisations. The information is the result of a PEST analysis and can be used as part of the input for scenarios, five forces analysis and strategic group analysis, which will be discussed later.

### 3.2.1  Political

Not surprisingly, political influences are of major importance for the public sector.

One of the most relevant factors for the public sector will be the trend towards deregulation and privatisation. Looking back some 20 years, in many countries, one will be surprised to see how many tasks that were considered to be typical public sector tasks have been deregulated or privatised. In almost all cases there has been pressure on public sector organisations to increase effectiveness and efficiency. Examples are the production and distribution of electricity, the water supply, telecommunications, railway services, broadcasting, etc. Before the 1980s such services were considered to be in the public domain, at least in many European countries.

Now in most countries they are deregulated or have been sold to the public. Comparing this with the situation in the USA, we can note that private companies have always provided many of these services there. This philosophy is now gradually being adopted in Europe, but with many differences in speed and direction (UK: the 'third way') between countries. (See Eleanor Doyle's chapter in this book.)

Just to illustrate this, in the early 1980s companies that provided temporary employees were not looked upon very favourably in the Netherlands. There was even a ban on new companies for some time. The politically correct view was that regional labour agencies should match supply and demand, rather than the free market. Nowadays the effectiveness and efficiency of companies such as Randstad, Vedior and Manpower are much applauded. In an issue of the *Financial Times* of July 1999 it was observed that even in a country such as France, with traditionally a large degree of government influence over the whole of society, the socialist government of Jospin is seriously considering the question of how to lower the level of government involvement in various aspects of society. In sum, what is regarded as a public sector task is as much the result of political choice and circumstances as it is of principle.

Another development that will indirectly affect public service organisations in the long run is the increasing trend to liberalise world trade. Now that the World Trade Organisation is in place, we will see a gradual increase in competition between countries, because subsidies will have to be lowered in the course of time. A similar development is already under way in Europe with the extension of the European Union in an easterly direction. With the much lower costs of land and labour in those countries, we can expect a gradual shift in agricultural production (primary as well as processing) from western Europe to the east. This is bound to have an impact on the type and structure of the agricultural production that is left. No doubt governments will have to deal with the consequences of this development, in terms of both employment and the use of land.

### 3.2.2 *Economic*

Against the background of the liberalisation of world trade mentioned above, the present internationalisation and globalisation of the economy will continue and even speed up. For countries with open economies such a development can seriously affect the trend in GDP. Some economists state that there is not much to fear from globalisation, since it impacts only a small portion of the economy. This may or not be true, but the effect of Japanese competitors on the production of cameras, television sets, motor cycles and automobiles in western economies has been dramatic. What can we expect to happen if the economies of large Asian countries such as India and China reach a stage comparable to that of Japan 25 years ago? Many people think technological and educational levels are not high enough in those countries. That impression is wrong: in a recent issue of *Business Week* it was mentioned that the CEO of McKinsey & Co., the international management consultants, was educated in India, as was the CEO of US Airways and another group of leading high-tech US entrepreneurs. Many of the world's largest software companies have development laboratories in Hyderabad, where there is an abundance of highly educated engineers willing to work at pay rates of slightly over 1,000 dollars a month. The products they make can be instantaneously delivered through telecommunications to the place where they are used. The differences in education levels and geography have disappeared for such products. During a visit to China in *1984*, one of the authors met an American industrialist who mentioned that he was outsourcing the production of microchips to a Chinese company in the Beijing area!

The pictures we see of the deprivation in countries such as China and India are far from representative of what those countries are capable of now and in the future. Such developments will not fail to have an impact on the level and type of employment as well as affordable pay levels for certain types of work in western economies. One of the great dangers in strategic management is to underestimate the potential of the other competitors. It would be a grave mistake to underestimate the future economic potential of emerging countries. The result may be that, just as with the arrival of the Japanese on the world market, individual companies and maybe even entire industries will come under pressure. This will change the industrial structure of countries, with many consequences for levels of employment and other social issues. Clearly, the public sector in each country should consider the impact of this development and think of possible (re)actions, and create the conditions for such reactions.

On a more national level one can expect income levels to be more differentiated than in the past because of the emergence of new international competitors. On the one hand one can see a scarcity of highly educated people, the people Drucker called 'knowledge workers' as far back as the early 1960s, and on the other hand groups of people who are less talented or motivated and for whom it may be more difficult to find a satisfying job with reasonable pay. In view of the more international labour market for knowledge workers than for less educated employees, it will not be surprising to see larger differences in pay developing between the groups. In countries with a history of 'limitation' of differences in pay this may lead to social pressure to counter or slow the trend. In countries with traditionally a more open market philosophy the effect of this trend may be outright poverty, social unrest and maybe even increased levels of criminality. The public sector will have to anticipate these consequences and develop adequate responses.

Another difference in wages, in some countries, is developing between the private and the public sector, with the private sector paying considerably higher salaries than the public sector. Since the public sector depends to a large extent on knowledge workers for whom there is a big demand, the serious problem arises of how to attract high-level individuals for the public sector. We are moving in the direction of a knowledge society, but we see that it is increasingly difficult to pay teachers and researchers, who provide the fundamentals for that society, enough to make the public sector attractive for them.

In some countries one can expect relative increases in disposable income for people who retire. In many cases they have taken care of their retirement financially. Often the obligations of mortgages, education of children, etc., will have ended, leaving them well off for their retirement. In the past, in many countries, laws have been passed with the aim of providing the elderly with a decent living in that period of life. Such laws were drawn up with the idea in mind that this group was a vulnerable one. Many years later, this idea may no longer be true in all cases. The consequence in many countries is the privatisation of such benefits, with a smaller role for part of the public sector.

The trend towards globalisation has led to the rise of so-called 'mega corporations', for example oil companies (Shell), car manufacturers (GM, Toyota), producers of fast-moving consumer goods (Procter & Gamble, Unilever), makers of consumer electronics (Sony, Philips), telecom operators (ATT, BT), and many others. Because of the ongoing wave of mergers and acquisitions their number will no doubt increase in future. These companies employ large numbers of staff in many countries. A decision to invest or disinvest in a country can have an enormous impact in terms of levels of employment, tax revenue, technological development, etc. This gives these companies *vis-à-vis* some countries an enormous bargaining power in negotiations. Some nation states may have to think about whether they can still be effective against such global economic powerhouses.

### 3.2.3   Social

One important social trend is demographics, where there are various trends. One development that can be seen in various countries is an influx of people from abroad. In part, this can be caused by situations such as war in a region: Kosovo nearby and more distant African countries are current examples. Another factor is that the European Union makes possible the free movement of goods, capital, services and *people*. In some countries, in the past, inviting people to emigrate from countries around the Mediterranean Sea solved the shortage of labour. Later their relatives joined the early 'guestworkers'.

In some larger cities the consequence now is that between one-third and half of the population has its roots in another country. This sometimes leads to serious problems because of immigrants' low levels of education, poor command of the language, low income, etc. The public sector is held responsible for solving these problems, with sometimes limited resources available. The difficulties of the early immigrants are decreasing now, with in many cases the second generation integrating well both socially and educationally. Experiences in the Netherlands show that the influx of asylum seekers and other immigrants places much strain on the parts of the public sector that have to deal with it. If the EU decides to spread the influx more evenly among its members, the public sector in countries that so far have taken in relatively few people will have to prepare for this great challenge.

In Europe the population is ageing. In part, this is caused by longer life expectancy (10 years longer than some 20 years ago) but also by an overall decrease in birth rates. The effects of this are diverse. For state pensions this may mean that if no action is taken now, premiums will have to go up in future, since pensions are either paid out of the government budget, or are paid by those who are working at present and who hope that future generations will take care of them once they retire. This also affects commercial life insurance, but here the impact of living longer is less dramatic, since the insured build up capital that will be used later to provide pensions.

At the other end of the age spectrum, more than in the past, traditional family life is changing. More younger people want to follow their own careers, which leaves them with less or no time to raise their children, if they decide to have them at all. This development requires day care for children to be available. Some parents may be able to pay a commercial rate for it; in other cases the public sector may have a role to play here.

A trend that is less clear as to how far it will go and how it will affect the public sector is the individualisation of society. This leads to less solidarity between groups in society, and may be enhanced in its effects by a more materialistic mentality that is also developing. Many fear that if such a trend continues, it may cause a split in society, with serious consequences. The least the public sector can do is to make clear that in the long run such effects are detrimental to all people concerned, even to those who profit most from individualisation.

### 3.2.4 *Technological*

Technological developments can have direct and indirect influences on the public sector. The indirect ones may be less visible at first, but have their impact later.

In the medical field many new discoveries can be expected. The amount of money spent and the number of researchers involved are enormous. The research is done partly in the private sector in pharmaceutical and medical equipment companies and partly in the public sector in universities and laboratories financed by governments. Since there is an almost endless demand for new cures for diseases already known or only just discovered, the question of how these research efforts should be financed is a major one. Many of these research projects lead to an increase in expenses in the healthcare sector. Other projects have a different impact on costs. Research in diagnostics aimed at detecting deficiencies in unborn children may result in the number of people to be treated later being lower, but there are serious ethical aspects that are only now being discussed. There are also developments that will lead to a decrease in the number of days, if any, that patients stay in hospital for treatment. Such research projects, in the end, lead to lower overall costs for the healthcare sector.

Developments in the field of telecommunications can have a variety of effects. First, the distance between a client of the public sector and the agency may become less important. Depending on the infrastructure available in a country (cable networks, telephone lines, etc.) the client can get information or ask questions without physically visiting the agency. Where a public sector organisation has a sophisticated Internet site, the client can interact intensely with the organisation without visiting it, for those interactions where human contact is not necessary. If such systems are further developed, fewer people may be necessary to provide information or to interact in other ways with the client. This may also have an effect on the amount of office space that is required to provide a service. For universities, such developments make it possible for students from all over the world to follow courses without leaving home. Of course, not all educational interactions can be done electronically (Becker, 1999), but those parts of the process that are individual (reading books, working on assignments) do not require the physical presence of participants at the school's location. In a way, one could say that many universities may become more like Open Universities than they are now.

The use of the Internet has negative aspects as well. For example, the public sector will have to think about how to stop violation of privacy, child pornography, fraud in e-commerce transactions, etc.

In the medical field, advances in information and communication technology make it possible for doctors to ask colleagues on the other side of the world to give a second opinion by sending them all the available information electronically and receive a reply the same day. There have already been experiments with surgeons using a robot to perform an operation on a patient 1,000 kilometres away in another country. This may seem a scary idea, but the patient is still doing well. It might well be that diagnosis and treatment in the far future may also become possible at more than arm's length. If such methods become the norm rather than the exception they are now, questions arise as to who will be responsible and/or accountable in case of mishaps, since different countries may not have the same rules for such cases. Clearly, there are a number of issues that the public sector has to deal with in this respect.

The general trend towards a more high-tech society where knowledge workers play a dominant role seems to be at odds with observations that in many developed countries the level of 'virtual illiteracy' is alarmingly high. *The Economist* of 31 July 1999 stated that in the USA and the UK this is slightly above 20%. If this trend continues, the danger of an underclass is far from imaginary. Clearly, it is an enormous challenge for society and particularly for the public sector (edu-

Exhibit 3.1    *Global trends for the public sector*

| Political | Economic | Social | Technological |
|---|---|---|---|
| • Deregulation<br>• Privatisation<br>• Extension<br>  of EU<br>• Role of<br>  government | • Competitors<br>  from developing<br>  countries<br>• Trade liberalisation<br>• Income differences<br>  increase<br>• Mega corporations | • Demographics<br>• Lifestyles<br>• Individualism<br>• Split in society | • Breakthrough<br>  in life<br>  sciences<br>• Telecommuni-<br>  cations<br>• Internet<br>• Imaging |

cation, social work organisations) to prevent this disaster scenario from becoming reality.

Exhibit 3.1 summarises the above discussion.

In a few cases a public sector organisation will be confronting only one of the four groups of forces. In many cases there will be a combination of two or more. To investigate the impact of such combinations on the sector, scenarios are a useful tool.

## 3.3    Scenarios

The use of scenarios is especially useful in situations where it is important to take a long-term *view of strategy*; where there are a *limited number of relevant key factors*; and when there is a *high level of uncertainty*. A scenario is a plausible view of a possible future. Scenarios can be used to *test the sensitivity of strategies* for different conditions and also to *challenge generally accepted views* about the future environment (*Exploring Corporate Strategy*, Section 3.3.3).

Scenarios are different from trend analysis, which may be the result of a PEST analysis, in that external developments are built into consistent 'wholes'. Many books have been written about trends (e.g. Naisbitt and Aburdene, 1990) and scenarios in the private sector (Hawken et al., 1982; van der Heijden, 1996), but far fewer have been published about scenarios that are useful for the public sector.

Early examples of scenarios for the impact of global trends on the public sector were developed by the Organisation for Economic Co-operation and Development (OECD, 1979) in Paris.

Exhibit 3.2 shows the variables that were taken into account when building the different scenarios. The four dimensions were:

- the nature of the relations likely to be established between developed countries;
- relations between advanced industrial societies and developing countries and relations between developing countries;

*Exhibit 3.2*   *OECD scenarios.*[1]

| Relations between developed countries | Collegial management | | | Partial abandonment of free trade between the poles | |
|---|---|---|---|---|---|
| Internal dynamics of the developed societies | Consensus in favour of high growth | Rapid value changes and moderate growth | Conflicts between social groups and moderate growth | | |
| Trend in relative productivities / North–South relations and relations between LDCs | Convergence | | | Divergence | |
| Large growth of North–South economic exchanges | A | B1 | B2 | B3 | |
| Accentuation of divisions between North and South | | | | C | |
| Partial fragmentation of the South following regional alignments with the developed country poles | | | | | D |

[1] The fourth dimension concerning the internal dynamics of the various groups of developing societies has mainly been taken into account at the level of the regional analyses incorporated in the scenarios.

- the internal dynamics peculiar to developed societies;
- the internal dynamics specific to the different groups of developing societies.

In summary, the scenarios were arranged in four groups:

- the high-growth scenario (A);
- the moderate growth scenarios (B1, B2, B3);
- the North–South confrontation scenario (C);
- the protectionist scenario (D).

Each scenario was then analysed to identify the likely effects on the use of energy and on the agricultural and industrial sectors, as well as trade and capital flows.

From the scenarios a number of critical issues were derived, dealing with energy issues, national policies to come to terms with the new challenges, efforts to help the Third World develop further and new forms of international co-operation. These were then further specified into policy recommendations. One group of measures was aimed at facilitating development of the Third World. Another suggested that the discussion should begin on the effects of an ageing population in developed countries. Some demographers hold the view that the age structure of a population directly affects confidence in its own future. An ageing population in developed countries may have a greater negative effect on relations with developing countries than a larger population. Another recommendation deals with making international trade more transparent and stable by improving the organisational framework. An outcome of this was the creation of the World Trade Organisation in the mid-1990s.

Separate governments also undertake scenario planning. In 1992 the Dutch Centraal Plan Bureau, a think tank of the Dutch Government, published three scenarios relevant for the Netherlands (Centraal Plan Bureau, 1992a, 1992b). Here the focus was on what should change in the Dutch society and economy in order to keep its position as a major economic force.[1]

The first scenario was called *Global Shift*, in which the centre of gravity moves to the Pacific Rim. Under this scenario there is a lot of technological development, entrepreneurial behaviour, inventiveness and incentives for innovation. The second scenario is labelled *Balanced Growth* and is characterised by economic growth in various parts of the world, combined with moves in the direction of sustainable economic development. In the third scenario, *European Renaissance*, technology develops less fast than in the Global Shift scenario, but still requires enormous investments. This leads to the need for economies of scale, with monopolistic tendencies and strategic alliances as a possible consequence.

For each of the scenarios the main issues for Dutch society and the Dutch economy are pinpointed. The study identifies two ways to deal with these issues. The first is to keep the main elements of the welfare state and combine these with elements of a so-called co-ordination perspective (the now famous Dutch Polder model). The second way is to strengthen the market perspective, which in time will mean reducing or giving up several elements of the present welfare state. There is no denying the fact that the discussion on which approach to choose is still going on, both inside politics and among the public at large.

Both examples of scenarios for the public sector clearly show how great is the impact of developments on a global level for individual countries and lower levels of government. There is the beginning of a tendency for municipal authorities in border areas to co-operate with one another. One example of this is the Aachen–Maastricht–Liège area, where the Belgian, German and Dutch borders coincide. Authorities work together and universities co-operate, and Maastricht Airport has been rechristened Maastricht–Aachen Airport. This may be a sign that alongside national interests cities are developing multinational interests as well.

## 3.4 *Five forces analysis in healthcare*

It is not uncommon to find that healthcare takes up around 10 per cent of GDP in many countries. This makes it one of the largest parts of the public sector, with a major impact on the economy. This sector also attracts lots of attention in most countries because it touches on people's health, one of the most basic needs, and many customers are not entirely satisfied with the service (quality, waiting lists, etc.). Also, costs seem to be constantly increasing. One might say healthcare is a sector that has a strategic problem, both at the national level and at the organisational level (hospitals, etc.). These problems seem to exist irrespective of the system in use in a country. In most European countries governments have a direct controlling influence in healthcare. So spending on healthcare is seen as a cost, rather than as a market that is expanding. It can be useful to think about healthcare as a market with suppliers and customers even if it is not operating as a 'free' competitive market.

A parallel can be drawn with other areas that were previously public sector and now are in the private sector (e.g. electricity, broadcasting, railways, telecommunications, etc.).

Porter's five forces analysis as described in *Exploring Corporate Strategy*, Section 3.4 can be used to shed light on some of the issues in healthcare.

### 3.4.1 *Threat of entry*

Currently one of the most effective barriers to entry in most countries is legislation. Most governments have a final say in whether or not a new hospital can be opened. A subtler way of entering a new market is to try to get patients from other countries. This is already happening in some countries where patients, because of waiting lists, etc., decide to get treatment on the other side of the border. If the insurance company agrees, a new competitor can enter the market without going through the bureaucratic procedure of establishing a new hospital. In some cases, patients are prepared to go a long way to get treatment for rare diseases. A university hospital in Pamplona specialises in treatment for certain forms of cancer: patients come from countries as far away as Finland for cure and care. Besides the quality of the cure, the cost of a single room, with separate bathroom and sitting area as well as the possibility for a relative to stay over, is less than one-third of the rate for a bed in a four-person room in the Netherlands. Hospitals should not be too confident that new global competition of this type will not arrive, even under the present regulations.

Entry is not always on a large scale. Recently, *Het Financieële Dagblad* mentioned that a British pensioner is now buying his medicine through his cousin in Holland. The Dutch pharmacist who delivered the medicine has entered the British market, almost without knowing it. Rather than pay £400 per month, the pensioner now saves half of that amount by shopping abroad. If differences between countries exist in terms of prices, waiting lists, etc., and the distances can be overcome without too many problems (the Internet), the entry of new competitors may be not far away.

### 3.4.2 Bargaining power of buyers and suppliers

It is amazing that in a situation where hospitals have almost no money to pay nurses a decent salary, pharmaceutical companies make large profits, as do suppliers of medical equipment and beds, and medical specialists. It seems that money can be made in the so-called non-profit healthcare sector, but not by the organisation that ultimately takes care of the patient. The bargaining power of the hospital is apparently not big enough for it to get a slice of the pie that is going to other parts of the value chain.

The bargaining power of the suppliers is not reduced by other players such as insurance companies, which are paying the bill for the patient. Neither is the bargaining power of the government. In many countries governments try to contain the rise in expenses, but are not always successful. From a bargaining point of view this can be explained as follows. Where a government views healthcare as a major responsibility, it will have a bad bargaining position *vis-à-vis* profitable suppliers since democratic processes will require that in the end government will pick up the bill.

On the 'customer' side, we see that they are becoming more demanding, which also puts hospitals under more pressure to satisfy them. For patients, not only cure, but also care (comfort, service, etc.) is important. From recent discussions with some hospital managers the authors found that many of them still think of quality only in terms of techniques to cure the patient. Comfort is considered irrelevant. But governments are encouraging consumerism in public services, strengthening the bargaining power of buyers.

### 3.4.3 Threat of substitutes

Technological developments may lead to substitution of some of the services provided by the sector. New surgical techniques reduce the number of days a patient has to stay in hospital after an operation. Lower-cost hotel facilities may be used in some cases rather than far more expensive hospital beds. Diagnostic techniques may make possible a less drastic treatment in an early phase. In Section 3.2.4 some other technological developments were sketched that may lead to a reduction in the number of services rendered by the hospital.

### 3.4.4 Competitive rivalry

So long as the influence of government on the sector stays high, the level of competitive rivalry will not increase dramatically. For routine treatments patients may not be willing to travel long distances for nicer hospital rooms or more friendly nurses. But for more threatening ailments, this may change. Since patients are becoming more assertive and better informed, more rivalry will develop. Some (university) hospitals are already drawing up strategic plans to define their future competitive position. These are still early developments, but they will no doubt continue in the future. This may be even more the case when hospital management may expect more of a free market and less dominance by government. In the Netherlands, Nma, the watchdog against anti-competitive behaviour, decreed in September 1999 that agreements on fees between general practitioners, physiotherapists, dentists, veterinarians, etc., were illegal, since these would in future be seen as cartels. It may take time before there is true competition on price between such specialists, but the Nma statement is a clear signal that some of the cosy arrangements have to disappear. Since such actions will result in lower overall costs, the idea may also be adopted in other countries.

A recent publication from the Dutch consumer association made a detailed comparison of a number of hospitals in a region, looking at comfort of rooms, visiting hours, experiences of patients (cure and care), etc. Since these hospitals were within easy reach, consumers had much better information on which to choose the hospital to go to for a particular treatment. No doubt this will increase competition between hospitals.

In sum, the healthcare sector is still competitively not in a dynamic situation. The above five forces analysis indicates that there are already developments that hint at changes in the next decade. The analysis also shows the conditions for the lack of competitive behaviour. If these conditions disappear, the situation will change fundamentally. Managers in the healthcare sector are advised to monitor their developments explicitly to avoid being surprised. Experiences in other parts of the public sector have shown that competition comes much quicker than expected.

## 3.5    *Strategic group analysis in MBA education in the Netherlands*

Strategic group analysis aims to identify organisations with similar strategic traits, that follow similar strategies or that compete on similar bases. In the public sector, management often does not think in terms of competition. We will use the higher education sector in the Netherlands as an example to illustrate the use of strategic group analysis. The reader should be aware that the types of institutions in countries can vary. In the UK, for instance, all polytechnics are now universities, whereas in the Netherlands the distinction is still very much intact. In the Netherlands the MBA degree is not yet founded in legislation, which means that any institution or individual can start an MBA course without legal barriers. In other countries the situation is different.

A useful way to identify strategic groups in MBA education is to use the geographic scope and the orientation of the education provided as the axes of the diagram, as in Exhibit 3.3.

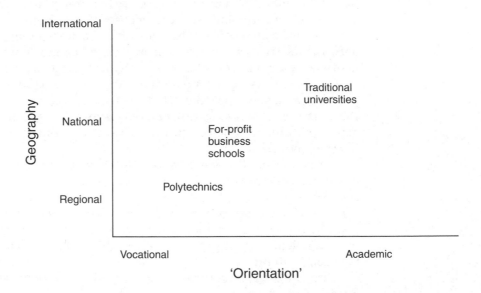

*Exhibit 3.3    Strategic groups in MBA education in the Netherlands*

The exhibit shows three kinds of institutions: traditional universities, for-profit business schools (FPBS) and polytechnics. Some traditional universities are centuries old, but others may have been established less than 40 years ago. A common characteristic is that they have a wide range of faculties, do research, attract students from all over the country, and provide education that is more academic than vocational. A number of the traditional universities have business schools that grant MBA degrees. FPBSs are relatively new, and provide MBA degrees only. Usually they are located close to the centre of the country. The students they attract are often managers who feel the need to broaden their perspective after several years' work experience. Many students have diplomas from a university or a polytechnic. The teaching is not as academic as in traditional universities, but often more academic than in polytechnics. Some of the schools already use the Internet as an integral part of the educational concept. The polytechnics (in the Netherlands named *HogeScholen*) often attract students from the region and provide education aimed more at application of theory than at developing conceptual thinking. Some of the polytechnics provide MBA degrees, in some cases in co-operation with universities from the UK.

The exhibit gives an indication of the direct competitors in MBA education. There is little competition between universities and polytechnics, since the types of training are quite different. Moreover, a university degree is generally valued more highly than one from a polytechnic. MBA education at FPBSs is generally more of the action learning type, which makes it attractive for practising managers. Several of these schools have recently received accreditation by the Dutch Validation Council.

The analysis can also give an insight into the barriers that prevent organisations moving from one group to another (they show the barriers *into* a group) (Exhibit 3.4). This does not necessarily mean that schools would like to move into other groups. For example, if the FPBSs tried to 'enter' the strategic group of traditional universities they would need to build up a reputation in research or innovation, which is not easy for the FPBSs. FPBSs may not be at all interested in doing research, since there would be high costs and little pay-off for the effort. Nor may they may find it easy to attract the right faculty to initiate such moves.

Conversely, for traditional universities to move in the direction of FPBSs may not be possible since the faculty may have difficulty adopting the action learning mode and working with generally much older students. The image of a traditional academic institution may be difficult to shed. Remuneration levels may make it difficult to find the right kind of faculty, since they can make more money outside than inside the business school. Compared to FPBSs, decision making is

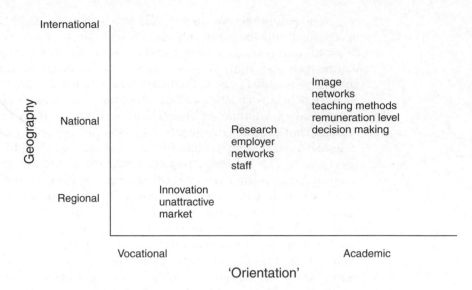

*Exhibit 3.4    Strategic groups in MBA education in the Netherlands: mobility barriers*

often time-consuming. When markets are changing quickly, this may be a serious drawback.

The positioning of the groups can give insight into what might be new competitive space (Exhibit 3.5), particularly if changes in the business environment are 'fuelling' changes in this 'industry' – particularly globalisation and information technology (see also Kim and

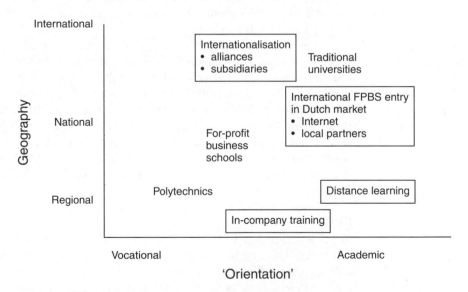

*Exhibit 3.5    Strategic space in MBA education in the Netherlands*

Mauborgne, 1999). One move could be for Dutch business schools to seek more international business. In the case of Bsn International, an FPBS, candidates from South Africa were coached by a faculty in the Netherlands in writing their dissertation. However, the reverse threat of international competitors entering the Dutch market is a major concern. Information and communication technology helps students study at their own place of work or at home, but also enables them to tap into an international network. So American or British schools could provide content over the Internet and local student support through partnerships with Dutch institutions. Finally, developing in-company programmes is also an option for further growth.

## 3.6   Summary

In this chapter we have briefly sketched some global developments that may affect public sector organisations. Often, the frame of mind is that such changes will not seriously affect the public sector or that legislation will take care of the issue. This is dangerous. Who would have thought some 15 years ago that one would not be able to watch a soccer game in the Premier League free of charge on the BBC or any other national public broadcaster? Certainly not managers in charge of then successful not-for-profit broadcasting organisations. Soccer on television was considered a public good that would always be available free of charge. This is no longer the case.

We have sketched how some techniques discussed in *Exploring Corporate Strategy* can be used to identify and analyse the impact of these global changes in the environment on public sector organisations. The PEST analysis is particularly helpful in identifying the global forces that have or will have an impact on the public sector. A number of global trends were briefly described. Scenarios are helpful to develop plausible views of possible futures by combining some of the most important trends from a PEST analysis. Two examples of public sector scenarios were given. The five forces analysis is useful to gain insight into the future structure of parts of the public sector. The analysis was applied to the healthcare sector and led to the conclusion that market forces will be felt more in future, and that organisations in that sector had better prepare strategies for the new context rather than try to block this development. Finally, strategic group analysis was applied to MBA education in the Netherlands. Three strategic groups and mobility barriers for each of the groups were identified, as was strategic space.

Even though these techniques were initially developed for companies, they can help public sector organisations better prepare for a future that will be drastically different from the past, even if one would like to think otherwise.

## References

Becker, G.S. (1999) 'How the Web is revolutionising learning', *Business Week,* 27 December.

Brews, P.J. and Hunt, M.R. (1999) 'Learning to plan and planning to learn', *Strategic Management Journal*, **20** (10), October.

Centraal Plan Bureau (1992a) *Nederland in drievoud*, Sdu Uitgeverij, The Hague.

Centraal Plan Bureau (1992b) *Scanning the Future*, Sdu Uitgeverij, The Hague.

Hawken, P., Ogilvy, J. and Schwartz. P (1982) *Seven Tomorrrows*, Toronto: Bantam Books.

Heijden, K van der (1996) *Scenarios: The Art of Strategic Conversation*, Chichester: Wiley.

Kim, W.C. and Mauborgne, R. (1999) 'Creating new marketspace', *Harvard Business Review*, Jan–Feb.

Naisbitt, J. and Aburdene, P. (1990) *Megatrends 2000*, New York: Avon Books.

OECD (1979) *Facing the Future: Mastering the Probable and Managing the Unpredictable*, Paris: OECD.

Ryan, W.P. (1999) 'The new landscape for nonprofits', *Harvard Business Review*, Jan–Feb.

## Note

1    The aim of developing the OECD scenarios was much wider: how to change the global social and economic fabric for future world-wide prosperity. This shows that in building scenarios it is of great importance to have a clear idea of the purpose of the scenario planning excercise.

# Trust and distrust in regulation and enforcement

## By Les Prince and Ray Puffitt

*This chapter is dedicated to the memory of Jane Louisa Puffitt, BA (Hons), Exeter (18th April 1978–25th March 2000), and her friend Stacey Jacqueline Parry (27th August 1979–25th March 2000), for whom misplaced trust exacted the ultimate price.*

> *I don't trust him. We're friends (Bertolt Brecht,*
> Mother Courage, III)

### Editor's introduction

An important part of the business environment of many organisations is the regulatory environment. This is particularly true for organisations in the public sector or those that have been recently privatised. The need for regulation for these organisations arises for two main reasons – the monopoly or quasi-monopoly status of the organisation and/or the 'sensitive' nature of their 'business' (in relation to impact on the public).

Les Prince and Ray Puffitt describe how regulation is an increasingly important issue between public sector organisations and their partners (public, private or voluntary sector) and between different parts of the same organisation (as customer/supplier philosophies prevail). So there are important links between this chapter and those on partnerships (Sandra Hill, Richard Butler/Jaz Gill) and with the Best Value chapter by Simon Speller.

This chapter explores the important practicalities of successful regulation – in particular the place of trust and distrust in regulation, hence relating strongly to the wider debate about contractual versus relational philosophies within and between organisations.

## 4.1 Introduction

Trust is usually presented as a positive and *defining* quality of good relationships, particularly where there are a strong interdependencies between actors (Coulson, 1998). Thus, trust is an essential aspect of relations between, for example, clients and contractors, purchasers and providers, and, although not always evident, between citizen and state. The immediate advantages of trust between actors is that it reduces the effort of maintaining all aspects of their relationship, allowing each to take some aspects simply for granted. But trust, or more precisely trusting, also bears a price – reduced vigilance. This is an inevitable corollary of trust itself. In many, perhaps most, relationships the loss of opportunity may be a price worth bearing for the sake of the benefits accruing from the relative security of a trusting relationship. In the special case considered in this chapter, however – relations and interdependencies between regulators and those they regulate – the reduction of vigilance implied by trust may actually compromise the ability of regulators to perform their duties fully, thus violating another important area of trust, that between society and those upon whom it relies for its protection. Thus, while it is not pragmatically or ethically acceptable to *advocate* the abandonment of trust as an essential aspect of regulatory relations, there are special aspects of that relationship suggesting that *distrust*, rather than trust, is the more likely quality defining the relationship.

## 4.2   *Defining regulation*

Regulation and control are at the heart of the concept 'government', especially local government. From 1946 onwards, however, with the establishment of various Acts of parliament such as the Local Government Acts of 1954 and 1958, the emphasis and role of local government shifted to the direct provision of services (Puffitt, 1968), and its role as a regulator was downplayed – even treated with some embarrassment. As a consequence, activities such as building control, environmental health and trading standards have been regarded within local authorities and elsewhere as somewhat tangential to the 'real' business of local government, while nevertheless remaining as core activities.

The broad political context of local government, however, has changed dramatically since the early 1980s with the requirement to adopt private sector business practices and values. The consequence of this has been that all local authorities were *required* to investigate ways of reducing direct provision of services, and to move instead towards contractual arrangements with outside businesses. This has placed regulation once more at the heart of local government activity. Once an authority decides, or is forced, to relinquish *in-house* provision of a service and secure it instead through a contract, partnership or by substitution (vouchers or direct payment), they move immediately and directly into a regulatory cycle and process, and therefore monitoring for compliance, burdens placed directly on other parties and *intervention* (whether by persuasion or coercion) become critical components. Where transparency, accountability and probity are primary values, as they are alleged to be in local government, then effective and, where possible, complete monitoring and appropriate interventions become paramount (see, for example, Hutter, 1986).

Using the term 'regulation' in Hood's sense of 'oversight' (Hood and James, 1996), it can be defined as:

> *the process of ensuring that standards and legal requirements are met for specific service or public activities, in order to ensure that policies are fulfilled. ... (Stewart and Walsh, 1992)*

This definition embraces both the role of external regulatory bodies overseeing the activities of *other* organisations and individuals, and also *internal* regulatory roles established by, *inter alia*, public service organisations for activities such as internal audit. Recent proposals from central government (DETR Circular 10/99 DETR, 1999) have given a new impetus to internal regulation (see Sandra Hill's and Richard Butler and Jaz Gill's chapters in this volume). Increasingly, activities are being undertaken under contract, service level agreements or partnership agreements with other agencies, whether private, voluntary or public. With the development of the so-called 'Best Value' regime in local government (see Simon Speller's chapter in this volume) and, at the time of writing, possibly also the health service, and its ultimate extension to other public service organisations, regulation and its attendant bureaucratic baggage is assuming a much higher profile and becoming a strategically more important aspect of public sector life. Moreover, the regulatory cycle is almost identical to the contractual cycle, thus, in many ways, conflating the two activities. This is important. Although contract and regulation are conceptually distinct, there nevertheless remains a significant overlap between the two, and in some cases the regulatory process itself may be characterised *as* a contractual relationship. Discussion about the place, possibility and appropriateness of trust in the regulatory cycle is thus linked irrevocably to the feasibility of moving from so-called arm's-length contractual processes to *relational* contracts. In many ways the issues raised by the two discussions mirror each other precisely.

It might be thought that regulation in the abstract is relatively straightforward:

- Standards defining a desired or desirable state are specified, including, perhaps, premises, processes, equipment, activities or behaviours.
- Inspection, sampling or other means of checking conformity with the standards are used to identify the actual state of affairs.
- Where there is a gap between the actual state and the desired state, then some activity takes place aimed at reducing the gap, using one or more of the available techniques and processes of social and political influence.

This, in crude terms, is the regulatory cycle. But of course it is not so simple in practice. Indeed, over a century-and-a-half of literature and debate demonstrates quite clearly how complex the process actually is (see for example, Lambert, 1963; MacDonagh, 1977; Rhodes, 1981; Hawkins, 1984; Hutter, 1986, 1988, 1997; Kagan, 1989; Kagan and Schultz, 1984). Regulation is not an activity isolated in its application or consequences. As an aspect of the political and *social* life of a community, there are complexities that can occur, some of which are practically impossible to anticipate. This is a direct consequence of being an activity involving *people* who assume and perform the *roles* of regulators and regulatees, not a mere set of interactions between the roles themselves. As a result:

- Specification of standards and definition of the desired or desirable state cannot always be clear and unambiguous.
- Adverse outcomes resulting from non-compliance cannot always be clearly identified.
- Methods of inspection, sampling or other means of gathering data are limited by the availability of resources, including, often, political will in the superordinate body overseeing the regulators themselves.
- There is a critical choice as to how, when and, more important, which of the social influence processes will be used to close the gap. An approach inappropriate to the regulatees may generate more problems than it solves.
- The application of sanctions and penalties alone is unlikely to ensure that the specified standards will be met and maintained, and, more importantly, their use by the regulatory body may preclude the principal from achieving other competing policy objectives of equal or greater importance.
- If the regulator gets close enough to the regulatee, so necessary for the establishment of trust, it runs the risk of regulatory capture, of co-option, collusion and possibly 'corruption' of, at least, its principal values.
- There may be unanticipated adverse consequences of compliance itself that may present problems of their own to the regulators.

It is the issues that flow from these problems that pose the major challenge to all regulatory bodies and expose the four primary dimensions of all regulatory and indeed, contractual activity, namely:

- the level of compliance sought;
- the social influence processes to be adopted;
- the regulatory situation;
- causes of non-compliance.

### 4.2.1 Compliance

The first decision a regulatory authority has to make is what level of compliance it is seeking for a particular regulatory activity, on a scale between 0 and 100%. In practice neither of the extremes on the scale is feasible. Total non-compliance is seldom acceptable, given that the reasons for regulation in the first place are established in laws of some kind. Where any public body, including regulatory bodies, allows such slippage, it can be compelled, by the power of *mandamus*, to fulfil its statutory responsibilities. On the other hand, insisting on *full* compliance has resource implications that few public bodies can muster. All resources are limited, and there is never sufficient regulatory or contract monitoring time to provide *exhaustive* and *continuous* information gathering on compliance.

### 4.2.2 Social influence processes

If, on inspection, it is discovered that a gap exists between the desired or desirable state of affairs, and those that actually exist, then an approach must be made with the intention of persuading the regulatee to take action to close the gap. The *choice* of how to make this approach is crucial, and must be taken in relation to other aspects of the case, including important cultural factors considered later. If an approach is itself *inappropriate*, the result can be a souring of the relationship, making future regulatory activities much more difficult. This is, perhaps, an issue of potent concern in a multi-cultural society.

There are several different models of the basic social influence processes (e.g. Chin and Benne, 1976; Dachler, 1990; French and Raven, 1959; Guest, 1984; Handy, 1985; Hosking and Morley, 1991; Kipnis et al., 1984; Lee and Lawrence, 1985, 1991). For our purposes these can be classified under the following six headings (O'Keefe, 1990):

- persuasion;
- activation of commitments;
- inducement;
- sanction;
- manipulation of the physical, social or informational environment;
- altering the decision-criteria.

From this a *strategy* can be formulated, comprising one or more of the basic influence processes that are considered most likely to bring about the chosen level of compliance (Kagan and Schultz, 1984). This in turn must depend upon the basic characteristics of the regulatory situation, what is known about the regulatee and, ultimately, the kind of relationship that is sought with the regulatee.

### 4.2.3    *The regulatory situation*

There are several aspects to the regulatory situation that must be taken into account in relation to the kind of approach and activity that might be appropriate. Is the situation defined as oriented to the future or the past; is it highly specified or general; is it about behaviour or physical circumstances; and is it about outcomes or processes? If oriented to the past, it may be about checking on whether specific standards or rules have been complied with, for example the design specification for a bridge. If future oriented, it may be about ensuring future safety, quality, and so on, as in, for example, fire prevention and the licensing of private hire vehicles. If highly specified, it will be characterised by detailed instructions and activities to be regulated, such as labelling foodstuffs. General situations are less easily specified, such as standards of care in residential homes. Behavioural situations are, obviously, to do with conduct, as in, for example, care in a nursing home. Regulation of the physical environment includes health and safety at work, such as provision of adequate equipment to deal with fires. Outcomes are to do with specific actions, such as the removal from sale of unfit food, and, finally, processes are related to continuous actions, activities or procedures such as quality assurance systems in factories, or the provision of emergency procedures. The reality of course is that in many regulatory situations there is a mixture of these elements.

### 4.2.4    *Non-compliance*

Non-compliance is not always, or even most often, the result of wilfulness on the part of the regulatee. In some cases the reasons may be simple misunderstanding, and although this is no defence in law, to maintain a healthy regulatory relationship it makes little sense to treat it as if it were the result of criminal neglect. Thus, understanding the causes of non-compliance, where it occurs, is critical to the regulatory relationship. These can be grouped under four general headings:

- Deficiency in knowledge on the part of the regulatee as to what is required. This may be due to unavailability of information, or ambiguity in information about what is required, or simply not knowing what sort of intervention to make to achieve the standards, for example no clear cause and effect relationship.
- Deficiency in resources available to the regulatee, for example inadequate premises, insufficient time, inappropriate equipment, insufficient staff numbers or skills, or insufficient financial resources to meet the standard.
- Deficiency in support from the regulator, for example,

- unclear standards; misleading or unclear instructions leading to uncertainty; inadequate control systems to provide appropriate feedback;
- attaching a different level of importance to the standards compared with that of the regulator;
- obstacles, constraints, internally imposed restraints, perverse rules, all of which create additional difficulty in meeting the required standards.

- Deficiency in intent, in which, although there is no obvious deficiency in knowledge, resources or support, the regulatee fails to comply with the required standards because of

  - different or misaligned values to those of the regulator – a difference in priorities;
  - an imbalance of power, where the power resides with the regulatee rather than the regulator;
  - a desire to act opportunistically to protect and enhance their own interests.

The probing and analysis of these causes of non-compliance will determine whether persuasion-based or sanction-based influence processes should be used to achieve compliance, and this in turn will influence the consequent relationship. However, this analysis must be coupled with experience and knowledge of the pre-existing relationship linked with the nature of the regulatory situation and, more particularly, consideration of the adverse results that may flow for all the individuals involved, any groups of which they are a part, the organisations by which they are employed and the community in general.

What then, in more detail, is the process of regulation? It is to this that we now turn because only when the process is clearly understood can we adequately establish the issues and questions relevant to the identification of situations where trust might be a viable part of the regulatory relationship.

### 4.3 The regulatory cycle

Regulation is a cyclical process (Puffitt, 1968; see Exhibit 4.1). The cycle begins when a critical mass of public opinion about a specific issue or issues persuades government at national or local level to develop a policy response. Policies are broad statements setting out what is to be achieved and how. These are supplemented by *policy instruments*, which are intended to bridge the gap between policy and its implementation. For example, a policy instrument might create a cadre of inspectors, who then may be subject to a *guidance note*, or *circular*, detailing the elements of quality they are to inspect. *Standards* are specifications of quality levels, or constraints to be observed, in

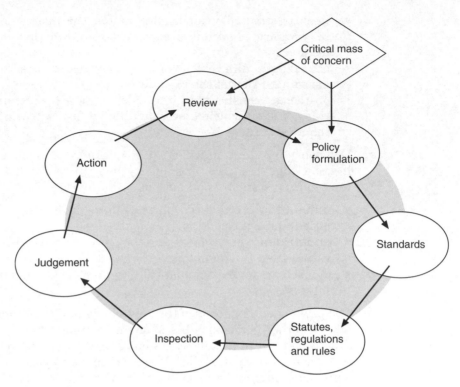

*Exhibit 4.1    The regulatory cycle*

pursuit of policy objectives. For example, a standard might specify space per employee in an office environment, whereas a constraint might specify a time limit within which certain actions must be completed. Such standards and constraints, and sometimes the means by which they are to be met, are then expressed in legislation, either statute or regulation, supplemented by rules formulated either nationally or locally. Taken as a whole, these define the desired or desirable state to be achieved or maintained by regulatory activity.

Inspection, sampling and other methods of gathering information are the means by which an actual state of affairs is evaluated and compared to the situation as specified by policy and standards; in other words, checking whether regulations, rules and standards are being attained. The regulator must then make a judgement about whether the regulatee is complying to a sufficient level. If not, some form of intervention or action is taken to achieve the desired state. Finally, to complete the cycle, knowledge gained during the regulatory process should, theoretically at least, be used to refine and reformulate policy, standards and often also remedial legislation. In this sense the process is not only cyclical, it is also iterative, with the ultimate aim of bringing the initial problems that stimulated the cycle in the first place under legal and administrative control. Nevertheless, it may not entirely eliminate the problems, because some problems are themselves cyclical or chronic. For example, issues of food hygiene can never be fully and finally solved because of the circumstances in which food is prepared.

Not all the stages identified above are necessarily under the control of the regulatory authority or agency. The development of a critical mass of opinion almost certainly proceeds independently of the action or involvement of even national government, even if professional politicians flatter themselves that it is otherwise. Environmental awareness is a case in point. For many years environmental pressure groups, such as Friends of the Earth and Greenpeace, acted on the margins of mainstream politics, and were regarded by many within government simply as a nuisance. In addition, policy may be formulated at national level, with only a limited input from local regulators. Similarly, standards may be set not by central government but by extra-national bodies such as the European Union (EU) or the United Nations. However, even where involvement by the regulatory agency in creating standards and policy is limited, the full regulatory cycle remains as the underlying template of the regulatory process, and therefore needs to be understood because it *illuminates* that process. Moreover, each stage in the regulatory cycle needs to be considered in its own right.

### 4.3.1   Critical mass of concern

Throughout the history of government, individual public authorities have often been involved not merely in responding to but also in stimulating concern regarding emerging problems. For example, the Clean Air Movement and the Noise Abatement Movement were both stimulated and given a boost when local authorities passed private act legislation (Puffitt, 1968). Sometimes local authorities have acted as a channel of communication between local and national pressure groups, thereby providing information and ideas upon which national government can build policy. Again, the Clean Air Movement is a case in point.

Today such activities continue in a variety of ways and through a host of forums and are a means whereby national government becomes aware of local problems and pressures which subsequently may require national attention. On the other hand, there is ample evidence in the historical literature of public authorities, at officer or elected member level, acting to suppress emerging protest, either because their own individual interests were implicated, or because such protests were considered to be subversive of the authority's ability to achieve objectives that it considered more important. Nowadays public authorities are supposed to try to match the services they provide to the needs or wants of their citizens (or consumers or 'customers'), thus requiring them to actively engage citizens in their decision making. Furthermore, citizen groups are now able to gather considerable amounts of information, due in no small measure to developments in information technology and computing, thus reducing their dependency on either the elected members or professional officers of an authority. In addition, many are developing sophisticated ways of using the media to expose their problems, including those they have with their local authority, and thus the opportunity for public authorities to suppress citizens' voices and interests is very much reduced. The information revolution will in the long run force (sometimes reluctant) public authorities to be much more responsive to problems in their communities. The central point here is that the development of a critical mass of concern is a necessary condition for the regulatory process to begin. Perhaps with further developments in information technology this critical mass may be achieved at a faster rate than hitherto.

One other aspect of critical mass needs to be noted here. This is what might be called the *loss* of critical mass. Clearly, over time social, cultural and political concerns change and develop. Thus, over time public concern over particular issues may diminish, until, perhaps, they cease to be an issue at all. In such circumstances, standards and regulations may become outdated, such that attempts to enforce them *themselves* become a matter of concern. In such a case the critical mass of public concern may serve to change, or abolish altogether, regulations and standards that were once regarded as important.

### 4.3.2   Formulation of policy

Often overlooked, but again a necessary condition, is that policy needs to be formulated with a view to *implementation*. There is nothing so useless as a policy that cannot be implemented, no matter how laudable. Much of the current debate on EU directives, for example, is not about whether or not they are laudable but whether they are attainable or realistic in the context of the United Kingdom (e.g. Alliston et al., 1993). If unattainable policies *are* formulated, the regulators may find themselves in an untenable position. At the very least they will lose credibility, which is essential for maintaining any basis of influence, as opposed to mere coercion (Aronson, 1988; Blackwell and Seabrook, 1993; Brown, 1963; Brown, 1965; Coulson, 1998; Gambetta, 1988; Kramer and Tyler, 1996; Luhmann, 1979; Lukes, 1974, 1986; Wrong, 1977); at the worst they will be seen as incompetent, manipulative, cynical, corrupt or authoritarian. They may be forced into trying to enforce the unenforceable. Aggrieved citizens have the power to go to the High Court to obtain an *Order of mandamus* to compel public authority to fulfil statutory duties, and this can sometimes create an entirely indefensible position. For example, if unattainable policies are adopted, say, for the control of markets or Sunday trading, regulators may simply ignore them, but at the risk of *mandamus*. Nevertheless, non-enforcement is a frequent and typical reaction to unrealistic legislative requirements, for example the requirement under the 1936 Housing Act for local authorities to inspect every dwelling in their area from time to time (Puffitt, 1968).

Equally, policy needs to reflect changes in circumstances, particularly the political and social climates. In recent years, with growing concern for the environment amongst the general public, policies that might have been unattainable at one time may now be realistic as they gain both public support and feedback from existing regulatory activities on related issues. Furthermore, ideas about what is and what is not acceptable change. Once heavily littered streets and fouling dogs became generally unacceptable, local authorities developed policies to deal with them. More recently, concerns about drinking alcohol and smoking in public places have begun to exert an influence on local policies. In summary, then, policies need to be:

- clear;
- capable of implementation;
- attainable;
- acceptable to the populace;
- durable, but responsive to changing knowledge and circumstances; and
- cost-effective.

If these conditions are met, then subsequent regulatory action becomes possible.

### 4.3.3 Standards

Standards are fundamental to the regulatory process. These will, in part, determine the way that regulation will be carried out. Broadly speaking, there are three types of standard:

- those that can be measured more or less objectively, such as the accuracy of a weighing machine or some other recording instrument;
- those that can be observed but cannot be the subject of detailed measurement, such as standards of cleanliness in a residential home or restaurant;

- qualitative, judgemental standards, such as the quality of care in a residential home, teaching in a school, commitment to food hygiene in a kitchen.

To be capable of application, they need to be discrete in the sense that they apply only to that which is controllable. For example, while it may be desirable for everyone to have good, positive attitudes towards others, it is actually *not possible* to control a person's attitudes directly, and any standard which required that they are would be completely unworkable. Moreover, it is desirable that those setting the standards state where discretion is possible and where it is not. Failure to do so leads inevitably to the long and costly process of building case law interpretations of ambiguous discretion. For example, it has taken many decades to refine understanding of what the term 'reasonably practicable' might mean in the context of Health and Safety legislation. This leads to confusion for both the regulator and the regulatee. Finally standards need to be stated as clearly and unambiguously as possible so that they may be understood by both the regulators and the regulatees.

### 4.3.4    Statute, regulation and rules

Rules, in their various guises, drive regulatory activity. Rules are different from standards because they specify prescriptions and proscriptions: *what has to be done* or *not done* to attain particular standards. They are constraints or restraints on unfettered action, or stimuli to overcome inaction, on the part of the regulatee, laying down limits within which they must operate and prescribing the conditions under which the regulator may or may not act. Good rules involve the detailed expression of standards which, if not met by the regulatee, will involve action on the part of the regulator. Bad rules, however, serve either to provoke resistance or to cause confusion. As Chinese philosophers noted, over 3,000 years ago:

> *Only such laws as are rooted in popular sentiment can be enforced, while laws violating this sentiment merely arouse resentment.* *(Wilhelm, 1951: 68)*

Statutes, regulations and rules need to be well drafted (see Exhibit 4.2). If they are subject to argument about interpretation, disagreement as to their intent and vagueness about their purpose, thereby encouraging 'creative compliance', then regulation is likely to be ineffectual. Fairness and justice for the regulatee require that they know *explicitly* the requirements that are laid upon them, burdensome though they may be.

Well-drafted statutes, regulations and rules exhibit the following characteristics they are:

- clear;
- capable of being understood by everyone who needs to, both regulator and regulatee;
- as complete as possible;
- practicable;
- acceptable;
- drafted so as to avoid 'creative compliance'; and
- non-discriminatory.

*Exhibit 4.2    Statutes, regulations and rules*

### 4.3.5    Inspection

The purpose of inspection is 'fact'-finding, or more generally research. This involves gathering information on the matters subject to regulation using a variety of methods, each having their origins in social research methodology (see Exhibit 4.3).

Inspection may be *open* in the sense that an appointment may be made in advance to undertake an inspection. It may also be *covert* as, for example, in the purchase of a product by a trading standards inspector to check whether required standards are being maintained or met. Or it may be *randomly episodic* to prevent regulatees from predicting when an inspection is likely to take place.

A key aspect of inspection is the degree to which it involves contact with the person or persons being regulated. In some cases, inspectors or contract monitors can gather information without any significant interaction with the regulatee. The sampling of food, air, water, and so on, are good examples. In other cases, such as inspection of a residential home, much of the information will be, and can only be, provided by the regulatee, by the servants of the regulatee, or by service users. The degree of interaction necessary may well determine the kind of social influence process that may used if subsequent to inspection some form

- observation;
- reviewing policies, records, processes, accounts;
- interviews;
- questionnaires;
- sampling;
- collection of statistics; and
- complaints and incidents data.

*Exhibit 4.3    Inspection methods*

- accurate;
- consistent across cases;
- equitable;
- relevant;
- focused;
- regular or purposefully random;
- cost-effective; and
- manifestly seen to be objective.

*Exhibit 4.4    Features of good reports*

of enforcement notice needs to be issued. It also has a considerable impact on the question of whether or not a relation of trust is feasible or necessary, or, indeed, if it might hinder the process of regulation.

Accurate recording of the information gathered is a crucial part of the process of inspection, because it ensures both that a clear history of a situation can be developed and that objectivity, insofar as this is possible at all, can be demonstrated should there be a later challenge. Accurate records are also essential to maintain levels of fairness and equity, for both regulators and regulatees.

Reporting is a further aspect arising from inspection in the simple sense that information needs to be put into a form in which it can be used and understood by both the regulatee and those who may wish to judge the regulator. This is part of the way in which inspectors and their support staffs are themselves held accountable. Accuracy is again important so that comparability in the approaches of differing inspectors can be ensured, and to avoid both inconsistency within and between regulatory bodies, and *charges* of inconsistency which are sometimes made against regulators (see, for example, Alliston et al., 1993; Genn, 1993; Hawkins, 1984; Wakely et al., 1994).

In such cases reports are likely to take a standard format (this may even be itself statutorily required). In other cases the type of inspection and the nature of the report will vary with circumstances and purpose, as, for example, in the inspection of a school. But, whatever form subsequent reports take, they should all demonstrate some fundamental features that, broadly, encompass the principles of clarity, simplicity and fairness (see Exhibit 4.4).

It is worth noting here that the whole issue of checking performance and enforcing standards is important in establishing so-called 'best value' regimes (see Simon Speller's chapter in this volume).

### 4.3.6    Judgement

The task of judgement is separate from that of inspection and the other means of gathering information. Essentially this is a stage of *data interpretation* in which the information that has been gathered must then be used to reach a decision about whether or not standards are being achieved or maintained. In some cases the judgement may be relatively straightforward, as when the data are simple statistical records. However, frequently the most important aspects of regulation are about things that cannot easily be measured, and these are often open to differing interpretations. Even with statistical data there remains an irreducible element of interpretation. (For an amusing treatment making important points about this issue see Huff, 1973. More conventional treatments can be found in Moore, 1980 and Waddington, 1977.) Great care, therefore, is required in these cases, both because of the need for fairness and consistency, and because conclusions need to be both justifiable and justified. Furthermore, in such cases the possibility of complaint or appeal is relatively high, and the strength of the evidence will be crucial in determining what intervention to make.

### 4.3.7  Action

Even in areas that are subject to tight statutory or contractual control, it is rare for there to be only one choice of action open to the regulatory authority. Having made a judgement based upon the information gathered during inspection, the regulator needs to decide what sort of action, if any, is appropriate. The first decision, therefore, is between action and inaction: is there a gap between the actual state and the desired state, and if so is it significant enough as to be regarded as a problem? It may be *so* insignificant as to make it perfectly sensible not to take action because, for example, the effort involved in closing the gap would not be worth the gain. Furthermore, taking action over a trivial 'offence' might also critically damage the reputation of the regulators rather than enhance it. Thus, this is a critically sensitive decision that requires careful consideration of the possible adverse results (the risks) that might, or might not, follow for the community if the gap is not closed.

If intervention is considered appropriate, then, as indicated earlier, a range of 'social influence' processes are available to help secure compliance (Kagan, 1989; Kagan and Schultz, 1984).

### 4.3.8  Review

The regulatory cycle needs to be a *learning* cycle. There is little point in securing compliance with standards that are unacceptable to society or out of date, especially when resources are constrained. Public perceptions, tastes and the law itself all change, however slowly. The review process involves assessing how effective a particular regulatory policy has been in meeting community needs or wants.

It may be that a particular set of regulations do not meet the changing needs of society, as when, for example, planning regulations were relaxed in enterprise zones. Equally, the authorities may decide in the light of public concern that certain situations need tighter regulation. For example, regulations on residential establishments have tightened in recent years as they have in many areas of food hygiene and food safety.

The work of those involved in regulation has traditionally been a valuable source of information for legislators and others, because over time they build up detailed knowledge, derived from direct practice, about the appropriateness and workability of legislation and the achievement of policy objectives in practice, and about emerging issues that may require remedial action. It is important that the regulatory authority has access to such information *and develops a systematic approach* to harnessing it to assist it in its contribution to the governance of the community. Such information is also critical to central government, because it provides important insights into whether, and how successfully, policy objectives are being met and whether there is a need for the redrawing of statutes, regulations, rules, notes of guidance, and so on.

## 4.4    *Trust or distrust?*

The relationship between a regulator and, for want of a better word, a regulatee is not voluntary, but enforced. It is a relation of interdependency in that the regulatee has no choice but to trust that the regulator will act in good faith and not abuse his or her position of power, and the regulator needs at some level to trust that the regulatee is being truthful and honest in turn. But, there is an essential quality to the regulatory relationship that implies not trust but *dis*trust as a defining feature. To understand this we need a working definition of the concepts. This is not altogether straightforward because, like so much else relating to the social life of people, it is not easy to capture every important nuance in a single definition (Kramer and Tyler, 1996). Nevertheless, although one might quibble with all its elements, the definition constructed by Mishra (1996), given in Coulson (1998: 14), is adequate for most of our present purposes:

> *Trust is one party's willingness to be vulnerable to another party based on the belief that the latter party is: competent; open; concerned, and reliable.*

For the regulatory relationship the aspect stressing the 'willingness to be vulnerable' is most important. However, it is also worth stressing that this willingness is based on an *active* consideration of the gains and losses that might arise in the situation, and *active* monitoring of whether trust is reciprocated; if it is *not* reciprocated it is unlikely to be maintained or maintainable. It is essential to realise that those who are being regulated are not merely passive pawns in the game of regulation, but are intelligent actors in their own right (Hosking and Morley, 1991), capable of construing the situation, making sense of it, and *taking action* on the basis of what and how they understand it. This is particularly important in situations where there are asymmetrical *authority* relations (Prince, 1998), as they are almost by definition in the regulatory relationship. But it is perhaps also important to note here that many of those subject to regulation also have their own resources, political and economic, which they can deploy to redress the asymmetries inherent in their relationships with the regulators. It is also important to note that the decision to trust another is, to a very great extent, a decision made under conditions of uncertainty; no one can ever be fully certain that their trust will not be violated.

### 4.4.1   Misplaced trust

Misplaced trust – trusting in those who cheat or betray – always has negative consequences. In war, it might be pointless deaths, lost opportunity, a battle lost. In peace, it might be financial loss, poor health or being cheated, and so on. In contract, it could mean the need for redress in the civil courts or the loss of reputation. In regulation, the adverse consequences may endanger the public health of whole communities or their economic well-being.

Regulators are appointed to act on behalf of society to control or prevent that which society, or more precisely *its legislators*, considers unacceptable and offensive. Given that trust implies, as noted at the beginning of the chapter, a reduced vigilance or lowering of monitoring, inappropriate or misplaced trust, therefore, carries the extra consequence that it may prevent regulators from establishing appropriate levels of influence or control over that which offends society, and for which they have been appointed to exercise oversight. The reduction of vigilance implied by trust allows those who are trusted the leeway to cheat – and this is the importance of the clause highlighting voluntary vulnerability in the definition of trust given earlier. It is therefore not surprising that distrust rather than trust might be both the more commoner and, according to some, a possibly more prudent response of regulators towards those whom they regulate.

### 4.4.2   Cultural aspects

Trust and trusting are, importantly, culturally bound (Hofstede,1994; Newman, 1998; Trompenaars, 1993). Gender, appearance, ethnicity, class, religion, sexual orientation and geographical location all bear

cultural codes of trust and distrust that may be specific to any reference groups or social categories allied to them (Baker, 1981; Harré,
1979; Harré and Secord, 1972; Kelley, 1952; Sherif, 1953; Tajfel, 1981,
1984; Tajfel and Turner, 1979; Turner and Giles, 1981). In each case
the propensity to trust and distrust, and more specifically *whom to*
trust and distrust, may be laid down as an aspect of cultural location
– an essential aspect of affinity to the cultural mores of a group. For
example, regulators dealing with close-knit agricultural communities
have a particular problem – to regulate such communities it is essential to establish their trust, otherwise they are unlikely to receive co-
operation. On the other hand, the means of establishing trust is often
to *join* the community as a member, and that clearly compromises the
ability to regulate because any enforcement notices might be construed
as betrayal. Successful regulation and enforcement *must* be based on a
consideration of such cultural factors, affecting the regulator's choice
of which social influence process to employ when faced with non-compliance. But when trust has not been established, or could be compro-
mised by the actions of the regulator, as noted above, then there is a
clear possibility for distrust, conflict and disorder, and all the negative
consequences that flow from them.

### 4.4.3   Hope and indifference

The choice between the two poles, trust and distrust, is not the only
one available to regulators. On the same continuum as trust and distrust lie intermediate positions that may be called hope and indifference, which in practice may be much more common responses than
either trust *or* distrust, particularly indifference (see Prince, 1988,
1998, for a similar model). For trust demands close *interdependence*, a
feature of relationships that is often overlooked, and it is only where
this is sought or established for psychological, economic, social or technical ends (for example, friend with friend, client with contractor, club
member with club member, principal with agent), or enforced, as with
regulator and regulatee, that the presence of either trust or distrust
becomes an issue of significance. But in the case of the enforced interdependence of the regulatory relationship, both regulators and regulatees may act to reduce their interdependencies, or transform them into
*dependencies*, in order to reduce the burdens implied by the relationship. Hope and indifference on the part of regulators are signs of this
process. These intermediate positions, therefore, need to be explained
even if not defined precisely.

'Hope' is, like trust, a situation of reduced vigilance, coupled with
the desire on the part of the regulator nevertheless to secure compliance with standards and regulations. This is the zealous regulator,
committed to the basic values of the regulatory role, who, recognising

the impossibility of constant, or even adequate, surveillance, due perhaps to the shortage of resources, including time, nevertheless believes that compliance is likely or at least possible.

'Indifference' again refers to a situation of reduced vigilance, but in this case implying a more or less complete withdrawal from the basic values and activities of the regulatory role. This is a situation where regulators, for a variety of reasons, but principally extreme resource restraint, protect themselves and their sanity by manifesting a complete lack of interest in the regulatee until such time as they are able to undertake the appropriate surveillance. It may also occur if repeated attempts at regulation are continuously thwarted, frustrated or undermined in some way. This may occur, for example, in situations where, despite statute, the elected members of an authority make clear their antagonism towards particular regulatory activities, or seek to divert regulators into activities that have political caché for the ruling party group, such as food inspection (see Prince et al., 1997, for an example). It may also occur where it appears that public attitudes render continued high-profile regulation in a particular regulatory sphere no longer valuable, desirable or popular.

With regard to hope and indifference, the principal determinants of which of these characteristics is the most likely response in practice are the level of regulatory resources available compared with the volume of monitoring work to be undertaken, coupled with levels of enthusiasm for and commitment to the values of the regulatory authority. Hope slides into indifference where resources are highly constrained, the volume of work to be undertaken excessively high and commitment to values eroded by the regulatory authority's inability to command sufficient support and resources to function as it was intended. This inevitably leads to increased non-compliance, increased volumes of work for the regulators as a group, and desperation or demoralisation on the part of the individual regulator. It is the classic negative, downward, self-fulfilling cycle. Where hope or indifference is the dominant response of regulators to high workloads and insufficient resources, clearly they are in no position to perform their regulatory functions adequately. In such circumstances all chances for the regulator to act so as to gain reasonable control and influence over that for which they were appointed to exercise oversight is lost. A terrible price is paid for the lack of trust, because where trust is possible the long-term cost of securing compliance is, relatively speaking, much less, in terms of both physical and human resources.

### 4.4.4  Distrust

Where absolute trust between regulator and regulatee exists, then the cost of ensuring compliance with standards will, theoretically, be less than otherwise, with beneficial results not only to the actors involved, but also to the public purse. Again, this is a direct result of the reduction of vigilance, indeed the reduced *need* for vigilance, where trust is a fully established aspect of a relationship, and respected by all actors. The dilemma is, of course, that the process of regulation is based in part on *deterrence*, *distance* and the availability to the regulator of *sanctions*. The use of the last, or even the implied *threat* of their use, undermines and limits the ability of regulators to establish a relationship based *purely* on trust.

Furthermore, trust does not necessarily ensure success, in any walk of life. That is to say, as noted earlier, no one can ever be fully certain that their trust will not be violated. It may appear cynical, but on observing the world and its workings, whether in academia, the public service, trade, industry, commerce or indeed any other human activity, it is often those individuals or agencies that act always to protect and enhance their *own* interests that ultimately achieve their goals. Indeed, this phenomenon is clearly recognised and articulated in the more recent literatures on the regulation of public service, and results in a hybrid regulatory mechanism which is a mixture of 'competition' with 'mutuality' (Hood and James, 1996).

Distrust can, of course, exist on both sides of the regulatory relationship. But perhaps the more important issue of distrust for processes of regulation is the distrust that may be harboured of the regulatee *by the regulator*. Here we are using the word to denote a circumstance in which opportunistic behaviours such as 'actively seeking self-interest with guile' are not merely anticipated but *expected* from the regulatee. It also covers fears of co-option by regulatees; the fear that if circumstances permitted, and the opportunity arose, the regulatee might seek to subvert the regulator by co-option, gain their collusion in concealment of their non-compliance, even make active attempts to corrupt them.

More than this, the greatest danger, at least in the view of many regulators, would be that the risk and the adverse results for the community following from a reliance on trust alone, or, worse, on naive or misplaced trust, is so great that only in the rarest regulatory situation can a *purely* trusting relationship be considered prudent or feasible. Which amounts to saying that distrust is pragmatically a better approach for regulators to adopt.

The crucial question then becomes what might the circumstances be where trust, rather than mere hope, indifference or distrust, becomes possible? To pursue this question further one has to refine and explore the basic elements of regulatory activity – the regulatory cycle, situation, choice and relationship, considered above – with a view to identifying the circumstances in which trust might be a valid *strategy* for regulators, and where it is not. For any regulatory authority this must be the starting point for discussion of trust in the regulatory relationship with those they regulate. The acid test is its effectiveness in securing compliance with regulations and standards, and in minimising any adverse results flowing from non-compliance to the community at large. Mere convenience for the regulators is insufficient grounds for the decision.

### 4.4.5   *Identifying the circumstances for trust and distrust*

One method for deciding where trust might be appropriate is the Maslin Multi-Dimensional Matrix developed by the authors (see the chapter by Prince and Puffitt in this volume). This is essentially a device for identifying and analysing significant dimensions underlying particular strategic decisions. The primary aim of the analysis is to identify where there is a good match, as opposed to a mismatch, between the organisation and what it provides, and elements of the relationship the organisation has to its environment. In other words, it identifies the 'matching service linkages'. The significant dimensions of the relationship between regulatory authority and the regulatee that have emerged from the earlier discussions (see Exhibit 4.5) can be located on the axes of the Maslin Matrix (see Prince and Puffitt in this volume), and thus provide a basis for analysis of the question posed earlier about when a trusting approach is appropriate, and when it is not. Plotting each of the dimensions individually against the axes 'trust, hope, indifference and distrust' reveals a relatively clear pattern (see Exhibits 4.6 and 4.7), although it should be emphasised that this pattern would benefit from further empirical investigation.

---

- level of compliance sought;
- availability of regulatory resources;
- specificity of standards;
- clarity of cause and effect;
- degree of non-compliance;
- significance of adverse results;
- strength of evidence;
- cause of non-compliance;
- risk of concealment, co-option, collusion or corruption;
- skills of persuasion and influence;
- skills of sanction and enforcement;
- pre-existing relationships; and
- desired future relationships.

---

*Exhibit 4.5   Dimensions of the relationship between regulators and regulatees*

Distrust is more likely when:

- a high level of compliance is sought but a low level of regulatory resources is available;
- cause and effect relationships are uncertain and therefore the regulatee can take action to maximise their own interests;
- standards are non-specific, involving behaviour rather than more concrete outcomes;
- a high degree of non-compliance is a common pattern among those who are to be monitored;
- the adverse results for the community as a result of non-compliance are highly significant;
- the strength of evidence is low, thereby allowing latitude to the regulatee to evade or obscure their real intent;
- the cause of non-compliance arises from a deficiency in intent on the part of the regulatee, occasioned by having different values, priorities or objectives to those of the regulator, rather than a simple deficiency in knowledge, resources or support;
- the risk of concealment, co-option or corruption is high;
- the regulator possesses low skills in the techniques of persuasion but has high skills in the use of sanction;
- there is a poor pre-existing relationship between regulator and regulatee; and
- the regulator is unconcerned about the quality of any possible future relationship.

*Exhibit 4.6    Distrust more likely*

There are, of course, many regulators who would suggest that the combination of characteristics denoting situations where trust might be appropriate (Exhibit 4.7) are, in practice, fairly rare. To quote from a long-standing and highly experienced regulator, 'fair law enforcement coupled with the extensive use of sanctions is overwhelmingly more effective and, more importantly, cost-effective, than any other approach that is available. When I took office I inherited an excellent team of people who had been giving advice, assistance and support for years and who could "trust and persuade for England". The consequences of this was that it was almost impossible to find any regulatee that complied with any of the legislation, let alone all of it. I have no doubt whatsoever that distrust and sanction work and that in the vast majority of cases, trust and persuasion do not' (private letter to Ray Puffitt).

In the terms introduced at the beginning of the chapter, this amounts to saying that, given the uncertainties involved, specifically

Trust is more likely when:

- a low level of compliance is sought and where there is a high level of regulatory resources available to monitor non-compliance;
- there is clarity of cause and effect;
- there is low specificity in the standards required;
- there is a low degree of non-compliance among those regulated;
- there is low significance in the adverse results flowing from non-compliance;
- there is considerable strength of evidence when non-compliance is found;
- non-compliance is due to deficiencies in knowledge, resources or support from the regulatee;
- the risk of concealment, and so on, is low;
- the regulator possesses substantial skills in persuasion as opposed to the use of sanction;
- there is a good pre-existing relationship; and
- the intention is to maintain a good relationship for the future.

*Exhibit 4.7    Trust more likely*

the uncertainties about the extent to which regulatees can be trusted not to 'cheat', so to speak, and given that the consequences of non-compliance might be very severe for the community, the only reasonable response on the part of regulators is to be almost hyper-vigilant in their oversight of regulatees. In other words, distrust is the only realistic response. The irony, of course, is that because distrust implies *increased* vigilance, this also implies increased strain on the regulatory system, specifically the regulators themselves and the resources, both physical and psychological, that they can bring to bear. In turn, this would exacerbate the problems of hope and indifference (and perhaps even of despair) amongst regulators.

## 4.5 Conclusions

In this chapter we have tried to consider the role and importance of trust in regulatory relationships. It is clear that, where it is possible, trust confers considerable benefits on all parties to the relationship, both regulators and regulatees, particularly in that it reduces the extent to which vigilance is required for the maintenance of the relationship, allowing all actors to take certain and specific features for granted. The particular circumstances of the regulatory relationship, however, suggest that, at least for the regulators, *distrust*, rather than trust, is the more likely defining characteristic of the relationship. Trust, properly speaking, allows a situation where either party in a relationship is allowed the *opportunity* to cheat, even if they never actually do so. But the consequences of allowing this situation in relation to regulations formulated, at least ostensibly, for the benefit of the community and its citizens could be significantly detrimental to the well-being of that community. For regulators committed to the basic values of regulation, and the ethos of protection for the citizenry, this is too high a price to pay, and the more pragmatic approach, therefore, is one of distrust. Ironically, the increased vigilance implied by distrust also implies an increased stress on the regulatory system itself.

On balance, while trust is clearly a desirable feature of most relationships, the citizen might prefer that those who regulate on their behalf be skilled and practised in the art of distrust rather than trust, for imprudent kinship with the latter may well result in no more than a 'dance with the devil' at the citizen's expense. On the other hand, it is worth reflecting that those who regulate, and those who are regulated, are themselves citizens, and in this regard to consider the words of Catullus:

*Trust, like the soul, once gone is gone forever.*

## References

Alliston, G., Bradley, R., Cullen, J., Denness, J., Murphy, A., Williams, K. and Page, M. (1993) *Review of the Implementation and Enforcement of EC Law in the UK*. Report commissioned by the President of the Board of Trade. London: Department of Trade and Industry.

Aronson, E. (1988) *The Social Animal*, 5th edn, New York: W.H. Freeman.

Baker, P.M. (1981) 'Social coalitions', *American Behavioral Scientist*, **24**, 633–647.

Blackwell. T. and Seabrook, J. (1993) *The Revolt Against Change*, London: Vintage.

Brown, J.A.C. (1963) *Techniques of Persuasion: From Propaganda to Brainwashing*, Harmondsworth: Penguin.

Brown, R. (1965) *Social Psychology*, London and New York: Collier Macmillan and Free Press.

Chin, R. and Benne, K.D. (1976) 'General strategies for effecting change in human systems', in W.G. Bennis, K.D. Benne, R. Chin and K.E. Corey (eds), *The Planning of Change*, 3rd edn, New York: Holt, Rinehart & Winston.

Coulson, A. (ed.) (1998) *Trust and Contracts: Relationships in Local Government, Health and Public Services*, Bristol: Policy Press.

Dachler, H.P. (1990) 'Ecological thinking as a relational phenomenon: integrating the contradictory cultures of the sexes'. Paper given to International Conference on Social Organisational Theory, *From*

*Methodological Individualism to Relational Formulations,* St. Galen, Switzerland, August.

DETR (1999) *Implementing Best Value: Circular 10/99,* London: Department of the Environment, Transport and the Regions.

French, J.R.P. and Raven, B. (1959) 'The bases of social power', in D. Cartwright (ed.), *Studies in Social Power,* Ann Arbor: University of Michigan Press.

Gambetta, D. (ed.) (1988) *Trust: Making and Breaking Co-operative Relations,* Oxford: Basil Blackwell.

Genn, H. (1993) 'Business responses to the regulation of health and safety in England', *Law & Policy,* **15** (3), 219–233.

Guest, D.E. (1984) 'Social psychology and organisational change', in M. Gruneberg and T.D. Wall (eds), *Social Psychology and Organisational Behaviour,* Chichester: Wiley.

Handy, C. (1985) *Understanding Organisations,* 3rd edn, Harmondsworth: Penguin.

Harré, R. (1979) *Social Being,* Southampton: Camelot Press.

Harré, R. and Secord, P.F. (1972) *The Explanation of Social Behaviour,* Oxford: Basil Blackwell.

Hawkins, K. (1984) *Environment and Enforcement,* Oxford: Oxford University Press.

Hofstede, G. (1994) *Cultures and Organisations: Intercultural Co-operation and Its Importance for Survival,* London: HarperCollins.

Hood, C. and James, O. (1996) 'Reconfiguring the UK executive: From public bureaucracy state to re-regulated public service'. Paper presented to ESRC Conference *Understanding Central Government: Theory into Practice,* University of Birmingham.

Hosking, D.-M. and Morley, I.E. (1991) *A Social Psychology of Organising,* New York: Harvester Wheatsheaf.

Huff, D. (1973) *How to Lie with Statistics,* Harmondsworth: Penguin.

Hutter, B.M. (1986) 'An inspector calls: the importance of proactive enforcement in the regulatory context', *British Journal of Criminology,* **26** (2), 114–128.

Hutter, B.M. (1988) *The Reasonable Arm of the Law? The law enforcement procedure of environmental health officers,* Oxford: Oxford University Press.

Hutter, B.M. (1997) *Compliance, Regulation and the Environment,* Oxford: Oxford University Press.

Kagan, R.A. (1989) 'Understanding regulatory enforcement', *Law & Policy,* **11** (2), 89–112.

Kagan, R.A. and Schultz, J.T. (1984) 'Criminology of the corporation and regulatory enforcement strategies', in K. Hawkins and J. Thomas (eds), *Enforcing Regulation,* Boston: Kluwer-Nijhoff.

Kelley, H.H. (1952) 'Two functions of reference groups', in G.E. Swanson, T.M. Newcomb and E.L. Hartley (eds), *Readings in Social Psychology,* rev. edn, New York: Henry Holt.

Kipnis, D., Schmidt, S.M., Swaffin-Smith, C. and Wilkinson, I. (1984)

'Patterns of managerial influence: shotgun managers, tacticians and bystanders', *Organisational Dynamics,* Winter, 58–67.

Kramer, R.M. and Tyler, T.R. (eds) (1996) *Trust in Organisations: Frontiers of Theory and Research,* London: Sage.

Lambert, R. (1963) *Sir John Simon, 1816–1904, and English Social Administration,* London: MacGibbon & Kee.

Lee, R. and Lawrence, P. (1985) *Organisational Behaviour: Politics at Work,* London: Hutchinson.

Lee, R. and Lawrence, P. (1991) *Politics at Work,* Cheltenham: Stanley Thornes.

Luhmann, N. (1979) *Trust and Power,* ed. T. Burns and G. Poggi, New York: Wiley.

Lukes, S. (1974) *Power: A radical view,* London: Macmillan.

Lukes, S. (1986) *Power,* Oxford: Basil Blackwell.

MacDonagh, O. (1977) *Early Victorian Government, 1830–1870,* London: Weidenfeld & Nicolson.

Mishra, A. (1996) 'Organisational response to crisis: The centrality of trust', in R.M. Kramer and T.R. Tyler (eds), *Trust in Organisations: Frontiers of Theory and Research,* London: Sage.

Moore, P.G. (1980) *Reason by Numbers,* Harmondsworth: Penguin.

Newman, J. (1998) 'The dynamics of trust', in A. Coulson (ed.), *Trust and Contracts: Relationships in local government, health and public services,* Bristol: Policy Press.

O'Keefe, D. (1990) *Persuasion: Theory and Research,* London: Sage.

Prince, L. (1988) *Leadership and the Negotiation of Order in Small Groups,* Unpublished PhD thesis, Birmingham: University of Aston.

Prince, L. (1998) 'The neglected rules: On leadership and dissent', in A. Coulson (ed.), *Trust and Contracts: Relationships in local government, health and public services,* Bristol: Policy Press.

Prince, L., Campbell, A. and Nanton, P. (1997) *Training for Health and Safety Enforcement.* Health and Safety Executive: Contract Research Report 155/1997, London: HSE Books.

Puffitt, R.G. (1968) *Development of Administrative Controls over Atmospheric Pollution,* Unpublished MA dissertation, University of Kent at Canterbury.

Rhodes, G. (1981) *Inspectorates in British Government,* London: George Allen & Unwin.

Sherif, M. (1953) 'The concept of reference groups in human relations', in M. Sherif and M.O. Wilson (eds), *Group Relations at the Crossroads,* New York: Harper.

Stewart, J. and Walsh, K. (1992) *Influence or Enforcement: The nature and management of inspection and regulation in local government,* London: Local Government Management Board.

Tajfel, H. (1981) *Human Groups and Social Categories: Studies in social psychology,* Cambridge: Cambridge University Press.

Tajfel, H. (1984) 'Intergroup relations, social myths and social justice', in H. Tajfel (ed.), *The Social Dimension, Vol. 2,* Cambridge: Cambridge

University Press; Paris: Editions de la Maison des Sciences de l'Homme.

Tajfel, H. and Turner, J.C. (1979) 'An integrative theory of intergroup conflict', in W.G. Austin and S. Worschel (eds), *The Social Psychology of Intergroup Relations*, Monterey, CA: Brooks/Cole.

Trompenaars, F. (1993) *Riding the Waves of Culture: Understanding cultural diversity in business*, London: Nicholas Brealey.

Turner, J.C. and Giles, H. (eds) (1981) *Intergroup Behaviour*, Oxford: Basil Blackwell.

Waddington, C.H. (1977) *Tools for Thought*, St. Albans: Paladin.

Wakely, R., Williams, T. and Points, G. (1994) *Local Government Enforcement: Report of the interdepartmental review team*. Report commissioned by the President of the Board of Trade, London: Department of Trade and Industry.

Wilhelm, R. (1951) trans. C. Baynes, *I Ching or Book of Changes*, Henley and London: Routledge & Kegan Paul.

Wrong, D.H. (1977) *Power: Its forms, bases and uses*, Oxford: Basil Blackwell.

# 5 Measuring up to the best: A manager's guide to benchmarking

*By Mik Wisniewski*

### Editor's introduction

An important part of competing successfully in the private sector is under-standing what best-in-class performance is all about and then trying to match or exceed that performance. Over the past decade this has led to a strong emphasis on benchmarking as a key management activity, as discussed in Chapter 4 of *Exploring Corporate Strategy*. This chapter by Mik Wisniewski of Audit Scotland takes a practical look at how benchmarking can be undertaken in the public services and how it is an essential ingredient of the public sector's efforts to improve quality of service or provide 'best value', as discussed in the chapters by Simon Speller and David Herbert which follow.

## 5.1 Introduction

Continuous improvement is a key element in both the Commission's Performance Management and Planning audit and the government's Best Value framework. Councils must demonstrate a commitment to identifying and introducing performance improvements in a significant and meaningful way. A critical part of such a commitment is ensuring that managers are constantly searching for better practice in other organisa- tions – both public and private sector – that can be integrated into their own service delivery.

This means that managers throughout every council need to be *benchmarking*. Councils thus need to ensure that they understand what benchmarking is about, that they are developing appropriate benchmarking strategies and that they are using benchmarking to drive continuous improvements in performance and service delivery. Although many councils have benchmarking activities under way, these vary considerably in approach, purpose and extent. As Keady (1998) comments:

> *Benchmarking – like many things tried in local government – is frequently misunderstood and has consequently been done badly.*

## 5.2   What is benchmarking?

There are probably as many definitions of benchmarking as there are organisations engaged in it. Benchmarking is best thought of as a structured and focused approach to comparing with others how you provide services and the performance levels you have achieved. The purpose of such comparison is to enable you to identify where and how you can do better. Benchmarking is concerned with finding and implementing better practice and performance wherever it is found.

This is not to say that you should be looking simply to copy approaches and methods used by others. Research has shown that such an approach rarely works because every organisation is different to every other in some critical way – in terms of leadership, culture, attitudes, resources, customer needs.

> *Benchmarking does not mean copying what other people do; it should be a learning process, challenging existing ways of working and identifying step-by-step changes that can close the gap between current performance and best practice. (LGMB 1997)*

Rather, you should be looking to understand what makes another organisation 'better' than your own in terms of service delivery or in carrying out specific activities. This will then enable you to assess how to improve your own performance so that you also can provide best practice service.

Equally, benchmarking should not be seen as a one-off, or quick-fix, solution to current problems or concerns. Benchmarking is a continuing search for, and implementing of, performance improvement. It requires considerable effort, motivation and good management to be effective but it does offer considerable payback.

> *Councils should ensure that a benchmarking approach is being developed throughout the organisation which not only includes examination of comparative data but also critically reviews service delivery and management processes. (Accounts Commission for Scotland, 1998b)*

And as CIPFA state

> *The cost of benchmarking need not be great; it need not involve external costs and it can be relatively quick and simple. Many organisations report at least a tenfold payback. (CIPFA, 1996)*

## 5.3 Benchmarks or benchmarking?

There is a degree of confusion for many managers as to what bench-marking actually involves. One of the most common misconceptions is that benchmarking is simply about comparing numerical performance *levels* across different organisations, with the notion of performance indicators and league tables then coming to mind. Comparison of such performance levels is important, but these numerical measures are best referred to as *benchmarks*.

> *League tables do not necessarily show whether a local authority is successfully meeting their customers' needs, responding to local priorities or performing efficiently or effectively. (LGMB, 1997)*

However, *benchmarking* is about more than simply comparing numer-ical levels of performance across councils. It is about understanding *why* there are differences in performance between organisations, and this involves looking in detail at the way services are delivered and managed and at the processes and activities involved in service deliv-ery that lie behind the benchmark measures of performance.

> *Benchmarking is much more than just focusing on performance measures since, at best, these will only serve to identify gaps that exist between one organisation and another. (Keady)*

The distinction between the use of benchmarks and the use of bench-marking is a critically important one. As a manager you will *not* be able to identify necessary performance improvements simply by look-ing at benchmarks. To deliver continuous improvement it is necessary to ensure you are actually undertaking benchmarking – comparing and challenging existing performance levels, practices and methods of carrying out activities and service delivery.

## 5.4 Why is benchmarking important?

> *Benchmarking is an integral part of best value. (Keady)*

Benchmarking is a structured approach to finding ways to improve your organisation's performance so that it conforms to – or moves towards – best practice. Any effective manager in any organisation is interested in continuous performance improvement: improving service delivery, reducing costs, improving efficiency, increasing effectiveness, increasing customer satisfaction. What frequently prevents a manager from improving performance is lack of knowledge: not realising that things could be 'better', not knowing how much 'better' things could be or not understanding exactly how to make performance 'better'.

Councils must adopt benchmarking so that their managers are looking constantly for better practice that they can adapt into their own service delivery. As such it can – and should – be used throughout the entire organisation at all levels of service delivery.

Benchmarking as a structured approach in the western economies was first developed by Xerox in part of their photocopy manufacturing business. The immediate catalyst for the company was that their technology patent rights had expired and they were rapidly moving from an effective monopoly position to one of fierce competition. As one of their managers commented:

> *Our patent rights ran out. We were attacked very heavily ... by American competition and then of course by the Japanese. We saw our market share decline from virtually 100 per cent to as low as 17 per cent. (FT/Longmans 1994)*

Xerox developed an approach to benchmarking to identify best practice methods and processes and to integrate these wherever possible into its own operations. The benchmarking investigation revealed a number of major performance gaps:

- Competitors were able to sell copiers more cheaply than Xerox could manufacture them.
- Assembly-line rejects in the manufacturing process were 10 times higher than some of the competition.
- Defects in finished products were 7 times higher than the competition.
- It took the company twice as long as the competition to bring in new designs and technical developments.

The critical issue for the company was that prior to benchmarking they were not aware of many of these performance gaps and how much better they needed to be to be truly competitive. Done properly, however, benchmarking can bring major benefits to performance and competitiveness. As a result of benchmarking Xerox were able to:

- increase customer satisfaction by 40 per cent over 4 years;
- increase incoming parts acceptance from suppliers to 99.5 per cent of goods received;
- reduce stock levels by 66 per cent;
- double engineering drawings per person;
- reduce service labour costs by 30 per cent.

## 5.5 *What are the different approaches to benchmarking?*

There is no single way to approach benchmarking but it is important to realise that there are different *types* of benchmarking that can be undertaken and there are different *ways* to benchmark. It is important to ensure that you are adopting the most appropriate type of benchmarking to meet your own needs and that you carry out this benchmarking in the most appropriate way.

To illustrate these we shall consider two managers who wish to develop benchmarking as part of their performance management and review. One is in charge of a local leisure centre. The second is a manager in the Personnel Department with particular responsibility for recruitment.

### 5.5.1   Types of benchmarking

**Data benchmarking**

Data, or metrics, benchmarking is not strictly benchmarking as such but an analysis of benchmark data (Exhibit 5.1). Data benchmarking involves numerical comparison of your performance in key areas (such as cost, quality, outcomes, customer satisfaction) against some benchmark. The benchmark might be a standard or target that has been established (internally, a nationally defined target or a target set by a professional advisory group) or it may be reported performance of other service providers. In the public sector such data benchmarking is often based on published performance indicators. It may also involve ranking organisations in league tables.

The personnel manager may express interest in benchmarks such as:

- recruitment costs;
- staff turnover levels;
- levels of application for vacancies;
- time taken to fill a vacancy;
- retention rates for new employees.

The leisure centre manager might be interested in benchmarks such as:

- operating costs;
- attendance levels;
- participation rates;
- customer satisfaction levels.

Data benchmarks can be useful in comparing performance with other organisations or between different parts of the same organisation. They provide a yardstick as to how you're doing compared with others

*Exhibit 5.1*   *This is a* benchmark *but it's not* benchmarking

|  | Our service | All councils |
|---|---|---|
| Average number of people per hour using |  |  |
| – leisure pools | 64.4 | 52.0 |
| – traditional pools | 32.3 | 28.9 |
| Income as percentage of operating expenditure | 24.7 | 35.3 |

in key performance areas and can be particularly helpful as a diagnostic tool – helping you to highlight areas where you appear to be doing better or worse than others.

However, such data benchmarks are really just the start of benchmarking for performance improvement. Whilst such data will help you identify performance gaps – *my centre's operating costs are 20 per cent higher than anyone else's* or *our staff turnover levels are 60 per cent lower than the average* – they do not in themselves help identify the causes of differences in performance or indicate how to improve performance. Indeed they are likely to raise more questions than answers – questions that the other types of benchmarking try to answer.

> *This kind of benchmarking has been used ... to help assess current performance and point up areas for investigation. (LGMB, 1997)*

It is also essential that the performance measures that are used for data benchmarking are not simply the ones that will make you look good but are realistically the ones that are of critical importance to your particular service. The Balanced Scorecard approach will be useful for managers trying to identify what these key measures are for their service area (Accounts Commission 1998a).

## Process benchmarking

In any organisation service is provided through completion of a set of interrelated processes. Process benchmarking involves the comparison and measurement of a specific process against a similar process in your own or another organisation. The purpose behind this is to help you decide how your own process might be improved.

> *Benchmarking involves an understanding of the processes and practices in your own organisation. (Keady)*

To deliver a best value service *all* the individual processes that make up the service delivery chain need to conform to best practice. You may have a state-of-the-art leisure centre with the lowest operating costs in the country but if some key processes are not conforming to best practice – the time taken to process customers through reception/admission for example – the service as a whole cannot be either. Process benchmarking involves developing a detailed understanding of how you complete a particular, specified process and comparing what you do, how you do it and what performance levels you achieve in that process with another organisation. Again, the purpose of process benchmarking is to see, by learning from others, how you can improve your own processes.

The concept of a process is a critical one for benchmarking. The

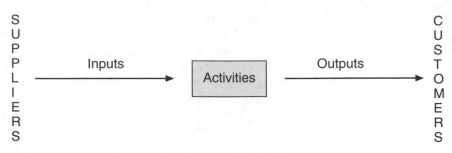

*Exhibit 5.2    A process*

technical description is that a process is a set of activities which con-
vert inputs into outputs which meet agreed customer requirements
(Exhibit 5.2). Every organisation delivers its services to its customers
through a set of interrelated processes which together make up a complete service delivery chain.

The leisure centre, for example, will have processes to ensure
that:

- publicity and advertising occurs;
- buildings and facilities are available;
- trained and qualified staff are available;
- customer services are provided;
- repairs and maintenance take place.

Similarly, key processes for the recruitment team will include:

- producing job descriptions;
- advertising vacancies;
- dealing with applications;
- organising interviews;
- organising induction of new staff.

There are three groups of processes common to any organisation
(Exhibit 5.3):

- *Core, or customer facing, processes.* Those processes that directly affect
  the customer (who might be external to the organisation or internal).
  Such processes are likely to involve the provision of customer service
  and service delivery in some form.
  For the leisure centre such processes will include:
  - dealing with customer bookings and enquiries;
  - customer reception;
  - provision of customer services.

  For the recruitment function core processes might include:
  - sending details to applicants;

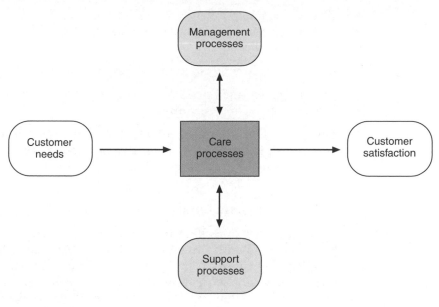

*Exhibit 5.3    Types of processes*

- arranging interviews;
- informing applicants of the outcome;
- agreeing terms and conditions.

> *Tower Hamlets has identified over 20 key processes suitable for benchmarking, including council tax collection, purchasing, case-load management, electoral registration, housing allocations. (Foot, 1998)*

- *Management processes.* Those processes required for effective management including strategy and planning, performance management and review. The leisure manager, for example, will be involved in the process of service planning and of monitoring the service's performance.
- *Support or enabling processes.* Those processes which support or help either core or management processes. These will include procurement, supplies management, systems management, financial management, asset management.

The key to successful process benchmarking is to understand and prioritise your processes. Realistically, you cannot benchmark all your processes at one time. It is necessary to decide which processes you will benchmark first and these will normally be those that are most critical to your success as a service provider. For the leisure service manager these might be:

- advertising and publicity;
- providing customer reception service;
- facilities management.

For the recruitment function the key processes might be:

- advertising vacancies;
- effective selective procedures.

The 'what–how' approach detailed in the Accounts Commission for Scotland's publication *The Measures of Success* (1998a) can be helpful in identifying key processes.

### 3 Functional benchmarking

Functional benchmarking involves comparing the structure and performance of an entire function in the organisation with a comparable function elsewhere. You could, for example, benchmark the entire recruitment function rather than simply some of its key processes. Functional benchmarking can be useful for reviewing alternative approaches to providing a service as part of option appraisal. For example, you might benchmark the in-house recruitment function with another organisation that has contracted out to a recruitment agency. This would enable benchmarking of comparable functions being delivered in different ways.

### 4 Strategic benchmarking

Strategic benchmarking is used to compare strategic approaches or initiatives across organisations. Organisations may have some strategic goals which are comparable and comparing approaches to achieving these can be productive. Most organisations, for example, will have a communications strategy of some sort regardless of whether they are public or private sector organisations. They will also have IS/IT strategies that could be benchmarked in terms of different approaches taken by different organisations. The leisure centre, for example, might benchmark its strategies for community participation in leisure. The recruitment function might benchmark its strategies relating to equal opportunities or to positive discrimination.

### 5.5.2   *Where to start?*

Managers and staff starting out on benchmarking can be confused about which level of benchmarking they should begin with. Many organisations start with data benchmarking because such comparisons are relatively straightforward and then move on to process benchmarking. With more experience functional and strategic benchmarking can then be undertaken.

For example, the recruitment manager might undertake data benchmarking of recruitment costs with a number of other councils. This might reveal that current costs are higher than most others'. As a next step the manager might then identify the key processes involved in recruitment and undertake formal process benchmarking with those councils with the lowest costs. This, in turn, might lead the manager to conclude that a major review of the entire function is needed using either functional or strategic benchmarking.

### 5.5.3   Ways of benchmarking

Just as there are different levels of benchmarking, there are different ways to benchmark. The way in which you decide to benchmark (effectively whom you will benchmark against) will be influenced by the type of benchmarking you decide to undertake.

### 1 Internal benchmarking

As the name suggests, this involves benchmarking against other parts of your own organisation and is usually undertaken as part of data or process benchmarking. Comparable processes are usually to be found in other parts of most organisations (notwithstanding the typical comment that '*we're the only ones who do this*') and seeing how someone else in the same organisation undertakes some activity can be productive. Internal benchmarking is particularly useful for multi-site organisations where similar functions may be carried out at the different sites and can help bring all parts of the organisation up to the same level of performance.

For the leisure centre, internal benchmarking might involve comparison with other centres run by the council. For the recruitment function there may be other recruitment teams in the larger departments or divisions within the council. Similarly, discrete processes may be being undertaken in other parts of the organisation. Dealing with customer enquiries, for example, is a process that can be found not just in the leisure centre but in most of the service areas in the council. Similarly, the recruitment team may decide to examine how it deals with written correspondence, a process it will have in common with many other departments and teams.

Internal benchmarking is an easy way of starting as it can be done fairly informally and quickly. It can also have the benefit of sharing good practices and innovation from one part of the council to another as there is likely to be less resistance to change than from 'importing' new practices from outside ('*that'll never work here*').

However, one of the drawbacks to internal benchmarking is that it is likely that most parts of the same organisation will be carrying out similar processes in much the same way (*'that's just the way we do things round here'*). This may limit the opportunity to learn about radically different approaches. As LGMB (1997) comment:

> *It is all too easy for organisations to become introverted and to take comfort from purely internal measurements. Where internal statistics show continuous improvement, and customer surveys give no cause for concern, an organisation can become out of touch with their users and out of line with their peers' costs and performance.*

### 2 Sector benchmarking

Sector benchmarking involves comparing yourself with other organisations in the same service sector. Typically, this will involve comparison with other local authorities – data, processes, functions, strategies. For example, comparing advertising processes in the recruitment sections in other councils or looking at repairs and maintenance costs in other councils' leisure centres. Such an approach allows for comparison with at least part of the outside world. However, there is a danger that this approach by itself can generate a congratulatory, 'cosy club' attitude about relative performance and identifying shared reasons why performance cannot be improved.

### 3 Competitive benchmarking

Competitive benchmarking is a form of external benchmarking which is focused on those organisations that are seen as 'competitors'. Competition may exist in the strict sense of the word where another organisation may be seeking to provide a service that you are currently providing. The in-house recruitment function may benchmark against private sector recruitment agencies. The leisure centre may benchmark against private sector health and fitness centres.

Such competitive benchmarking can be particularly productive at revealing new and innovative approaches to service delivery and achieving performance. However, it can also be difficult to gain access to competitor information – either data benchmarks or details of their processes.

'Competition' may also arise through comparison of your performance levels with those of other organisations even where these are not direct competitors. Customers will be comparing your performance in dealing with their telephone booking at the leisure centre with their bank or electricity company. Job applicants will be comparing the way you deal with their application with other organisations they have experience of.

Benchmarking in this sense can be easier although it implies that you have a detailed knowledge of your customers and an understanding as to which role models they are comparing you with. It requires you to identify who these organisations are and then investigate how they carry out activities and processes and the performance levels they achieve. However, such benchmarking can lead to changes you can implement that directly improve customer satisfaction.

## 4 Best-in-class benchmarking

Again, this is a form of external benchmarking but focusing specifically on those organisations that are judged to be best-in-class in terms of a particular process, function or strategy. Such best-in-class organisations could be in any public or private sector and will not necessarily be in the same business as yours. It is also important to know whom your customers regard as best-in-class.

Some of the best-in-class that Xerox benchmarked against included:

- Walt Disney – staff motivation and training;
- American Express – accuracy of invoicing and billing;
- Marriott Hotels – dealing with customer complaints.

Exhibits 5.4 and 5.5 summarise this section.

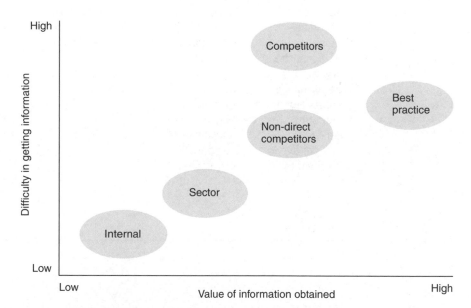

*Exhibit 5.4*     *The trade-off between the difficulty of obtaining information from different levels of benchmarking and the value of information obtained*

*Exhibit 5.5*   *Levels of benchmarking*

| Internal | | Sector | |
|---|---|---|---|
| • Easiest to do<br>• Establishes internal best practice<br>• Least threatening | • Limits focus to the way we do things here<br>• Often limited in practice to larger organisations<br><br>• Internal rivalry may prevent sharing of information and good practice | • Allows for direct comparisons<br>• Often uses already available information<br>• Can be less threatening<br>• Allows monitoring of performance improvements against others in a similar business | • Limited to sector current best practice<br>• Available information may have 'quality' problems<br>• Ignores emerging threats from outside competition<br>• May generate an attitude that we're not much worse than the rest |
| **Competitor** | | **Best-in-class** | |
| • Helps focus on core processes<br>• Helps reinforce the urgency of performance improvement<br>• Identifies current competitive disadvantages | • May be unwilling to share detailed information<br>• Available information may be indirect, third party<br>• May be unwilling to compare processes | • Allows for widest perspective<br>• Best option for identifying innovative practices | • Can be difficult to decide who is best-in-class<br>• Best-in-class may not be UK based<br>• Best-in-class may be suffering from benchmark visit overload<br>• May be difficult to transfer best practice into your own organisation |

### 5.6   How do you get started?

There are four key stages to successful benchmarking:

- planning;
- analysis;
- action;
- review.

#### 5.6.1   Planning

#### 1 Decide what you want to benchmark and why

Benchmarking works best when it is undertaken as a tightly focused project. Individual processes or activities need to be identified and agreed for benchmarking. Benchmarking the whole of Social Work or Roads and Transportation is unlikely to be productive, particularly if you have little current experience of benchmarking. As Keady comments:

> *Time spent in planning and developing a systematic approach will be time well spent. Avoid immediately diving out the door.*

Deciding on the key areas for benchmarking requires an understanding of what your critically important processes and activities are. Benchmarking is intended to tackle important issues with a high value (such as high spend, cost or priority) and a high opportunity for improvement (such as high return, low risk, quick benefit). The definition of 'important' might relate to processes or activities which are critical to:

- survival or development;
- achieving customer satisfaction;
- improving efficiency;
- improving effectiveness.

> *Virtually anything can be subject to benchmarking. It is therefore important to concentrate on those things that are critical to organisational success and the delivery of best value. (Keady)*

Equally, it may be that one process or area has become important because of a recognised need for improvement. It may be that customer complaints about some aspect of your service – leisure centre customers not able to book facilities at the time they want, for example – have increased. Similarly, perhaps through data benchmarking you have realised that some aspect of your performance is considerably worse than another organisation's – perhaps retention rates of new employees in the case of recruitment or high energy costs for the leisure centre.

It is also important to be clear about *why* you are undertaking a benchmarking project. The value of benchmarking lies in identifying the potential for performance improvement and then implementing change to make that improvement happen. Benchmarking should not be used simply to show that your current level of performance is adequate or to justify why you intend to do nothing or because it's seen as flavour-of-the-month.

## 2 Decide what type of benchmarking you're going to start with

Your decision as to whether to benchmark internally, against the rest of the sector, against competitors or against best-in-class will be influenced by a number of factors. Amongst these will be your previous experience in benchmarking and the resources that can be devoted to the project. It is advisable to see these levels of benchmarking as sequential and incremental to your own learning process. That is, to start with internal benchmarking and move on to the other levels as you build up expertise, experience and information.

A logical approach would be to:

- try internal benchmarking first. It's usually an easy way to get started and there are likely to be other parts of the organisation carrying out similar processes to yours.
- try other councils. You will probably have contacts there already, you'll know some of the things they're doing and you'll have some idea of their relative performance compared with your own.
- try other public sector organisations. The NHS, police and fire services, central government agencies will all have comparable processes and activities. They may also have comparable functions and strategies.
- try other organisations which have established a reputation for excellence in some part of their activities, even if these activities are not identical to your own. Such activities and processes may still have much in common with yours, enabling you to learn from others. For example, Chichester District Council benchmarked their system for responsive housing repairs with BT's system for repairing telephone faults.

## 3 Decide who's going to be involved

A variety of people should be involved in benchmarking. You can't benchmark by yourself. It has to involve those staff who are directly involved in the process or activity to help generate ownership of what you are trying to do. It is important to ensure that staff at all levels are involved. At its worst benchmarking can provoke a defensive attitude with staff seeking to justify the current position or query the validity of benchmark comparisons.

You will also need to organise the training and support that those involved in benchmarking will require and the communication that will be needed at all stages of the benchmarking project for those involved and those affected. Without adequate communication the most likely response from staff will be that it's just another cost-cutting exercise that's being imposed from the centre of the council.

You will also need to consider:

- *The use of external consultants*. For a variety of reasons you may wish to consider the use of external consultants in the benchmarking strategy. Whilst this will increase the visible costs of benchmarking, they can bring useful benefits in terms of:
  - instant expertise and experience;
  - access to other benchmarking data;
  - contact with potential benchmarking partners;
  - additional credibility as independents.
- *Involving customers / users of the process or service*. Without a detailed understanding of customers' expectations, their perceptions of your current performance levels and their views on where you need to do better, there is a danger you might focus on the 'wrong' processes to benchmark or you may select the 'wrong' organisations to benchmark against. Depending on the process or activity you are looking at, such customers might be external or internal.
- *Involving elected members*. Given the importance of benchmarking in Best Value the role of elected members needs to be carefully considered by managers. Their role will include deciding on appropriate performance standards for a service, reviewing actual performance against standards and targets set and ensuring that the service compares favourably both with other councils and with other service providers. Members may also have to approve innovative – and different – ways of service provision that have emerged through benchmarking.

At least one Scottish council has organised benchmarking training for elected members.

### 5.6.2   Analysis

#### 4 Understand your own performance

Before you can sensibly compare your own performance with someone else's you need to ensure that your own performance is adequately understood. This implies that you have identified what your key performance measures should be and that you have good performance information relating to these. Measures might include:

- *Inputs* – the resources used in a process: people, equipment, facilities, money.
- *Throughput* – efficiency measures which are usually ratios of outputs to inputs. These could also be 'quality' measures relating to a process – accuracy, timeliness, etc.
- *Inputs* – the results or end products of the process.
- *Outcomes* – the impact of your outputs on customers, end users, citizens, the wider community. These may include satisfaction measures.

### 5 Undertake data benchmarking

Data benchmarking will be useful at giving you an understanding of where your own performance lies in comparison with others. The data you need will depend upon the level at which you intend to benchmark (internal – best-in-class).

A number of councils have organised informal benchmarking clubs or grouped into 'families'. Whilst this approach is often a useful starting point for benchmarking it will not be sufficient by itself. Care needs to be taken that such clubs do not develop into data benchmarking sessions with the prime focus on agreeing common sets of performance measures, often after considerable time and effort has been put into agreeing definitions. Equally, although such groupings are typically on a council basis (based on profiles, demographics, etc.), on an individual service basis the group may not provide the best sector comparators. Even where such a group does provide good comparators there is also a danger of benchmarking becoming too introspective and forgetting that other organisations not in the club – public and private sector alike – may have radically different approaches to processes and service provision.

The sources of data will depend largely on the area being benchmarked. Data may be available through internal management information systems, through the statutory performance indicators, through VFM studies that have been conducted, through informal benchmarking clubs, through published sources, through personal contacts, through consultants. You are unlikely to be able to obtain all the data benchmarks that you would like. However, incomplete benchmark data is not an excuse for not progressing further. Even incomplete or inadequate data will help you assess your own and others' performance.

### 6 Assess key performance gaps

Through data benchmarking you should be able to determine the key gaps in your performance compared with your benchmark partners – remembering that such gaps may indicate where you are doing 'worse' than others but might also show where you are doing 'better'. You are not looking for a rigorous assessment at this stage – you are simply trying to establish in broad terms where the key performance gaps occur. Is it in terms of inputs, efficiency, effectiveness, quality, customer satisfaction or throughputs?

This will help you determine where to focus attention for the benchmarking project proper.

## 7 Understand your own processes

The next stage is to complete what are known as *process maps* for the areas you are benchmarking. As Foot (1998) comments:

> *Process mapping is an essential but time-consuming part of benchmarking.*

Process maps are detailed diagrams comprising a flowchart of tasks and activities that make up some defined process together with information for each step in the process about:

- key input requirements;
- resource requirements;
- critical controls and constraints on the process;
- required outputs;
- performance levels or standards;
- customer requirements.

Only by comparing process maps between and within organisations can meaningful performance improvements be identified (Exhibit 5.6).

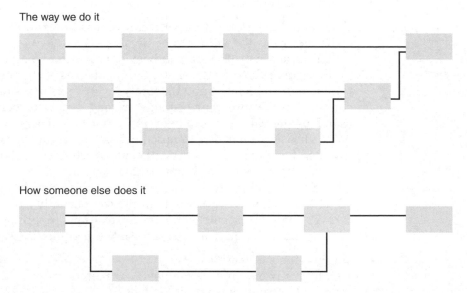

*Exhibit 5.6    Comparing process maps*

Audit Scotland's publication, *The Map to Success* (2000), details how process mapping can be used in benchmarking.

## 8 Choose your benchmarking partners

Once the process maps have been developed it's then time to look for specific benchmark partners. These are other organisations – or other parts of your own – where processes, functions or strategies can sensibly be benchmarked. It is important to see this level of benchmarking as being of mutual benefit to all organisations involved – benchmarking must be seen as being of mutual benefit if it is to succeed at this level. The choice of benchmarking partners will be influenced by a number of factors:

- the level at which you have decided to benchmark;
- the extent to which potential partners have developed their own process maps and a detailed knowledge of their own performance;
- the extent to which potential partners are willing to share detailed information on performance and processes;
- resource costs involved in working with particular partners in other geographical areas.

  *In trying to choose a partner, have in mind:*

  - *ease of access*
  - *whether you will be able to build a long-term relationship*
  - *whether you can offer something as well as gaining something yourself (CIPFA, 1996)*

You should resist the temptation to choose partners simply on the basis that they are willing to be involved. You need to consider which organisations will provide the best partners for your benchmarking project, particularly in the context of the degree of change that you can realistically implement and the likely level of resources to support that change. The leisure centre manager may decide to benchmark customer phone calls for bookings and enquiries. There would be little point choosing as a benchmark partner an organisation which had invested heavily in the latest call centre technology if leisure services realistically cannot afford comparable technology.

You should try to select partners against clearly set out criteria which you judge will assist in genuine comparability between you and others. The recruitment manager, for example, might set key criteria for benchmarking partners as those organisations with:

- similar levels of recruitment;
- a similar mix of grades of employee recruited;
- comparable equal opportunity policies.

## 9 Complete benchmarking

Once benchmark partners have been organised the benchmarking of agreed processes, functions or strategies can take place. This will normally involve:

- organising a benchmarking questionnaire so that there is clear, systematic agreement and understanding about what data and information will be collected and shared. One of the key success factors in successful benchmarking is ensuring that the right information is collected and then used.
- agreeing a code of conducts between partners. The 'ground rules' about access to potentially confidential information and the use of such information needs to be properly agreed by all the partners. A European Benchmarking Code is available.
- gathering information. This may involve the use of questionnaires, internal reports, site visits, interviews with key staff.
- analysing the information. Adequate consideration needs to be given in advance as to how the information collated will be analysed and used. Without this there is a danger that benchmarking becomes a form of 'industrial tourism' with considerable time and resources expended but with little visible result.

### 5.6.3   Action

## 10 Decide what you want to improve and how you're going to do it

The key purpose of your analysis of your benchmark partners is to help you identify where and how you can do better. Proper analysis will have helped you decide – in the context of your key processes – how your performance compares with others'. Proper benchmarking should also have helped you determine what actions you need to take to bring your performance up to best practice. It is important to develop a detailed improvement plan using a project management approach to plan for the improvement changes. Roles and responsibilities need to be clearly set out as to goals and targets for improvement.

## 11 Implement the improvement plan

Implementing the planned performance improvements will usually require careful change management. Such change often requires staff to adopt new approaches, processes and ways of working to deliver best practice. Frequently, the people who have to make the changes work will not have been directly involved in the benchmarking project.

They may need to be convinced as to what you want to do, why you want to do it and what it is intended to achieve. Communication, training and support will all be required.

### 5.6.4   *Review*

**12 Monitor progress and achievements**

Part of the implementation should build in timely monitoring of progress against your improvement plan. There is no point waiting until the end of the project to find out that it didn't work. You will need to build in progress reports through the life of the improvement plan.

**13 Decide what's next!**

Benchmarking is not a one-off activity. It is part of a continuous review of service delivery. You don't just do benchmarking once. So decide which area of your activity you're going to look at next.

## 5.7   *Making benchmarking a success*

While there are no guarantees of success in benchmarking, experience of a variety or organisations suggests that the following need to be in place.

### 5.7.1   *Planning*

- Make sure you're focusing on the key performance areas. There's no point putting a lot of effort into benchmarking something that will have little payback.
- Ensure a focus on what the customer thinks is important, and that includes internal customers – the whole point of benchmarking is to help you improve customer service.
- Ensure senior management commitment at the start of the project. There's little point coming up with radical plans for change as the result of a benchmarking project if senior management are not committed to making that change happen.
- Communicate at all the key stages of the project to all the key stakeholders. None of us likes too many surprises so keep people informed of what you're planning to do, why you're planning to do it and how it will affect them.
- Encourage staff to recognise and admit to problem areas or service failures. Benchmarking only works in a genuine no-blame culture.
- Make sure you've got the right people involved at each stage of the project and give them the support they need.

- Don't see benchmarking simply as a way of cutting costs or as something that's flavour-of-the-month.
- Start with areas where you're likely to be able to deliver some 'quick wins' otherwise staff will lose interest in something that's not going to help them for a long time yet.

### 5.7.2   Analysis

- Allow adequate time and resources for those involved – proper benchmarking is a time-intensive activity.
- Provide people with the skills and training they'll need. Tools and techniques such as process mapping, Pareto analysis, failure mode effect analysis and statistical process charts will all prove beneficial if people are aware of them and know how to apply them.
- Involve the whole team in analysing your performance and that of others and in looking for ways of improving your performance.
- Ensure you have accurate and reliable performance measures yourself before you look at anyone else.
- Be honest with yourself about your own performance.
- Try to create a learning culture encouraging staff to see alternative approaches positively rather than as a threat.
- Keep the benchmarking project tightly focused on agreed processes and areas.

### 5.7.3   Action

- Use a project management approach to change.
- Set challenging but achievable improvement targets.
- Build up from small wins – see benchmarking as incremental not as big bang.
- Involve staff – and where you can customers – at all stages.
- Ensure that benchmarking is fully integrated into your other activities – service reviews, service planning, performance improvement – and is not seen as stand-alone initiative being done for its own sake.

### 5.7.4   Review

- Check improvement progress regularly and take corrective action as soon as it's needed.
- Learn from your own experience for the next time you benchmark part of your service.
- Communicate what's been achieved to those who've done the hard work.
- Accept that further improvements are always possible.

## 5.8    *How ready are you to benchmark?*

If you answer *No* to any statement, consider how this might affect your ability to benchmark properly and consider what you might be able to do about it.

|  | ✓ Yes | ✗ No |
|---|:---:|:---:|
| We see benchmarking as a way of improving service delivery and not of simply cutting costs | ☐ | ☐ |
| Our senior managers are genuinely committed to achieving major change | ☐ | ☐ |
| Our elected members are genuinely committed to achieving major change | ☐ | ☐ |
| We have no fixed or rigid views about how things should be done | ☐ | ☐ |
| We have put a good benchmarking team together involving staff from different levels | ☐ | ☐ |
| There is a genuine commitment to provide the resources we need to benchmark properly (time, people, training, etc.) | ☐ | ☐ |
| Staff are willing to admit to poor practice and performance | ☐ | ☐ |
| We have told our staff what we are trying to achieve through benchmarking | ☐ | ☐ |
| We are willing to share information with others about our own good and bad practices | ☐ | ☐ |
| We have identified our key processes and activities | ☐ | ☐ |
| We know what our customers see as the important aspects of our service and our performance | ☐ | ☐ |
| We understand our own performance in these processes and activities | ☐ | ☐ |
| We're good at project management | ☐ | ☐ |
| We've identified – and planned for – the barriers that might prevent us from making change happen | ☐ | ☐ |
| We know how the results of our benchmarking will be built into our service plan | ☐ | ☐ |

## 5.9   Conclusion

This chapter provides an overview of what benchmarking involves when it is used as a meaningful part of the continuous improvement process.

In spite of the words of caution expressed here, don't be put off. There's no single way to benchmark and the best way to learn what works for you and your service is to start now.

Remember: it's all about improving the service you want to give to your customers by learning from others.

## References

Accounts Commission for Scotland (1998a) *The Measures of Success: Developing a balanced scorecard to measure performance*.

Accounts Commission for Scotland (1998b) *Planning for Success*.

Accounts Commission for Scotland (1999) *Performance Management and Planning Audit: Manager's Guide*.

Audit Scotland (2000) *The map to success: Using process mapping to improve performance*.

Bendell, T., Boulter L. and Gatford, K. *The Benchmarking Workout*, FT Pitmans.

Burns, T. (1992) 'Researching customer service in the public sector', *Journal of the Market Research Society*, **34**, 55–60.

Camp, R. (1989) *Business Process Benchmarking: Finding and Implementing Best Practices*, ASQC Press.

CIPFA (1996) *Benchmarking to Improve Performance*.

Cook, S. (1997) *Practical Benchmarking*, Kogan Page.

DTI (1995) *Best Practice Benchmarking: Managing in the 90s*.

Foot, J. (1998) *How To Do Benchmarking: A Practitioner's Guide*, Inter Authorities Group.

FT/Longman (1994) *Benchmarking to win: A Manager's Guide*.

Geber, B. (1990) 'Benchmarking: Measuring yourself against the best', *Training*, **27** (11), 36–44.

Keady, C. (1998) Measuring up to expectations, *Municipal Journal*, Sept 18, pp. 37–39.

LGMB (1997) 'Benchmarking: measuring up to the best', *Management Briefing No. 1*.

### Web sites

| The Accounts Commission for Scotland | http://www.accounts-commission.gov.uk |
| The Audit Commission | http://www.audit-commission.gov.uk |
| Audit Scotland | http://www.audit-scotland.gov.uk |
| The Benchmarking Centre | http://www.benchmarking.co.uk |
| The Benchmarking Exchange | http://www.benchnet.com |

| The Business Processes Resource Centre | http://bprc.warwick.ac.uk |
| Government Information Service | http://www.open.gov.uk |
| Local Government Association | http://www.lga.gov.uk |
| Public Sector Management Research | http://psm.abs.aston.ac.uk |
| The Quality Network | http://www.quality.co.uk |

# Strategy in action

*Illustration 1*

### The ABC benchmarking partnership

In Scotland, 32 unitary local authorities provide services – including primary and secondary education, social work services, housing, leisure services, road maintenance, cleansing and refuse collection, food safety – to around five million citizens and are responsible for annual expenditure of almost £10 billion. The pressure on local authority managers to ensure they are providing effective and efficient services has probably never been as intense.

In May 1997, the new Labour government was elected in the UK. Part of its manifesto related to modernising local government and part of this related to the introduction of a Best Value regime with the government announcing that 'achieving best value will not just be about economy and efficiency, but also about effectiveness and the quality of local services'. In England and Wales best value was initially applied to a small number of pilot authorities. In Scotland, the Secretary of State announced that best value would apply to all 32 Scottish local authorities, and a small task force of officials from the Scottish Office, the Convention of Scottish Local Authorities (COSLA) and the Accounts Commission for Scotland was created. The task force had a remit to develop a framework for delivering best value across local government services in Scotland, with an immediate aim of identifying the key principles and essential elements underpinning best value.

There was a particular necessity for the latter since councils were expected later that year to provide a submission to the Scottish Office demonstrating their commitment to best value, the extent to which they were already complying with best value and their plans to achieve best value across all services. The task force produced a report in the summer of 1997 setting out what were described as the essential elements of best value. These were:

- *Sound governance.* There were four aspects to sound governance set out: ensuring a customer/citizen focus to service provision; sound strategic management; sound operational management; sound financial management.

- *Performance measurement and monitoring.* Robust performance information was seen as a key element of best value both for internal management purposes and for external scrutiny and accountability.

- *Continuous improvement.* Delivering continuous improvement in both the management and delivery of services was seen as a further key element of best value. Again, there were four aspects of this set out: developing detailed cost information about council activities and service provision; the use of performance benchmarking; the use of competition; the use of rigorous option appraisal in deciding how services could best be provided.

- *Three-year budgeting.* The development of three-year budgeting linked to councils' long-term priorities and targets.

Although benchmarking was explicitly set out as a key element of the Scottish Best Value, it is clear that the use of comparative information was expected to play a role in a number of other aspects of the regime. Demonstrating evidence of sound operational management could only be done with some element of comparison of performance; comparison of strategic performance would clearly be essential; performance measurement would require some comparative aspect to be useful to managers and key stakeholders; the development of detailed cost information for comparative purposes is clearly a type of data benchmarking. However, the intent behind benchmarking was not simply to create a data benchmarking industry in local government but rather to ensure that comparative information helped identify and disseminate good practice and ultimately helped improve service delivery.

   Councils in Scotland took differing approaches in their response to the requirement to use benchmarking. Seven councils (Clackmannanshire, East Lothian, East Renfrewshire, Inverclyde, Midlothian, North Lanarkshire, Perth and Kinross) formally set up the ABC Partnership in June 1997 specifically in response to the Best Value requirement. The councils involved felt that meeting Best Value requirements was likely to be resource intensive and a key objective of the benchmarking Partnership from the outset was to enable participating councils to help each other with the workload and to share good practice. From the start, the Partnership realised that benchmarking projects would need to involve relatively large numbers of people in the various councils and yet, at the same time, would need to be properly project managed in order to ensure they actually delivered performance improvement. It was decided to set up a parent group made up of one officer from each of the partner councils. This group would then facilitate and sponsor benchmarking between partners, oversee the progress of each benchmarking project and ensure information was shared between the partners. Once a topic area for benchmarking had been agreed, a sub-group would then be established involving other officers from the partner councils.

   It was also recognised from the outset that a code of benchmarking practice would need to be adhered to by all partners given the nature of some of the information to be shared. A detailed code was developed around nine key principles but with two central requirements:

- absolute confidentiality with regard to all information collected and/or received;

- no communication of data or identity of individual councils without the written permission of the councils concerned.

Initially, seven service areas were agreed for benchmarking: building cleaning, catering, fleet management, payroll services, personnel services, service planning, statutory performance indicators. A benchmarking sub-group was formed for each area comprising those partner councils with a particular interest in that service area, together with a small number of additional councils co-opted onto that particular sub-group.

The Partnership, by its own admission, has enabled a greater level of benchmarking activity than might otherwise have been the case and many of the findings and recommendations arising from the Partnership's benchmarking activities have been adopted by the partner councils. Some of the recorded achievements as a result of the benchmarking work include: cost savings in payroll services as a result of reductions in error rates and staff costs; the adoption of more environmentally-friendly fuel purchasing in Vehicle Maintenance together with cost savings in vehicle servicing; the production of a service planning guide summarising best practice.

All of the benchmarking projects were completed as planned, with some moving into a further, more detailed phase. The Partnership has also agreed the next set of benchmarking projects it intends to undertake, covering a further 13 service areas. The Partnership has acknowledged the learning that had to take place in the early stages in order to enable the projects to move forward successfully. However, it has also reported the wider benefits that benchmarking has brought the partner councils, including the development of professional skills, widened experience and the spread of learning.

I am grateful to the ABC Partnership for the information provided.

# 6

# *The Best Value Initiative*

*By Simon Speller*

## *Editor's introduction*

The ability to provide 'best value' products or services is the key ingredient of long-term strategic success for all organisations. This is emphasised throughout *Exploring Corporate Strategy* but particularly in Chapter 4 when discussing strategic capability. Behind this quest to provide best value lie some difficult issues for managers. First, there is the problem of under-standing what best value means to the different groups of customers or potential customers. Most 'markets' are not homogeneous in their require-ments, so there will be a variety of answers to this question. Second, there are often stakeholders other than customers who have a view on what best value should mean – this is particularly true in the public sector context. Third, there is a need to establish some standards or yardsticks about best value – concerning product/service features, quality and prices (or unit costs in the public services). Finally, there is a need to establish a regime that will deliver best value rather than just tell about it!

These are issues faced by all organisations. In the private sector the mechanisms of competitive markets ultimately resolve these questions. Those who do not provide best value will not survive in the long term. The challenge for the public sector has been to deliver this pressure to perform in other ways. The Best Value initiative (described in this chapter) and clini-cal governance (in David Herbert's chapter) need to be seen as part of a rev-olutionary process in attempting to improve best value in the public sector. For a long period of time – up to the major public sector reforms of the 1980s – the view largely was that professional and political judgement would determine and sustain best value. This was found to be wanting and in many cases became, at least in part, more like professional and political arro-gance – the paternalistic welfare state. The reforms of the 1980s attempted to tackle this through market and quasi-market mechanisms such as dereg-ulation, compulsory competitive tendering, market testing and internal mar-kets, as discussed in Chapter 10 of *Exploring Corporate Strategy*. It was some of the downsides of these reforms that led the Labour government in the UK to introduce the Best Value initiative described in this chapter. The philosophical shift is from a contractual/market mechanism approach to improving performance, to one of benchmarking best practice and ensuring that mechanisms are in place to meet that best practice. So there is an important link between this chapter and Mik Wisniewski's chapter on benchmarking.

## 6.1   Introduction

This chapter discusses and illustrates how the 'Best Value' initiative introduced by the UK Labour government in 1997 (immediately after the General Election) fits in with the desire to achieve better performance from public sector organisations – in this case local public services provided by local councils and voluntary organisations. This is paralleled by the 'Clinical Governance' initiative relating to health services (see David Herbert's chapter).

Local government in the UK is provided by over 450 local councils (also called local authorities) which have statutory responsibilities for a range of services and for democratic representation at the local community level. These services include primary and secondary education, social services, planning, waste management, roads and highways, social housing, and fire and rescue services. Councils responsible for the full range of services in their areas are called 'unitary' councils. These 'unitary' councils usually serve metropolitan areas and conurbations (with populations of around 400,000 or more).

The trend over the past five years has been to create more unitary authorities from the traditional Victorian 'two-tier' system of non-metropolitan county councils (the 'upper tier' with strategic responsibilities and education and social services in particular) and district councils contained within county areas (the 'lower' tier responsible in particular for local planning, refuse collection, social housing). Since 1995, 46 new unitary authorities have been created in England alone (19 in 1998). There are still 34 county councils and 238 district councils in England under the 'two-tier' system. All 32 local authorities in Scotland and 22 in Wales are now unitary authorities.[1]

The drivers for change in the way local authorities and their services are managed are both *internal* and *external*. *Internal* drivers and pressures for change and 'modernisation' include the adoption of management ideas, concepts and practices from the private sector by public sector managers and professionals. This particularly includes quality management ideas such as Total Quality Management (TQM) and Quality Assurance (QA) that became popular in the 1980s following the UK Conservative government's programme of Compulsory Competitive Tendering (CCT), which introduced market testing on the basis of cost comparison between competing tenders for specific contracts such as refuse collection and street cleansing services.[2] Another internal driver for change can be local policy and political initiatives set up and brokered by local leading elected councillors.

Far more significant are *external* drivers for change. These include:

- Government policy, e.g. on CCT and 'market testing', to open the public sector to competition and to encourage or make the public sector behave more like the private sector. This includes government campaigns such as the DTI quality and competitiveness campaign launched in 1986.
- General social and economic changes, including the growth of more assertive and demanding customers from the 'baby boomer' generation downwards as major users of public services, and the corresponding decline of elderly people simply 'grateful' and acquiescent in their consumption of public services.[3]
- Promotion of consumer interests, e.g. the National Consumer Council (NCC) and the Consumers' Association.
- Greater awareness of private sector practices through contacts as supply chain partners in service delivery and through purchasing and procurement (especially new technology).

These external pressures have gradually been forcing significant and fundamental changes on local authorities, as described by John Stewart:[4]

- A shift from being service-led to being customer-led, and from an emphasis on inputs to outputs and outcomes of services.
- A move away from professional cultures (e.g. in education, social services, environmental services) towards corporate cultures.
- A move from direct service provision and a sole supplier approach towards an emphasis on a facilitating and enabling role, and towards a joint provision and partnership approach.
- A shift from only meeting minimum standards towards a concern for cost efficiency and effectiveness in service delivery.
- A change from a non-competitive culture towards a competitive approach in providing services, together with an emphasis on licence generation in more areas of activity (beyond leisure and television services).

Best Value has been introduced as part of a wider national agenda for modernisation. The related themes of democratic renewal and an ethical (and credible) regime also need to be considered.

At the heart of the government's approach is a desire to ensure that local councils genuinely serve their communities and that local people see their councils and councillors as relevant and meaningful (hence the language of 'engaging').[5] Much of the inspiration for this approach comes from the experiences of the New Labour Party (many

Ministers and MPs were themselves Councillors or Officers in the local government system). Much of the language and ideas come from the USA, e.g. the ideas of 'reinventing' government.[6] As with many of the ideas from private sector management, one acid test is whether public sector managers have sufficiently customised some of these imports, relating them as appropriate to a UK public sector setting.

## 6.2    What is 'Best Value'?

### 6.2.1    The purposes of Best Value

The introduction of Best Value reflects the 'voices' of diverse stakeholders interested in local government, e.g. central government departments, national political parties, consumer pressure groups, as well as the network of local government bodies representing councillors, professionals and trade unions.[7] These have promoted Best Value in at least four ways:

- Best Value as part of democratic renewal;
- Best Value as part of Quality and Quality Management;
- Best Value as driven by hard-edged performance indicators;
- Best Value as a respectable way of developing CCT.

Best Value, since its inception in the Labour Party manifesto before the 1997 General Election, has deliberately been defined broadly and in an open-ended way. The 'official' definition of Best Value, set out in the Government White Paper *Modern Local Government – In Touch with the People*, is:

> *Best Value will be a duty to deliver services to clear standards – covering both cost and quality – by the most effective, economic and efficient means available.*

The 'duty' of Best Value is related to a local authority's need to be 'accountable to local people' and 'to have a responsibility to central government in its role as representative of the broad national interest'. As with the government's Chartermark scheme, introduced in 1991, to promote customer care in the public sector, the emphasis is on 'openness' of information about services and service standards as a key means of promoting accountability.

Although local authorities have a 'duty' to promote and progress towards Best Value, it is defined and described largely in terms of the processes and programmes involved to which councils are expected to subscribe. This is, in large part, a conscious reaction to the previous government regime of Compulsory Competitive Tendering (CCT) for local public services that operated from 1980. This was widely perceived to be over-prescriptive and rigid, not to say negative in its assumption that the private sector was inherently better at service delivery than the public sector. This contributed in large part to a public sector management inferiority complex and defensiveness amongst public sector managers when their services have been compared to the private sector.

Compared with the CCT requirement that local public services be provided to the tenderer with the lowest bid in terms of cost of contract, Best Value has been introduced to promote 'pluralism' in service delivery. The emphasis has been on pragmatism ('what matters is what works') and on the primacy of service outcomes to customers, users, clients and the wider community. The one 'E' of 'economy' under CCT is enlarged to the three 'E's of 'economy, efficiency and effectiveness'.[8]

### 6.2.2   Local versus national needs

There is also an understanding that essentially two basic levels of assessment apply:

- local assessments – what matters in one locality may not be so significant elsewhere;
- national assessments – that all people in their role as users, clients, customers or other stakeholders have a right to expect reasonably equitable treatment for many services wherever they live.

This is one of a number of ambiguities and dilemmas that public sector managers and executive and political leaders at local level need to grapple with. The first three years of the Best Value regime have encouraged local councils and their partners to innovate and experiment, to be unafraid 'to do the right thing' (a 'carrot' approach'). The new Beacon Council scheme[9] introduced in the Government White Paper, in which excellence and innovation will be recognised and rewarded, is a good case in point. At the same time, however, there has been an explicit statement that 'failing' councils and services (as with schools or social services departments) will lead to direct government intervention (the 'sticks' approach). This is implicit in the stress on independent audit/inspection and certification in Best Value. Some of these ambiguities and dilemmas will be discussed further below.

## 6.3   The architecture of Best Value

The government White Paper *Modern Local Government – In Touch with the People* sets out the key pillars of Best Value:

- A Best Value Performance Management Framework and outline programme for all local authorities, recognising the need to address national requirements and local aspirations and differences.

- Local Performance Plans linking up community, corporate and service planning with the reviews programme for every local authority, outlining future work and priorities as well as reviewing past performance.
- Performance indicators, standards and targets – both national and local.
- Fundamental Performance Reviews of services and the key elements of the four 'C's – Challenge, Compare, Consult, Compete – against which all reviews will be assessed for rigour and thoroughness. (See Section 6.3.3 below.)
- Audit and Inspection arrangements to scrutinise and assess whether best value is being obtained by local authorities. These are to be undertaken by existing specialist inspectorates (e.g. Social Services, OFSTED), with the Audit Commission undertaking this role in those areas not previously subject to inspection.
- Intervention by central government where there is failure in services, as a last resort. The prime consideration will be the interests of local people and users of services in such cases.

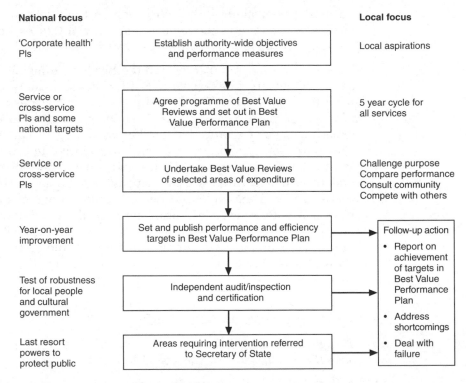

*Exhibit 6.1*  *Best Value Performance Management Framework*

### 6.3.1   *Best Value Performance Management Framework*

Exhibit 6.1 illustrates the duality of focus of Best Value – the local focus relating to service improvements at local level related to local needs and aspirations, and the national focus relating to nationally related standards, e.g. for schools and social services, where the government states it has 'key responsibilities and commitments'. It also illustrates the outline of a process and programme local authorities are expected to follow, starting with setting authority-wide objectives and performance measures (performance indicators), agreeing a programme of fundamental performance reviews (FPRs) of services set out in a Best Value Performance Plan (BVPP) and carrying out a range of these reviews each year. Each local authority is expected to undertake reviews each year of 20–25 per cent of its services (or their value/cost). Exhibit 6.2 shows how the Best Value Framework should connect with planning which would already be in place – such as corporate plans, plans for separate service departments and broader community and economic development plans. Ensuring that Best Value approaches 'joined up' with these various efforts was an important challenge.

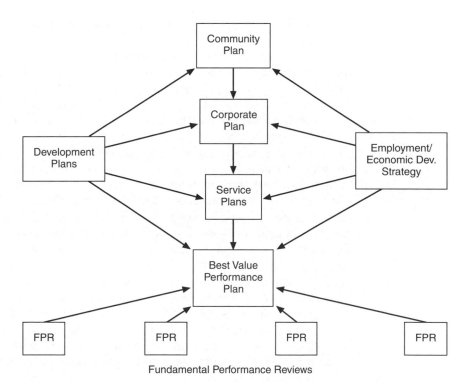

**Exhibit 6.2**   *Models of joined-up thinking and action – levels of planning and strategy*

Each year the BVPP will look forward in identifying the future reviews programme, and look backward to the performance in undertaking reviews and meeting targets and standards in the previous year. The BVPP looks ahead for a five-year period, and is 'rolled forward' annually. It is the BVPP that is subject to external audit and inspection, a crucial element in the government's strategy for introducing Best Value. It correctly perceives that many local authorities, skilled in the dark arts of evasion during the years of the CCT regime, will only develop Best Value because they must comply and because such compliance can be assessed and enforced. This also reflects the relatively slow development of Quality Management ideas and tools from the private sector during the 1980s and 1990s.[10]

### 6.3.2    *Performance indicators, standards and targets*

The Best Value initiative places great stress on developing national and local performance indicators. Although the idea of local authorities assessing their performance via a series of performance indicators is not new, the Best Value regime aims to ensure they are used with a degree of rigour and are subject to external as well as internal scrutiny. The degree of external audit and inspection is perhaps quite different from the private sector, although this is changing as bigger businesses in particular open themselves to external assessment in terms of their corporate social and environmental responsibility. The other key purpose of performance indicators (PIs) is that they enable comparisons of performance to be made. Thus 'benchmarking' (see Mik Wisniewski's chapter in the book) is being introduced, ostensibly to promote improved performance. A key feature of PIs in the Best Value regime is that, where possible, they focus attention on what services have delivered (outputs) and on the perception and impact of these (outcomes), rather than what resources have been devoted to them (inputs). This emphasis is markedly different from the CCT requirement to focus on cost issues almost exclusively, which necessarily are inputs and process focused. Strictly speaking, 'data benchmarking', or the comparing of numerical performance indicators or levels between organisations or specific services, is about 'benchmarks'. Benchmarking proper is about a rigorous and continuous organisational process of making appropriate comparisons to enable the organisation or service to identify where and how to improve performance. This may involve 'process benchmarking', where key processes for a service (and their related sets of inputs and outputs) are compared with any other comparable processes that may suggest scope for service improvements.

Such comparisons are *not* limited to similar services, organisations or sectors, and in fact significant process improvements may be inspired by comparisons of analogous processes in other industries.

The emphasis in official guidance on Best Value has been on the continuous improvement of services, similar to that proposed under Total Quality Management (TQM) and by management frameworks and tools such as the European Excellence Model (revised in 1999). This is entirely consistent with a proper understanding and application of benchmarking, with the target set for council services to aim to be in five years' time as good as the current top 25 per cent.

What is significant, and indeed may be typical of a great many councils, is the rush into benchmark-related activity, exchanges of data for services of similar councils, without the related competence to ask the questions of why and how such differences occur, or the commitment to make suggested changes to processes. There is anecdotal evidence of 'benchmarking clubs' for the exchange of data and ideas that run out of steam and energy through lack of proper partnering and planning (see Mik Wisniewski's chapter on benchmarking).[11]

### 6.3.3  Fundamental Performance Reviews

Perhaps the key requirement of the Best Value initiative is the fundamental performance review of services. Local authorities are required to look at their poorer performing services early in their five-year programme. They are also expected to look at 'cross-cutting' service and programme areas, e.g. community safety, local competitiveness and enterprise, health, cultural facilities. These are the kinds of services provided by a range of providers, often in formal partnerships, and are not the responsibility or province of one sole department or agency. Other programme areas for review that cannot be 'pigeon holed' very easily for public sector managers include urban regeneration, social exclusion and sustainable development. These do not relate conveniently to discrete service delivery 'packages', and raise complex issues of stakeholder management, planning and strategy beyond the scope and control of a single department, agency or organisation.

In such an operating environment, the government expects local councils to be 'community leaders', co-ordinating and facilitating partnership working, and carrying out Fundamental Performance Reviews. This fits the wider 'modernisation' agenda of 'democratic renewal' – of councils engaging with and leading their communities.

The four key questions for Fundamental Performance Reviews are known as the four 'C's of Challenge, Compare, Consult and Compete. Over the last year many councils have added a fifth 'C' of Collaborate. Exhibit 6.3 outlines what each of the four Cs relates to. These key questions are useful to ensure that fundamental service

*Exhibit 6.3    The four Cs (or five?)*

| | |
|---|---|
| Challenge | Questions about justifying the service. Why is the service provided? Also about the way it is provided. There may be other organisations better placed to supply the service, even if current methods are considered adequate. |
| Compare | Comparing performance of the service against similar services and with the best. External comparisons recommended, outside of local government. Links to data benchmarking in various ways, and sometimes process benchmarking. |
| Consult | Consulting internally with front-line staff and trade unions, and externally with organisational and community stakeholders. This fits in with well-established networks most councils have, as well as area/neighbourhood forums and other relatively new mechanisms for 'listening' to the community. |
| Compete | Continued from CCT regime, and related to 'challenge', this is expected to be more positively and imaginatively embraced, e.g. via public–private partnerships for service delivery. |
| Collaborate | Working in partnership with organisational stakeholders from the private, voluntary and public sector, and community and neighbourhood-level groups |

Source: Government White Paper *Modern Local Government 1998,* DETR

reviews stay on course and address the 'wicked issues' and choices in the design and delivery of council services. The 4Cs or 5Cs feature strongly in Best Value training for officers and councillors, and in the presentation of reports.

Interim progress reports on fundamental service reviews being undertaken by councils suggest that the Cs for Consult, Compare and Collaborate have been reasonably successful. However, there is considerable evidence that the Cs of Challenge and Compete are addressed far less thoroughly and rigorously at present. Exhibit 6.4 shows how one Local Authority (Stevenage) was putting together these elements of Best Value.

### 6.3.4    Audit and inspection

The audit and inspection arrangements have deliberately been introduced nearly two years later on in the process of developing Best Value. This is, in part, of necessity because of the time to set up the appropriate mechanisms with the DETR, the Audit Commission, the Local Government Association (LGA), which represents the various types of councils in England and Wales, and the Improvement and Development Agency (I&DeA), set up to promote Best Value and other parts of the modernisation agenda.[12]

The later introduction of audit and inspection arrangements also provided time for local authorities to demonstrate their capability to adapt to and guide change to the new Best Value and 'modernisation' setting. A chance to 'do the right thing' as opposed to 'doing things right' in what is often described as a conformance and compliance-only culture and environment.

The key features of audit and inspection arrangements promoted by the government are:

- the rigorous external check on information supplied by local authorities in BVPPs, and on council management systems.
- external inspection of services (analogous to OFSTED inspection of schools and Social Services Inspectorate (SSI) inspections of social services). These to be undertaken by a new BV Inspectorate.
- annual external audit undertaken by District Audit, as at present. Feedback is provided via a Management Letter which is presented to local councillors.
- guidance and advice on internal systems of control and audit via the Audit Commission.

These arrangements are intended to serve a dual purpose – to improve local public services by ensuring that councils develop, manage and control services to achieve 'continuous improvement', and to identify and act upon failures of services and whole councils, as with central government intervention into 'failing' schools. Since audit and inspec-

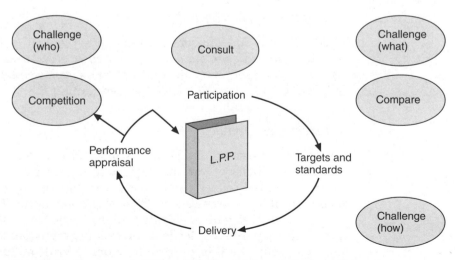

*Exhibit 6.4    Best Value Framework* (*Source*: Stevenage Borough Council)

tion arrangements have traditionally been a feature of local government in the UK, the significance of the new regime is the emphasis on
supporting local councils to promote continuous improvement and, at
worst, to remedy 'failing services', a marked contrast to an emphasis
exclusively on 'naming and shaming' poor performers in the public
sector.

Audits will essentially focus on the processes of local councils in
developing and delivering best value as set out in a council's Best Value
Performance Plan, rather than on the outputs and outcomes for service
users and other stakeholders. Having said that, the DETR and Audit
Commission guidance stresses the need to bear these in mind. For
example, the Audit Commission 'is committed to designing an inspection
service that acts as a catalyst for change' in order to make 'real improvements to the quality of local services and to the quality of people's lives'.

## 6.4   *The experience of Best Value*

Analysing and evaluating the Best Value initiative is interesting as a
sector-wide case study of the management of change and the need to
align strategy to a quite significantly different operating environment.
In this section the context of introducing Best Value is reviewed,
together with an assessment of organisational responses from a range
of related stakeholders. In particular, the differences between the CCT
environment and BV environment are important to recognise, and the
influences of management ideas, theories, tools and practices from the
private sector into the voluntary and public sectors since the early
1980s.

### 6.4.1   *A new mindset and culture?*

What all these 'stakeholders' share is an agreement on the basic need
for local authorities to change not only their structures but also their
corporate 'mindset' and culture. This was previewed by J. Stewart of
INLOGOV and others 15 years ago (see Exhibit 6.5).[13]

### 6.4.2   *A stakeholder approach*

A useful way to examine this change of mindset and culture is to evaluate the positions of various key stakeholders within a local community and local council. Stakeholder mapping is an effective tool for
such an evaluation (see Kevan Scholes' chapter in this book).

An acid test will be whether there is greater 'listening' to the
community by council leaders to other groups, better 'engaging'
between groups and, in particular, more 'pluralism' and diffusion of
power at a local level.

*Exhibit 6.5*   *Changing the corporate mindset for Best Value*

| From | To |
| --- | --- |
| Inputs/Processes | Outputs/Outcomes |
| Internal focus | External focus |
| Administrative approach | Managerial approach |
| Control | Consensus |
| Directive | Participative |
| Closed systems | Open-ended |
| Rigid | Flexible |
| Reactive | Proactive |

Source: Speller, based on Stewart

Similarly, for managers and front line staff who deliver services, the uncertainties of Best Value represent a challenge of a different kind to that presented under CCT. As mentioned above, CCT created an art of evasion of the 'rules of the game'. They also gave managers power versus local councillors in that CCT was defined as a 'technical' and 'professional' activity, and contract specifications (the lifeblood of the CCT 'contract culture') were perceived to be beyond a lay member's comprehension and scope.

Under Best Value, such technical considerations remain important, but not central. What is crucial is the test of what is 'best value', and for whom? As Exhibit 6.5 suggests, a focus on outputs and outcomes creates conditions for a wholly different approach to local governance and to management of services. Over three years into the Best Value initiative it is clear that political leaders and senior managers understand better the requirement not to presume to either 'externalise' all services or keep them all 'in house'. The test is – which (currently) is likely to deliver 'best value'?

### 6.4.3   Developing an 'outside-in' approach

Best Value has frequently been characterised as requiring an 'outside-in' approach, as opposed to an 'inside-out' approach by internal stakeholders (both councillors and officers). The acid test of 'listening', referred to above, can be more precisely identified as the capability of the organisation to be 'client/customer-led' rather than 'service-led'. The experience of the Best Value initiative to date is that the 'Consult' part of Best Value is reasonably well developed but has a long way to go if local councils are to move up Arnstein's ladder of participation from tokenistic information giving and 'public consultation' to meaningful empowerment (see Exhibit 6.6).[14]

Speller and others have recognised the problems of developing a customer-led approach as not only an issue of cultural style and

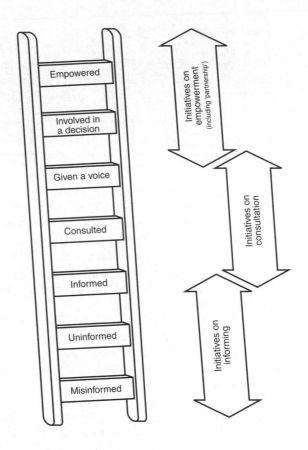

*Exhibit 6.6    The ladder of participation*
Source: C. Brigham LGMB/S. Arnstein (1967)

leadership type and style, but also a technical/managerial problem of simply not knowing how to go about collecting the right kind of data. Useful tools recommended for public sector managers include gap analysis of service quality (ref. Parasuraman, Zeithaml and Berry) and the European Excellence Model, which emphasises the need to assess 'customer results', 'society results' and 'people results'. Both these approaches are more external customer focused than Investors in People (IIP) or Quality Assurance systems like ISO 9000.[15]

## 6.5 Conclusions

This chapter has explained how the regime of Best Value is being developed for UK local councils, to deliver a central government 'modernisation agenda' for the range of local public services. The development of Best Value follows a traditional pattern of local government conformance and compliance to such external pressure, backed up by legislation and guidance. Central government has led with a 'carrot' approach, offering local councils far more leeway in managing their own affairs (and finances) provided councils modernise their structures (a traditional local government obsession at all levels) and their practices. The aim has been to encourage local councils to take up the challenge and responsibility to 'open up' their organisation far more to external stakeholders such as local residents, community groups, local business groups, etc., and in general to be more in tune and in touch with their communities and electorate (e.g. so that turnouts of local voters rise from the 30–40 per cent common in UK elections).[16]

This chapter has looked at the 'managerialist' emphasis in the modernisation agenda and Best Value regime. The six pillars of Best Value, including the Performance Management Framework (see Exhibit 6.1), underline the need for council officers as managers to perform better for their customers and stakeholders. The trend towards larger and 'unitary' councils reflects a long-standing search for greater efficiency and economies of scale.[17] The traditional committee system is giving way to smaller 'cabinets' of key councillors, and these councillors are clearly becoming more 'managerial' and 'strategic' in their roles *vis-à-vis* their officers, other councillors and stakeholder groups inside and outside the council.

The other side to the central government approach is the 'stick' of ensuring that performance in sevice delivery improves via enhanced external audit and inspection arrangements. These are to supplement new internal scrutiny roles for 'backbench' councillors (somewhat on the lines of a UK parliamentary select committee), and to ensure that local councils are more accountable for the quality of their services.

UK local councils constitutionally derive their powers only from central government at Westminster. Under Best Value, councils are expected to set and meet local performance levels and indicators as well as a considerable number of national performance indicators (e.g. over 190 for London Boroughs). This reflects traditional tensions between focusing on local needs and providing equitable services nationwide (e.g. the performance of local schools).

The introduction of Best Value is an ambitious programme. Key to its eventual success, apart from critical matters such as the tenure of the Labour government and the agenda of any successor governments, is the timescale central government is prepared to accept for effective and sustained change towards adopting Best Value require-ments. A parallel may be drawn with private sector large organis-ations such as Rank Xerox, ICL, TNT, Motorola and others adopting TQM/Excellence programmes towards quality award/'world class' standards. It takes a long time, and requires a long-term view, some-thing not noted in central or local government. This suggests that the leadership style and cultural changes needed will have to be prompted, at least in the short and medium term, by the external pressures of central government, social expectations and market com-parisons as well as by the eventual recruitment of a different breed of councillor and officer.

## *Notes*

1    See the *Local Government Association Year Book 2000* or the *Municipal Year Book*.
2    David Garvin and others have explained the rise in popularity of TQM-related initiatives and programmes in terms of 'waves' of devel-opment, e.g. from Japan, to the USA, to the UK, to the rest of Europe. One 'wave' is from manufacturing to services to public services.
3    Paul Corrigan, a UK public sector management specialist, uses an anecdote of the post-war generation being simply 'grateful' in their attitude to receiving public services, in contrast to the greater assertiveness of later generations and their higher expectations. See also S. Speller and A. Ghobadian (1993) 'Change for the public sector', *Managing Service Quality*, July and Sept.
4    See J.D. Stewart (1986) *The New Management of Local Government*, Allen & Unwin.
5    Similar phrases (or 'sound bites') recur in Labour Party documents before and after the 1997 UK General Election, e.g. The Labour Party (1997) *New Labour – Because Britain Deserves Better (Party Manifesto)*, esp. pp. 32–35.
6    Many of the key policies and proposals in the early Clinton Administration found their way across the Atlantic into New Labour, many to be absorbed into Tony Blair's 'big idea' of the 'Third Way', somewhere in between complete privatisation on one hand and complete public ownership and management in relation to public services on the other.
7    Steve Martin headed up the Warwick University Team responsible for monitoring and supporting the national Best Value pilot programme for the DETR. There are regular reports published on progress.
8    This language of the three 'E's began to appear in UK local govern-ment management discussions in the late 1980s, specifically in an Audit Commission Management Paper on Performance Reviews (the precursor of Best Value service reviews).
9    See *The Beacon Council Scheme*, DETR, 1999.

10    See the comment under (3).

11    See also *Measuring up to the Best – A manager's guide to bench-marking*, Accounts Commission for Scotland, 1999.

12    *Seeing is Believing*, Audit Commission, and DETR Circular 10/99 *Local Government Act 1999: Part 1 Best Value*, DETR

13    See 4 above.

14    The Arnstein 'ladder of participation' and other similar ideas were extensively discussed in the late 1960s, and examined in the *Skeffington Report* on participation in planning matters.

15    There are currently six mainstream models/frameworks promoted in the UK public sector. Three originate from the private sector: Investors in People (IIP), ISO 9000 Quality Management Systems and the EFQM European Excellence Model. Three frameworks/schemes specific to the public sector are the Chartermark, the Local Government Improvement Project (LGA/I&DeA) and the Beacon Scheme (DETR). All of these are extensively used.

16    Turnout at local elections is explicitly discussed in the *Modernising Local Government* Consultation Paper (March 1998).

17    The quest for greater efficiency, and its linkage to 'bigger is better', dominated public sector management debates in the 1960s and 1970s, e.g. the Fulton Report on the Civil Service and the Bains Report on Local Government Management.

# 7 Clinical governance

## By David Herbert

### Editor's introduction

The performance of healthcare organisations in terms of their quality of service and the outcomes (for patients and society) from these services was historically governed largely through professional judgement of the clinicians. Clinical governance in the NHS described in this chapter and the Best Value initiative in the UK (in Simon Speller's chapter) need to be seen as part of an evolutionary process in attempting to improve best value in the public services. For a long period professional and political judgement were the dominant mechanisms. In many cases this came to be regarded as professional and/or political arrogance – the paternalistic welfare state. The reforms of the 1980s attempted to resolve this through market and quasi-market mechanisms – such as privatisation, deregulation, compulsory competitive tendering, market testing and internal markets (particularly in the NHS). These brought problems too, as relationships between and within organisations became contractual rather than collaborative. Clinical governance and the Best Value initiative were attempts to move the approach forward – with a major emphasis on benchmarking, as discussed in Mik Wisniewski's chapter. Clinical governance moves the efforts for quality enhancement and control to a more systematic regime of benchmarking, setting performance standards and clinical audit. These are issues that are covered in Chapter 4 of *Exploring Corporate Strategy*.

### 7.1 Quality improvement in healthcare

Quality improvement in the National Health Service is the objective of the UK government and clinical governance is the term given to the means to that end. This chapter discusses the issues around clinical governance and proposes a model to give focus to that discussion. It is, however, apposite to consider how the drive for quality in the public sector has reached the point it has.

Over the past 20 years British governments have had a stated aim to improve the quality of public services but the journey has taken a circuitous route. Initially they took the view that quality would best be achieved by creating private sector situations such as a competitive environment within which quality would naturally follow. Hence the Compulsory Competitive Tendering (CCT) policy was applied to much of the public sector in the 1980s and an internal market set up in 1992 in the NHS. Both these policies had an implicit assumption of quality as 'conformance to requirements', but such a definition is now old fashioned because it does not take into account the implied needs of the customer. Further, it does not include a commitment to continuous improvement. In the mid-1980s public sector organisations had begun to use quality system standards such as ISO 9001 (ISO, 2000) and sought external accreditation for the management system, usually for part of the organisation. This allowed a wide and unco-ordinated diversity of approaches to achieving quality which made it difficult to judge overall progress.

Until the 1990s the measurement of performance quality had been carried out in a haphazard manner largely through the professional judgement of individual clinicians. In the early 1980s the NHS had established its first Performance Indicator package with 145 assorted measurements. This had risen to over 2,000 by 1996 and covered Health of the Nation, Outcome, Purchaser, Provider, Secondary, Background and Direct Access. The package lacked acceptance to a certain extent because staff tended to believe its aim was to measure their mistakes and not place them in an improvement culture. In addition, the package was not structured to show how the data should be used. In 1996 (Department of Health, 1996) the intended use of performance indicators was reaffirmed to:

- raise questions and highlight issues for further discussion and investigation and not simply provide answers;
- place local activities in a national context;
- make comparisons over time;
- monitor effectiveness of actions and interventions;
- be used in conjunction with each other to tell a complete story.

In 1994 the Chartermark scheme had begun a shift in emphasis towards total quality management by emphasisng excellence in public service and putting people first, rather than solely relying on 'conformance to requirements' and an accredited quality system, where these existed.

In 1997 the UK government decided to accelerate change by requiring by statute the introduction of two major initiatives based on increased 'customer' orientation. These initiatives are called 'Best Value' in the majority of the public sector (see Simon Speller's chapter) and 'Clinical Governance' in the NHS. In the latter the new approach has been facilitated by the replacement of the competitive climate by a partnership approach. Both initiatives share three underlying principles: accountability, ownership and continuous improvement. Most of the essential elements in Best Value of sound governance, performance measurement and evaluation, and continuous improvement are also to be found in Clinical Governance. Sound governance in Best Value includes citizen focus, strategic management, operational management and financial management.

The government compares clinical governance with corporate governance in the private sector. The latter had been introduced by statute in 1992 to solve a perceived need for better governance at Board level but it is at least debatable that that initiative was introduced to solve a political need and affected only those at Board level rather than other staff. This is not the case with clinical governance, which will depend for its success on ownership at lower levels in the organisation.

The government has assisted the progress of clinical governance by including in the 1997 changes the setting up of support organisations which are to ensure/guide the generation of clinical standards and/or act as inspection organisations. They will also act as centres for benchmarking information. These organisations are listed in Exhibit 7.1.

A further reorganisation in the NHS on 1 April 1999 reduced the number of NHS Trusts (and therefore the span of control of health authorities/boards) and gave their chief executives statutory responsibility for clinical governance, i.e. responsibility for the clinical performance of the Trust. The importance attached to clinical governance is demonstrated by requiring NHS Trust boards to have a clinical governance committee with a status equal to that of their finance committee.

A significant feature of the NHS is the large number of different

*Exhibit 7.1*   *NHS supporting organisations*

| Organisation | Purpose |
| --- | --- |
| National Institute for Clinical Excellence (England) | To develop national service frameworks (standard setting). |
| Commission for Health Improvement (England) | To monitor the implementation of service frameworks and local quality systems participate in clinical audit, review local action in respect of poor clinical performance. |
| Clinical Standards Board (Scotland) | As a statutory authority for standard setting, and accreditation of managed clinical networks. |

stakeholders, all of whom need their hopes and aspirations to be satisfied. These stakeholders include doctors, nurses and professions supplementary to medicine (PSMs) in each of the acute and primary sectors; patients; the public at large; NHS Trusts; health authorities/boards; health councils; and politicians. Additionally, NHS customers have very variable expectations of the service. For example, most patients in a hospital are happy to have their condition cured, but there are others who place more importance on receiving a cup of tea precisely at 5pm or on having a separate room. Expectations vary with education and social background. This means that it is vital to explain to patients what they should expect and, therefore, more difficult to find a basis for measuring the difference between expectations and perceptions. Each of the stakeholders must be committed to clinical governance for it to succeed. The starting point is that clinical governance, like quality, comes from well-trained staff performing cost-effective routines.

One drawback of the 1997 changes has been doubt over the definition of clinical governance. For example, the official definition is

> *A framework through which NHS organisations are accountable for continuously improving the quality of their services and safeguarding high standards of care by creating an environment in which excellence in clinical care will flourish. (HMSO, 1997)*

Other views see clinical governance as almost one and the same thing as a quality system:

> *About accountability, structures and processes. It is a structure framework linked to the corporate agenda – corporate accountability for corporate performance and providing a framework linked to the corporate agenda. (Scottish Office, 1998)*

A quality system is a framework but which, as has been the case with earlier versions of ISO 9001/2000, does not necessarily result in quality improvement on its own. However, ISO 9001/2000 does have the objective of redressing that balance.

This chapter develops a model for clinical governance, discusses the benefits for the many stakeholders, outlines the effect of new NHS structures on clinical governance and provides advice for public sector managers on the issues they face.

## 7.2 Developing clinical governance

Clinical governance has to move the NHS from a blame culture to one where performance is reviewed in a routine manner without the extremes of goodness and badness which sometimes pervade these discussions. This requires the NHS to be a learning organisation but in particular to possess a framework which enables all stakeholders to understand, and be committed to, the role of the others. This needs to be carried out in a decentralised, team-based, open environment where collaboration replaces hierarchy. These new values have to overcome potential conflicts as seen by some clinicians since they perceive other stakeholders as receiving more power with the advent of clinical governance. Some opinions, which have to be countered, are:

- Quotations at the Scottish Office (1998) have been described (Smy, 1999) as the politicians' definition of clinical governance and that the correct definition should be 'doing the right things right'.
- A fancy way of reminding clinicians of their statutory duty (Goodman, 1998).
- The initiative is there to reduce medical freedom by increasing the use of performance indicators (Taylor, 1998).
- The intent is to use evidence-based care for rationing decisions.
- It is not clear whether the real aim is quality improvement or cost reduction.
- Improving the quality of healthcare or exposing bad practice (Dunning, 1998)?
- An attempt to undermine the self-governing status of health professionals and the ability of clinicians to question when they judge it right to overrule management decisions (Dunning, 1998).

Therefore the overriding requirements for successful implementation of clinical governance must also include the need for managers and clinicians to develop a systems approach to the quality of healthcare. There is a need for it (Heard, 1998) to be a reflective, iterative ongoing process involved with continually assessing and evaluating how care can be improved for patients, and the creation of an environment in which clinical excellence can flourish. If these conditions are met, the uncertainty and tension which exist in a large organisation at a time of great change will diminish or be removed. Such a system must enable the ability of Trust chief executives to influence clinical policies and ensure the commitment of clinicians to procedures initially unfamiliar to them. The question is how to achieve this.

Exhibit 7.2 shows the link between clinical governance and quality improvement, but the underpinning conditions have to be in place before improvement will take place.

Experience shows that improvement will not follow unless from a solid base. This means attention to various situational factors beforehand:

- a definition of quality which fits the work of the organisation;
- a quality system/framework understood by all;

*Exhibit 7.2*    *Framework for quality improvement*

- knowledge of the current quality level;
- benchmarking data for comparison with other Trusts or medical specialities.

In essence, these factors answer the question 'where am I now?' before setting off on the improvement journey.

These four points are discussed in turn below.

### 7.2.1   *Definition of quality*

The differing needs and responsibilities of stakeholders in the NHS force a more complex definition for quality to reflect their situation. Ovretveit (1992) decided that quality in the NHS had a number of dimensions, acknowledgement of which would provide better focus:

| | |
|---|---|
| **Patient quality** | Whether the service gives people what they want. |
| **Professional quality** | (a) Professional views of whether the service meets patients' needs as assessed by a professional (outcome being one measure), and<br>(b) whether staff correctly select and carry out procedures which are believed to be necessary to meet patients' needs (process). |
| **Management quality** | The most efficient and productive use of resources to meet client needs, within limits and directives set by higher authorities. |

The difficulty is that different stakeholders may meet some of these dimensions in their duties but not all. This is why there can be tensions in such a large organisation. The service may be patient centred but that should not invariably take precedence over professional issues or the need for the efficient use of resources. The legitimacy of this is a very difficult concept to justify to patients and the public at large.

### 7.2.2   Quality system

Most organisations have a de facto quality system: the organisational structure, processes and resources to implement quality. The question is whether to formalise the system and whether to seek (external) accreditation for it. The major systems used in the health sector are of different types (Exhibit 7.3).

Previous issues of ISO 9000/2000 have been in use in the UK health sector for 10 years for particular services within Trusts rather than for the complete organisation. The new version is expected to assist quality improvement but its predecessors have not been so helpful. In this writer's experience, the most effective use of the standard has been to act as a technique for telling management whether they were in control of the organisation.

The European Business Excellence model (European Foundation for Quality Management, 2000) has the advantage of self-assessment and wide use in both the private and recently the public sector. Hence it is very useful as a benchmarking tool. The model is based on nine criteria divided into two sections termed 'enablers' and 'results':

*Exhibit 7.3*   *Types of quality system*

| Type | Basic concept |
| --- | --- |
| ISO 9001/2000, Quality Management Systems – Requirements. (ISO 2000) (Commences early 2001) | Quality system based on management responsibility, resource management, product and/or service realisation, and measurement, analysis and improvement. No self-assessment. |
| The Health Quality Service Accreditation Programme (King's Fund, 1999) | Quality system plus self-assessment based on the management of 52 standards. |
| The European Business Excellence Model (2000 version) (European Foundation for Quality Management, 2000) | Self-assessment model which accepts the de facto quality system. |

| **Enablers** | **Results** |
|---|---|
| Leadership | People results |
| People | Customer results |
| Policy and strategy | Society results |
| Partnerships and resources | Key performance results |
| Processes | |

Each of these is divided into a number of 'sub-criteria' which are subject to a scoring mechanism. For example, leadership is divided into

1a Leaders develop the mission, vision and values and are the role model of a culture of excellence.

1b Leaders are personally involved in ensuring the organisation's system is developed, implemented and continuously improved.

1c Leader is involved with customers, partners and representatives of society.

1d Leaders motivate, support and recognise the organisation's people.

The disadvantage is that it does not include all the components of clinical governance and clinical audit is excluded. Whilst some pilot exercises have been carried out, it has only recently come into wider use. However, in Health Service Circular 1999/123, May 1999 (Department of Health, 1999), support has been forthcoming from the NHS Executive on the grounds that it is a 'logical, systematic framework to the process of self-assessment'.

The Health Quality Services method is prescriptive and relates only to the management system.

The self-assessment component of the second and third models tells the organisation more about itself and hence contributes more to corporate self-learning, which is particularly important for clinical governance. It is proposed that one of the self-assessment models be adopted but a clinical governance model also be developed to increase focus within a particular organisation.

### 7.2.3 Knowledge of the current quality level

Knowing this level enables the organisation to be clear about whether the corporate performance is acceptable before it sets out on the journey to quality improvement. In this, the role of performance indicators is key because they will eventually provide proof that progress has been made. Historically their adoption within the NHS has been beset with difficulties because of the perceived difficulty of justifying the difference from the norm of any particular measurement. Justifications for these variances included:

- measurement indicates past as opposed to present performance;
- demand factors as opposed to hospital performance;
- supply factors that are peculiar to the locality in question;
- national resource figures indicating inefficiency;
- inefficient use of resources in the hospital which has remained unidentified or uncorrected.

At the risk of being provocative these are issues to be met and managed along the path of service improvement, not reasons for not using the data.

### 7.2.4   Benchmarking data

The same arguments against the use of PIs have been used in respect of benchmarking data, i.e. cross comparisons are difficult to the point of being impossible. This is one of the reasons why the UK government set up the organisations listed in Exhibit 7.1.

### 7.2.5   The Stirling Model

This new model extends the work of Ovretveit (1992), who suggests that the definition of quality should not only include dimensions but also identify 'inputs', 'process' and 'outcomes', i.e. a 3 × 3 matrix. It also includes Heard's (1998) definition of the components of clinical governance:

1. Clinical leadership
2. Complaints
3. Continuing health needs assessment
4. Changing practice through evidence assessment
5. Continuing education
6. Clinical risk management
7. Clinical performance
8. Clinical audit
9. Culture of excellence
10. Clinical accountability

The Stirling Model (Exhibit 7.4) argues for the development of a local clinical governance model to force attention on the detail so that an understanding is gained of what is realistically achievable.

Adopting this approach provides a model shown in Exhibit 7.5 which will provide very clear focus on the components of clinical governance (the 10 components are numbered in **bold**). The inputs and processes are equivalent to the enablers in the EFQM model and the outcomes equivalent to the results. The Stirling Model needs further research but it can be developed into a focused learning tool.

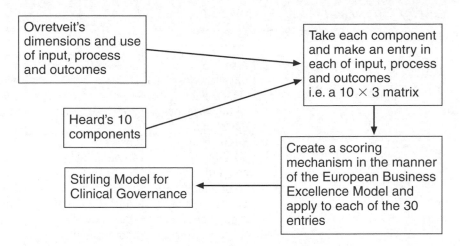

*Exhibit 7.4*    *The Stirling Model for Clinical Governance*

## 7.3   *Benefits to stakeholders*

The many stakeholders will rightly look for potential benefits from clinical governance, but these will be different depending on the role of the stakeholder within the organisation and their ability to influence events. Success requires those such as lead clinicians and Trust directors to include in their planning for clinical governance specific benefits for other stakeholders, particularly nurses, who form a large part of the staff and whose co-operation is essential. Research shows that there are a number of benefits that will increase the support of the clinical staff provided that the plans reflect their importance. These benefits do not appear by management edict. Exhibit 7.6 provides a summary of the benefits that are available to different stakeholders.

*Exhibit 7.5*    *The Stirling Model for Clinical Governance*

|  |  | Inputs | Process | Outcomes |
|---|---|---|---|---|
| **Patient** | **2.** | Complaints. | Investigate complaint. | Monitored improvement in patient satisfaction. |
|  | **3.** | Continuing health needs assessment. | Delivery of care. | Prove adequate response to needs assessment. |
| **Professional** | **7.** | Set up internal system to collect clinical performance data. | Assess performance data and identify improvements. | Prove the data have been used effectively for identifiable improvements. |

*Exhibit 7.5 (continued)*

|  |  | Inputs | Process | Outcomes |
|---|---|---|---|---|
|  | 8. | Plan subject and time schedule for clinical audit. Obtain evidence base data. | Carry out clinical audits. | Manage corrective actions and contribute data to evidence base. |
|  | 10. | Set up clinical governance committee at Trust Board level. Set up routine report scheme to CG committee. | Ensure accountability by discussion of data with board, public and patient input. Agree any improvements. | Annual report to health authority/board. Carry out agreed improvements. |
|  | 4. | Collect clinical data from benchmark sources and within the Trust. | Agree identifiable practice changes and plan their implementation. | Prove that that changes in practice have been made. |
|  | 5. | Suitably qualified, trained and co-operative clinicians. | Identify and provide further training within continuing professional development basis. | Prove the effectiveness of continuing education. |
| Management | 1. | Suitably trained, knowledge of objectives. | Drive forward clinical governance system. Involved with, and enthuse, appropriate stakeholders. | Effective clinical leadership |
|  | 6. | Carry out risk assessments. | Manage risk. | Prove reduction in risk. |
|  | 9. | Obtain evidence of clinical standards elsewhere. | Plan and implement clinical improvements leading to excellence. | Prove improvements. |

*Exhibit 7.6*   *Benefits to clinical governance stakeholders*

| Stakeholder | Benefits |
| --- | --- |
| Health Authority/Board | Clearer accountability for clinical performance. |
| | Improved knowledge of performance. |
| Management | Conditions set for improved ownership by clinical staff provided the management give the clinical governance programme a high enough profile. |
| | More integration with clinical staff. |
| | More effective standards. |
| | Increase in resources due to the cost-effective use of standards. |
| Doctors | Improved framework for medical audit. |
| | Improved applied research framework (i.e. outside medical schools). |
| | Improved patient focus. |
| | Participative involvement in the generation of realistic and achievable targets. |
| | Better clinical effectiveness in primary care due to enhanced monitoring procedures. |
| | Better teamwork with other stakeholders. |
| Nursing staff/PSMs | Improved framework for their participation in standard setting. |
| | More common paperwork systems within and between Trusts. |
| | Effective use of their resource due to standardised work practices. |
| | More involvement in patient care projects at ward level. |
| Patients | Better able to see if service delivery tallies with expectations. |
| | Better control over the variability in expectations among different patient groups. |
| | Opportunity for element of involvement in their own care. |
| | More effective listening to the voice of the patient. |
| Health Council | Improved monitoring. |

## 7.4   *Strategy and structures in the new NHS*

The new (1999) governance chain in the NHS is shown in Exhibit 7.7. The changes mean that Area Health Authority/Boards are responsible for managing a structure that is easier to command and control. It is also a structure that allows greater devolution of power and authority, which is an opportunity that must be grasped if ownership of clinical governance is to be achieved.

The aim of the new structure is to support the achievement of certain objectives within a changing environment, in other words to:

- ensure Trust chief executives have statutory responsibility for clinical quality;
- reduce the span of control of most Health Authority/Boards by reducing the number of Trusts;
- establish Primary Care Trusts on a more viable basis starting with the status of general practitioners;
- move away from resourcing inputs to resourcing against outputs – a step towards resourcing outcomes.

The achievement of these objectives and the benefits to stakeholders begin with a workforce that includes individuals with strong professional values developed over many years in the absence of cost pressures and outside administrative influence. Indeed the pursuit of

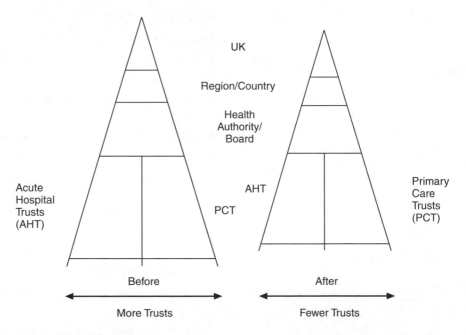

*Exhibit 7.7   New governance chain*

quality was once seen as the province of the professionals. The structure is there to serve the general public. The Trust boards have the responsibility for:

- setting up an effective clinical governance committee;
- ensuring clinical governance is monitored at board level and an appropriate annual performance report is prepared for the government;
- introducing structures, standards and processes;
- involving patients and the public;
- empowering staff to improve standards;
- empowering staff so that they undertake ownership of clinical governance activities;
- ensuring the highest possible standard of care is achieved;
- building partnerships and collaborations with other agencies.

The advent of greater political devolution in the UK in 1999 has given some freedom to tailor the implementation of clinical governance slightly differently across the United Kingdom. For example, in Scotland the Government White Paper (Scottish Office, 1997) stated that the chair of the clinical governance committee would be a non-executive director of the Trust, whereas in England the committee should be led by 'a lead clinician'. The potential effect of this Scottish arrangement is to introduce an element of independence where the chair can question the clinicians and present more forceful support of the patient point of view. Also, the participation by general practitioners in Primary Care Groups (Local Health Care Co-operatives in Scotland) is voluntary but in England duties are more prescriptive because GPs are already more closely concerned with running services in the community and community hospitals.

These new structures will not in themselves reduce the complexity which causes confusion amongst people who work in the governance chain without the assistance of a framework such as the Stirling Model.

## 7.5 *Managing in the public sector*

Managing for Best Value or Clinical Governance imposes a certain discipline on public sector managers. Success requires marketing these initiatives relentlessly in large public sector organisations, something that is perhaps done less well than in the private sector. The challenge is to make the changes permanent rather than temporary. The new initiatives will achieve this if they are based on a continuous and mature approach that allows evolution rather than a 'big bang'. This will avoid 'death by initiatives' and a corporate weariness towards them. A champion is required to establish momentum but that must not prevent the staff taking ownership, which means that there must be an exit mechanism planned for the champion from the outset. Improvement is established through the study of processes rather than the performance of individual departments. In the NHS, for example, a holistic approach needs to be applied to the study of patient pathways and managed clinical networks – processes which cross departmental boundaries. The management needs to facilitate constant interaction between stakeholders, perhaps based on informal structures rather than the hierarchical nature of much of the public sector. The overall objective is to seek innovative ways of becoming better by translating national frameworks into local application. It is for that reason that a local clinical governance model based on the Stirling Model is recommended to force attention on the detail so that an understanding is gained of what is realistically achievable.

## References

Department of Health (1996) *Health of the Nation Update*, London: Department of Health.

Department of Health (1999) Health Service Circular, No. 1999/123.

Dunning, M. (1998), 'Another chance to make real progress or another opportunity to be missed?', *British Journal of Health Care Management*, **4** (12).

European Foundation for Quality Management (200) *Improved EFQM Model*, Brussels.

Goodman, N.W. (1998) 'Clinical governance', *British Medical Journal*, **317**, 1725–1727.

Heard, S. (1998) 'The risk of missing the point of the quest for continuous improvement', *British Journal of Health Care Management*, **4** (12), Supplement, 2–3.

HMSO (1997) *The New NHS: Modern, Dependable*, London: HMSO.

ISO (2000) *ISO 9001/2000, Quality Management Systems – Requirements*, Geneva: International Standardisation Organisation.

King's Fund, (1999) *The Health Quality Service Accreditation Programme*, 3rd edn, London.

Ovretveit, J. (1992) *Health Service Quality*, Oxford: Blackwell Scientific Publications.

Scottish Office (1997) *Designed to Care: Renewing the NHS in Scotland*.

Scottish Office (1998) Several speeches by Sam Galbraith, Minister for Health, Scottish Office.

Smy, J. (1999) 'So what does clinical governance mean?', *Hospital Doctor*, 15 April, p. 30.

Taylor, D. (1998), 'New quality, new danger? Political pipedream is gaining critical mass', *British Journal of Health Care Management*, **4** (12).

# 8

# The Maslin Multi-Dimensional Matrix: A new tool to aid strategic decision making in the public sector

## By Les Prince and Ray Puffitt

> The way to deal with an impossible task [is] to chop it down into a number of merely very difficult tasks, and break each one of them into a group of horribly hard tasks, and each one of them into tricky jobs, and each one of them ... (Terry Pratchett, Truckers, p. 119)

## Editor's introduction

Managing the portfolio of products or services over time is an important strategic management task in all organisations. Many managers have been guided in that task by the use of the Boston Consulting Group Matrix and similar analytical tools, as described in Chapter 4 of *Exploring Corporate Strategy*. This chapter takes the principles of product portfolio analysis to develop a new matrix which better reflects the context within which portfolio issues are decided in the public sector – particularly the political context and priorities.

## 8.1 Introduction

The Maslin Multi-Dimensional Matrix (MMDM) is a tool that has been developed to aid strategic decision making. It was initially designed by Ray Puffitt as a tool for marketing decisions within public sector organisations in response to evident shortcomings in the Boston Matrix when applied to the public sector. Once formulated, however, it rapidly became apparent that the MMDM had applications far outside the scope of mere marketing, and that it could be adapted readily for broader questions of strategic planning. It has since its genesis been used on management development programmes for senior public service managers in Britain, and *in situ* in several British local authorities. Within these contexts it has already proved useful both as a tool and as a method of approach, for generating and identifying important and relevant questions that arise in the strategic planning process. Nevertheless, the MMDM is still under development; evidence of its utility remains, in the strictest scientific sense, anecdotal, and as we write there is still need for a systematic empirical examination. We are confident, however, that any such future examinations will vindicate the MMDM, and its associated method, as a powerful aid to decision making. Furthermore, although developed primarily for public service managers, specifically those working within British local government organisations, we also believe that the MMDM has utility within other sectors as well.

The MMDM differs from many decision-making tools in that it does not take either a normative or a prescriptive stance in relation to the processes of arriving at decisions. As explained below, the principal dimensions that form the core of the analysis are derived directly from the decision context within which the decision maker must work. The MMDM, therefore, integrates fully within the decision maker's own frame of reference, and does not require awkward redefinition of key terms in order to be useful.

In principle there are infinitely many dimensions that define the relationship between a public service organisation and the environment in which it operates, although in practice there will effectively be between four and ten that most adequately define the decision space, depending on the primary issues that must be taken into account. This makes the MMDM a very flexible tool capable of providing important insights into a wide range of decision problems that arise not only at the strategic level but also at more tactical levels of management. Ultimately it is limited only by the analyst's, that is, the decision maker's, imagination.

## 8.2   *Limitations of the Boston Matrix*

The Boston Matrix has been an influential tool, developed by the Boston Consulting Group (BCG) specifically for marketing within the private sector (Johnson and Scholes, 1999; Richardson and Richardson, 1989; Walsh, 1989). It is exceptionally well known, but because it was materially important for the initial development of the MMDM it is important here to provide a necessarily brief description and critique of it. A more detailed critique can be found in the companion to this volume, Johnson and Scholes (1999).

In essentials the Boston Matrix is very simple. Rooted in the economic model of the so-called 'rational' actor, it comprises two predefined dimensions, 'Market Share' and 'Market Growth', arranged on a $2 \times 2$ matrix (see Exhibit 8.1). Against these axes, the products or services offered by an organisation are evaluated. The dimensions themselves are, strictly speaking, not dimensions at all, but a simple binary or bipo-

**Market share**

|  | High | Low |
|---|---|---|

<table>
<tr><td></td><td>High</td><td>Stars</td><td>Question marks</td></tr>
<tr><td>**Market growth**</td><td></td><td></td><td></td></tr>
<tr><td></td><td>Low</td><td>Cash cows</td><td>Dogs</td></tr>
</table>

*Exhibit 8.1    The original Boston Consulting Group Matrix (BCG)*

lar scale consisting of two values: high and low, although it should be noted that the *x*-axis is eccentrically labelled right to left rather than left to right as is more conventional in figures of this type. By allocating these notional, and possibly subjective, values to each axis of the matrix, four cells can be identified. In the standard Boston Matrix these are labelled: Dogs, Cash Cows, Rising Stars and Prospects (or Problem Child, or Question Mark – see Johnson and Scholes, 1999). These refer to goods or services provided by the organisation. The roots of this tool in *selling* are obvious from the label Prospects. Thus, a 'rising star' would be defined as something provided by the organisation that has shown an increase in market demand, and shows the potential for development as a significant source of income for the organisation, or, probably more appropriately for the public service, for the achievement of its primary objectives (Puffitt, 1993). 'Dogs', by contrast, are those aspects of the organisation's activities in relation to its publics that either have a declining market share, or are in danger of becoming, in economic jargon, a net cost to the organisation – something that costs more to produce than it derives in income. For the public service a 'dog' would be an activity that fails significantly to help the organisation achieve its primary objectives, statutory or otherwise. The implications for decisions in respect of these are, respectively, development and promotion in the first case, and abandonment in the second, although, as Johnson and Scholes (1999) observe, the situation is generally not always so straightforward, either because of political pressures within the organisation or because, in some cases, there may be other good reasons for maintaining 'dogs' within the overall portfolio of the organisation.

The issue of 'primary' objectives is an important one for the public sector, where 'market share' may not be an appropriate evaluation, especially in relation to statutory duties. Puffitt (1993) discusses the issue in detail, and has developed a set of tools for examining a raft of objectives that may be important for an organisation and breaking them down into Primary and Secondary objectives, and then further into Critical and Non-critical secondary objectives. One aspect of this discussion that is particularly important in relation to Maslin analysis is the recognition that public sector organisations, especially, have multiple and often *competing* objectives that are not easily captured in a simple analysis such as that offered by the Boston Matrix.

Simple though it is, the Boston Matrix has embedded within it several highly dubious assumptions. First, the rational actor model upon which it is based. This model *asserts* that a 'rational' actor, whether an individual or an organisation, will always act to maximise 'utility', defined here in narrow economic terms as a contribution to the objective of making a sufficient profit to satisfy the owners of a business. This is often interpreted crudely in terms of money – 'the bottom line' – although it is important to note that 'utility', and even 'profit', is often better conceived in broader terms as 'advantage' of some kind. This immediately introduces a complication into the calculations implied by the Boston Matrix that cannot be encompassed within the matrix itself. A 'dog' that provides no immediately obvious monetary benefits, according to Boston Matrix analysis, *may* provide important advantages of other kinds by a different analysis – prestige, for example (Johnson and Scholes, 1999). The trouble is that it is not at all clear whether the 'rational' actor model underlying the Boston Matrix is intended to be normative or descriptive – whether it is meant to assert that 'rational' actors *ought* to maximise their utility as a broad ethical prescription, or whether it is claiming that *empirically* actors *do* act to maximise their utility. In practice there is a fudge between the two, both positions being implicit in the use of the model, and it is frequently impossible to be clear about what is being asserted or claimed. In either case, however, the underlying model presents problems. If it is intended as a normative model, then it demands a level of rationality that is impossible to attain, and which, in any case, is a very poor approximation of human rationality as opposed to that of the computer (Allison, 1971; Cohen et al., 1972; Eisenberg, 1984; Hickson et al., 1986; March and Simon, 1958; Simon, 1960; Weick, 1979); if it is intended as a descriptive model, it is, simply, wrong – no such creature as the rational actor, in these terms, has ever existed, except in the imaginations of economists and Gene Roddenberry. And in the latter case the Vulcans are simply a dramatic device. Of course one way out this dilemma is to treat the Boston Matrix simply as a *descriptive* device without implications for action (Johnson and Scholes, 1999).

Second, as noted above, it is implicit within the Boston Matrix that economic return is the primary criterion upon which decisions are made, ignoring the importance of other considerations, such as the political and social context (Johnson and Scholes, 1999).

Third, as with many normative models of decision making, there is an assumption that perfect information will be available, and that it can be processed fully, adequately and continuously in order to inform the final decision. But, as is by now well known from studies of naturalistic decision making (e.g. Lipshitz, 1993; Orasanu and Connolly, 1993), information is usually incomplete and ambiguous, and therefore subject to interpretive constraints. Furthermore, people are *very bad* at processing such information as they have to hand, and decisions are often based not on *maximising* utility, but on a strategy of *satisficing* (Janis and Mann, 1977; Simon, 1960). Taking these in turn, information flowing to and from the environment is not, in and of itself, *meaningful*. The meaning that is derived is, to a *very* great extent, *supplied* by those interpreting it. This is true even of financial and statistical data (Huff, 1973; Moore, 1980; Waddington, 1977). In deriving the meaning of information, interpretive strategies are deployed, and these often involve not so-called 'rationality' based on statistical, logical or economic principles, but political considerations, broadly understood, and other 'non-rational' factors such as simple preference for one thing over another (Hosking and Morley, 1991). This is attributable to several fundamental features of human psychology. In the first place our ability to deal with information is severely constrained by cognitive limitations, and beyond certain well-known limits we begin to experience cognitive overload (Hosking and Morley, 1991; Steinbruner, 1974). Once the limits of attention and processing capacity have been reached, information is processed more cursorily, and sometimes ignored altogether. Second, human beings cannot entirely divorce their *rational* capacities from other features of mentation such as *affect* (emotion) and *conation* (will); indeed, recent arguments from neurology suggest that were we able to overcome the emotional component of our humanity altogether we would not be able to function rationally in any sense (Damasio, 1994, 1995). Vulcans, from the *Star Trek* universe, the ultimate (and indeed the *only*) known examples of fully rational actors in the economic sense, may be able to function without emotion; human beings cannot. This inescapably introduces an element of the 'non-rational' into *any* decision, even strategic decisions. Partly as a result of these factors, plus others from the context such as time constraints, it has been observed that *real* decision makers, as opposed to the fictional ones of the rational actor model, tend to settle on decisions that fall short of maximisation. This aspect of real-life decisions was called *satisficing* by Herbert Simon, by which he meant that people on the whole tend to settle for decisions (or outcomes) that are overall *satisfactory* and *sufficient* to their purposes (Simon, 1960).

Fourth, the Boston Matrix implies, mainly by omission, that organisations operate in only one context – that strange abstraction called 'the market' – in which they are in perpetual competition with other inhabitants of the same context. This is simply not true. Even private sector organisations operate in a broadly political and social context, as much as the market. Put in crude terms, all organisations are obliged to operate within the law, and sometimes are required to act contrary to what their management might regard as their own best interests as a consequence. Regulation is a case in point. More broadly, the implication of permanent and ineradicable competition, with the injunction to capture competitive advantage, rather overlooks the importance of *co-operation* between individuals and organisations. Many organisations could not survive without such co-operation.

Thus, to take the prescriptions of the Boston Matrix at face value is not very helpful, especially in the public sector, as a guide either to how an organisation *should* act, or to how it *will* act. Even in the private sector, where the injunction to 'watch the bottom line' might be expected to have most force, it is not at all clear that dealing with the 'dogs' is, or can be, a simple matter of abandonment. In the public sector it may not be possible to abandon the 'dogs' at all (Johnson and Scholes, 1999).

The public sector works in an overtly political environment. Most organisations within the public sector are either arms of, or delegated services of, government, and therefore, at least in the West, subject to various forms of direct and indirect 'democratic' control. In practice this means being subject to various partisan political pressures. In particular, many public services are established as an outcome of political commitments to various social values, regardless of economic costs. Many of these are also enshrined as statutory duties. Undoubtedly many of these might appear, under Boston Matrix analysis, as 'dogs', but the scope for abandonment is very severely constrained, and even impossible if they fall under the remit of statutory duty – any public body can be forced, by *mandamus*, to fulfil its statutory duties regardless of prevailing circumstances, in which case the market becomes entirely irrelevant. An example will serve to illustrate the point. In the matter of public transport, while it *may* be possible for a private contractor to abandon 'uneconomic' routes (depending on the nature of the contracts they have to supply the service), a *publicly owned* transport company may well find itself obliged to continue operating, as a public service, despite the lack of economic viability.

## 8.3   *The Montanari Matrix*

Montanari and Bracker (1986) (cited in Johnson and Scholes, 1999) have also developed a matrix, similar to the Boston Matrix, for use in the public sector (Johnson and Scholes, 1999). This is also a 2 × 2 figure, comprising two dimensions: 'Ability to serve' on the x-axis and 'Public need and support + funding attractiveness' on the y-axis. Like the Boston Matrix, both these axes are measured by the simple evaluations of low and high, arranged on the x-axis in the same eccentric order as the Boston Matrix (i.e. right to left).

In broad terms this matrix is clearly an improvement on the Boston Matrix for use in the public sector. The ability to serve is of paramount importance, especially in relation to statutory requirements, and draws attention to the resource implications, both human and otherwise, that are necessary to fulfil public duty. As a shift away from the language of 'markets' towards that of 'service' this dimension more clearly identifies one of the major preoccupations of the public sector.

The same is true of the other dimension of the matrix. But, as labelled, this dimension presents problems of its own. In point of fact it identifies, and then conflates, three distinct variables: public need, public support and funding attractiveness. It is difficult to see how one could make a meaningful evaluation of all three simultaneously. That people might *need* something does not necessarily imply either that they are *aware* of the need, or that they will be supportive of attempts to fill the need. Part of the problem is the question of *who defines the need?* Using public health issues for examples, it is now held that people in general *need* to take more exercise. It is also generally held that those members of the public who smoke *need*, for their health's sake, to give it up. In both cases, however, there remain substantial numbers of people who either dispute the need itself, or simply fail to support attempts to fulfil the need. The reason is obvious: it is a need that has been defined by the public authorities, not necessarily by (some) members of the public itself. On the other hand, members of the public may define for themselves a need (say, the reduction of speeding traffic in their area) that the authorities are either unwilling or unable to recognise.

Funding attractiveness, while important, is independent of the other two aspects of the dimension, as labelled, that this matrix uses. It is also problematic in that it begs the question of 'attractiveness for whom'? High levels of public support *may* make it attractive to fund a particular service, but then again, *central government approval* might be the key criterion of attractiveness, even in the *absence* of general public support.

It would have been better had the y-axis dimension been presented as three distinct aspects of analysis. True, in this case any particular analysis may then contain contradictions, but, as noted above, this is actually a reflection of one reality that the public sector often faces – multiple *competing* objectives (Puffitt, 1993). This, ultimately, is what led to the development of the Maslin Matrix.

### 8.4    *The Maslin Multi-Dimensional Matrix*

The fundamental principle behind the MMDM is what may be called 'creative clarification': a process of approaching difficult problems of strategy systematically, but without expelling the creativity essential to 'good' decision making. Using the language of formal decision theory, the MMDM is a tool that assists in the maintenance of vigilant decision making, as opposed to non-vigilant (garbage can) decision making (Hosking and Morley, 1991; Janis, 1972, 1982, 1989; Janis and Mann, 1977; Lindblom, 1952), without prescribing all aspects of the process. In its basic form the MMDM looks similar to the Boston Matrix: it comprises a $2 \times 2$ matrix of four cells, with two evaluative axes. It differs fundamentally from the Boston Matrix, however, in one important respect: very little of the MMDM is predefined, and in principle all aspects of it can be redefined to accommodate the user's context. Furthermore, the normative aspects of the Boston Matrix have been deliberately excluded, and although some aspects of the MMDM remain mildly prescriptive, its primary orientation is towards *descriptive* analysis, and clarification of situations, rather than the provision of ready-made categorisations that contain implicit prescriptions for action. At each stage of MMDM analysis, the analyst is in complete control of the decision processes – what to include and exclude; what to prioritise; and, most important, the *interpretation* of any results. At no stage does MMDM analysis tell the analyst what he or she *should* think, nor does it prescribe preset courses of action. Indeed, in many ways MMDM analysis resembles a sort of 'Socratic dialogue', in which the method provides prompts to which the analyst seeks his or her *own* answers.

The one predefined element of the MMDM is the *x*-axis: *Needs or wants of the client group*. Note, however, that even the definition of this dimension is not fixed *a priori*, but is subject to analysis and, in many cases, may require some form of research. From our experience, this is a primary dimension for evaluation of options in the public sector, and almost all MMDM analyses proceed as a comparison of this dimension with various other 'user-defined' dimensions that are plotted on the *y*-axis. Nevertheless, in principle this, too, can be redefined according to circumstances, although in what follows we will consider it a 'fixed' element of the MMDM (see Exhibit 8.2).

### 8.4.1    X-*axis: needs or wants of a client group*

Derivation of the 'needs or wants of a client group' is extremely important, and requires very careful consideration. In general, however, the needs of any particular client group of a public service organisation are laid down in some form of rule, whereas wants are simply desire.

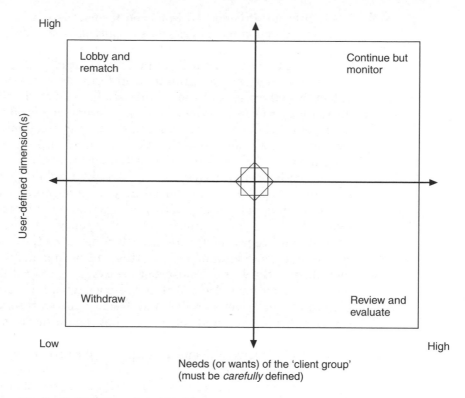

High

Lobby and
rematch

Continue but
monitor

User-defined dimension(s)

Withdraw

Review and
evaluate

Low

High

Needs (or wants) of the 'client group'
(must be *carefully* defined)

*Exhibit 8.2*   *Maslin Multi-Dimensional Matrix*

Wants exist solely in the mind. One wants a house, or a car, or the latest fashions, and so on, and in this case the final criterion as to whether the want can be satisfied is preparedness or ability to meet the market price, or persuade someone else to meet it on one's behalf (notwithstanding other more direct methods of acquisition such as theft). Needs, on the other hand, as understood within public services, are derived from *rules* of some sort: legal, political or, sometimes, moral. Quite obviously these implicate particular sets of values and interests as well. To illustrate, consider the following example.

A person may *want* a house, but if that person is unable to pay the market price, either by way of purchase or rent, then they cannot have the house *unless* they are able to establish their *need* for a house. In the latter case they will need to satisfy the criteria, as laid down by statute or local policy, for the award of social housing or housing benefit, and therefore fall within the remit of the appropriate public authority. It should not be imagined, however, that the *wants* of a citizen or client group are somehow always irrelevant. On the contrary, if there is sufficient demand from the population for a particular service, whether or nor it is needed in formal terms, there are occasions when that can become a policy priority as politicians or public service managers respond (see Puffitt and Prince in this volume).

Using this example to illuminate the status of the labels high and low on the *x*-axis, these evaluations in terms of need are generally set out in formal criteria of some kind. High and low, in this case, may mean that government, the ruling party group of a local authority, the management team of a particular service, or some other body with the authority to set priorities of this kind has decided, *for whatever reason*, to define a need as real and of a particular weight.

Questions of priority *within* a particular public agency are, however, quite separate. That a need may have been defined as high by, say, the ruling party group of an authority does *not* mean that it automatically has a high priority for the agency itself. That decision depends on aspects of the relationship between the agency (or cost centre) and its environment, and this will be clarified by dimensions identified on the *y*-axis. To use a crude example, the ruling group of an authority may have decided that the poor among its citizens have a high need for poverty relief, but because of statutory limitations, scarcity of resources, and rules about how an authority may dispose of what resources it has, the local authority as a whole is unable to accept poverty relief for its citizens as a priority for action.

The importance of this is that needs are *defined by some group in relation to some particular sets of priorities*. Clearly there is scope here for levels of need to be defined differently by significant groups party to related decisions; for example, elected members and officers within an authority may set the levels of need for a particular group at different levels, and this alone immediately draws attention to the political process. Again, the emphasis here is *not* on the technical aspects of a decision, but on the political and social aspects (to which one would also add cognitive elements – Hosking and Morley, 1991), and this highlights the importance of the negotiated features of resultant decisions.

### 8.4.2   Y-axis: user definitions

The *y*-axis is purely user-defined, according to requirements. In a detailed analysis several such dimensions will be defined, and the resulting diagrams compared with one another to provide a 'thick' textured analysis of the situation, or problem, under consideration. As noted above, there are infinitely many possible relevant dimensions, although the scope will in practice be restricted by particular salient aspects of the context and the issues under consideration. Again, different parties may disagree on what is or is not salient, but this is irrelevant to the overall analysis. Indeed, the fact of disagreement may itself become an important aspect of the analysis.

Given the statement above, it is clearly not possible to give any-thing like a definitive list of the kinds of dimensions that may be used. Instead, therefore, we will list a representative sample of the kinds of dimensions that users have in the past deployed in using the matrix:

- level of concern by elected members;
- level of concern of the community;
- level of concern by national government;
- level of provision by other agencies;
- level of finance available;
- level of (non-financial) resources available;
- level of staff expertise;
- level of statutory duty (mandatory or discretionary);
- level of activity currently undertaken.

Several of these dimensions, it will be noted, are concerned with bodies other than the one making the decision, and this again highlights the principle that in the public sector decisions are generally made in the light of another group's priorities. Some of these other groups also represent a 'higher' authority: national government; elected members; a management team.

### 8.4.3 Measurement of dimensions

As with the Boston Matrix, the dimensions of the MMDM are, in their usual form, measured by a simple two-point scale, providing four cells. Depending on circumstances, however, it is perfectly feasible for users to adopt a true continuous scale for both axes, if they wish, providing a more fine-grained measurement of the issues under consideration, but in practice we cannot envisage many situations where a scale of more than about five points would give any particular advantage; most of the questions likely to be approached using the MMDM are not really amenable to precise measurement, and using a spurious accuracy could create more problems than it solves.

### 8.4.4 The quadrants

Although much of the MMDM is open to creative and flexible definition or redefinition, it has become clear through use that the quadrants generated by the 2 × 2 form of the matrix can be given general labels that apply in a wide variety of circumstances. These are: *Withdraw*; *Lobby and rematch*; *Continue but monitor*; and *Review and evaluate* (see Exhibit 8.2). In some ways these are similar to the *kinds* of prescriptive conclusions generated by the Boston Matrix, but they differ in several important respects. First, they have been labelled so as to place political context at the centre of the analysis. This is critical. Many public sector organisations, especially local government and associated agencies, are not free to act in ways that their private (or even voluntary) sector counterparts are. Of course this feature of the public sector should not be over-exaggerated; *all* organisations are restricted to some extent, and their management groups are certainly not free to act as they like. Nevertheless, in the public sector, because, at least in theory, the actions of an organisation are subject to direct, and partisan, political control, much of what they can do is restricted in a way unlike those of other sectors.

The second point follows from the first. Unlike the Boston Matrix, the labels for the MMDM do not identify strictly 'market-oriented' decisions, but instead identify *actions of engagement with the political process itself*. That is to say, the actions denoted by these labels necessarily imply the need at some point to engage with partisan politics, recognising that not all decisions can be, or indeed ever be, optimising in a strictly commercial sense. Engagement with the political process, of course, also implies the need, on the part of managers engaging in this kind of strategic decision making, to have and develop political skills themselves, as well as the more generally recognised managerial skills. Of course it has been recognised for some time that political skills are requisite for managers, and others, in *all* organisational settings (Hosking and Morley, 1991; Lee and Lawrence, 1985, 1991), but here, again, these skills need to be in many ways to the fore. Specifically, what are needed are highly developed skills of perception and negotiation (Hosking and Morley, 1991).

The final point relates to the flexibility of the MMDM, and the need for 'engaged intelligence' in interpreting appropriate responses to MMDM analysis. Although the labels are themselves fairly clear, they nevertheless are also subject to interpretation, specifically interpretation rooted in a full understanding of the context. For example, *Lobby and rematch* may be easier in some circumstances than others. Approaching a particularly convinced and inflexible ruling party group, for example, may not be altogether wise if the issues address deeply held convictions within the group. Again, this highlights the principle that not all decisions can be treated as purely technical matters, but sometimes need to be regarded more as an extension of diplomacy. Thus, in such a case, while the analysis may identify the *need* to lobby and rematch, in practice this will have to be taken alongside some fairly robust knowledge of the context, and adjusted accordingly. In this sense the creative and intelligent deployment of skills, knowledge and experience is inseparable from the analysis itself.

### 8.4.5   *Interpreting the diagonals*

In using the MMDM, it became apparent that not only were the cells analytically useful, but so were the diagonals. The more it is used in practice, in fact, the more important the diagonals appear to be. On the basis of *a priori* consideration, we labelled the two diagonals as *Equilibrium* and *Disequilibrium* (see Exhibit 8.3). These seem to highlight some fundamental tensions that may underlie issues under analysis, and have considerable implications for any subsequent decisions. Significantly, this feature of the matrix has much in common with mapping techniques of 'negotiation space' in what Morley (1996) calls utility models of negotiation and bargaining. There, in a similar analysis, Morley observes that a bottom left to top right diagonal represents a line of 'common interest' between negotiating actors, whereas a top left to bottom right diagonal represents a line of conflict between the parties (Morley, 1996: 340). This is important here because, as noted earlier, the MMDM is a model of decision

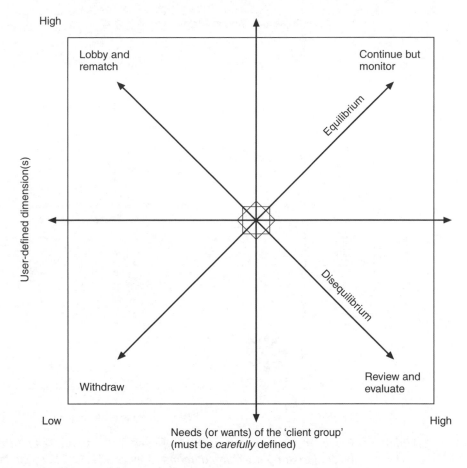

*Exhibit 8.3    Maslin Multi-Dimensional Matrix*

space taken in relation to a political context, and the essence of that context is the implication that final decisions must be made on the basis of negotiation and bargaining, even if this is implicit.

## 8.5    Some examples

One of the best ways to show how a Maslin analysis proceeds is to use simple examples. In each of these the *x*-axis, needs or wants of the client group, is considered to be defined according some rule laid down by authority. The *y*-axis in each case is defined separately by two dimensions: 'level of elected member concern' and 'existing level of provision'.

To begin, because they are the easier examples, it is useful to consider the quadrants located on the line of equilibrium: bottom left

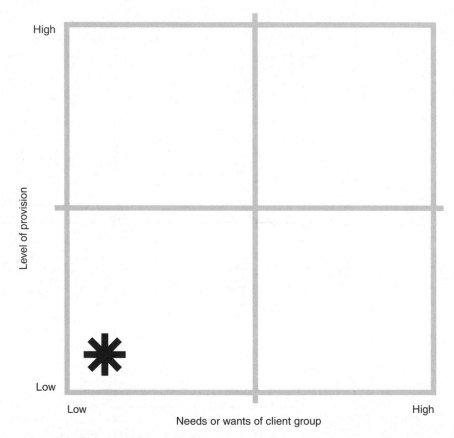

*Exhibit 8.4    Provision of wash houses. Level of need for wash houses plotted against level of existing provision demonstrates equilibrium because both are matched*

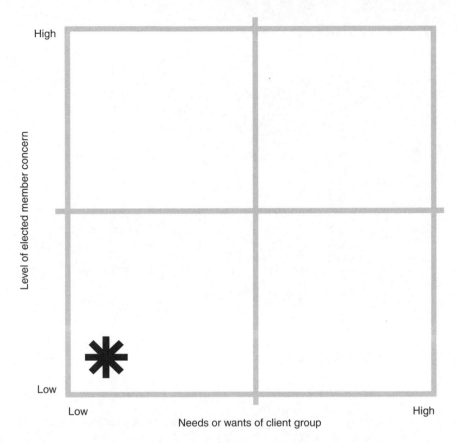

*Exhibit 8.5*    *Provision of wash houses. Level of need for wash houses plotted against level of political concern also demonstrates equilibrium*

(withdraw) and top right (continue but monitor). Equilibrium here denotes a situation which is politically unproblematic; activities, resources and requirements are fairly well matched.

### 8.5.1   Example 1: Bottom left quadrant (See Exhibits 8.4, 8.5, 8.6)

With the advent of baths in private houses the need for public wash houses *for the general community* has declined, and there is no statutory requirement on local authorities to provide them. Thus, on level of need (x-axis), wash houses would fall on the left of the Maslin Matrix. Because public baths are not a pressing political concern, levels of elected member concern are low, and thus wash houses fall into the lower left quadrant by this analysis. Taking the levels of current provision as a separate analytical dimension, it is clear that cur-

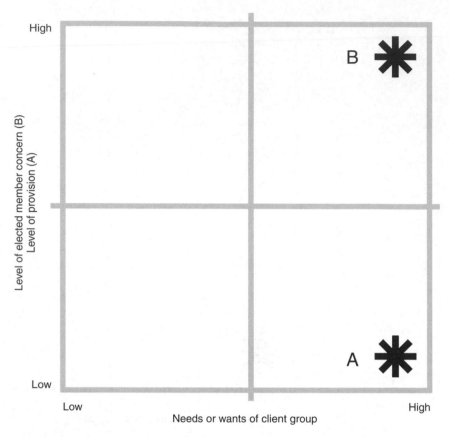

*Exhibit 8.6*   *Provision of wash houses. When the client group is defined differently, in this case as members of the vagrant population, the level of need for wash houses may become high. Plotting this against level of provision (A) and level of local political interest (B) may thus generate a complex anaylsis in which one part of the plot shows equilibrium and the other disequilibrium*

rent provision is also low. Thus, in these analyses of this issue (there could be others), it is clear that wash houses are not a priority. If there is *any* existing provision, it is also clear that it could perhaps be abandoned without very much difficulty. But note here that had the client group been defined not as the general population, but as members of the *vagrant* population, the analysis might have turned out differently – perhaps as high need, low member interest, and low provision (bottom right-hand quadrant), or high need, high member interest (perhaps a lobby group), and low provision (top right-hand quadrant *and* bottom right-hand quadrant). Quite clearly in both these cases there would be a need to act, and ultimately the action would have to be directed towards revaluing one of the dimensions, either by increasing provision from low to high, or redefining the level of need as it applies to the organisation from high to low – perhaps by persuading another agency to take on the problem.

### 8.5.2   Example 2: Top right quadrant (See Exhibit 8.7)

The top right-hand quadrant has values of high on both dimensions. A good example here would be child protection services. Here there is a high need, as defined not only by statutory duty, but also in a general sense because there is widespread political and moral assent to such provision. Thus in terms of need child protection would fall on the right-hand side of the matrix. Local authority social service departments expend considerable resources in pursuit of child protection, so

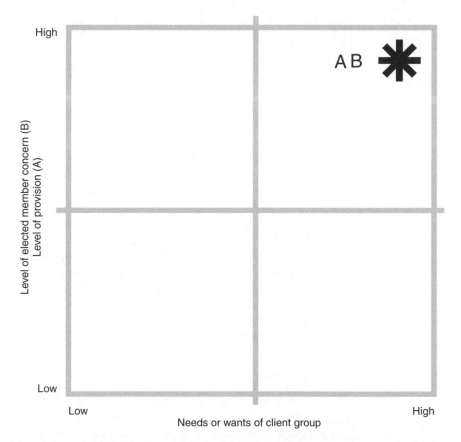

Exhibit 8.7   *Provision of child protection services. Need for child pretection services is defined as high, by statute. Levels of provision and local political interest are also high, and therefore both plots demonstrate equilibrium*

in terms of levels of resourcing it falls in the upper half of the matrix, and intersecting with the *x*-axis therefore falls in the upper right-hand quadrant. In terms of elected member interest or concern, this is also likely to be high, although not necessarily actively so. Individual elected members, perhaps even a majority of them, might not be personally interested in the issue. But politically their levels of concern are high when the issue is made salient. Thus, while it is possible to conclude in general that elected member concern is high, this does not denote any kind of ongoing active preoccupation. In this case the label 'continue but monitor' is clearly appropriate: there is a match between need, priority and resources. But monitoring continues to be necessary not only to ensure that the levels and kind of provision remain appropriate, but also to monitor whether there is a significant change in need for the provision.

### 8.5.3   Example 3: Top left quadrant (See Exhibit 8.8)

This quadrant is labelled, for convenience, 'Lobby and rematch', but it could equally well be labelled 'Why are we still doing it?', whatever 'it' is. Any examples for this quadrant are likely to be controversial, so, at the risk of upsetting someone, we tentatively suggest that municipal golf courses might be an issue falling into this quarter. In statutory terms the provision of municipal golf courses is a low need, and yet many authorities continue to provide if not high then at least substantial provision. If levels of elected member interest or concern are low (thus falling into the bottom left quadrant), it might be possible to abandon the provision altogether. But here we need to ask further questions regarding member interest, and the *meaning* of a high or low evaluation. If their concern is high, this implies they are somehow focused on the issue, but it is necessary to ask whether they are committed to *keeping* the existing provision or *abandoning* it. Thus, in this case it is insufficient merely to know that members have concerns; the nature of those concerns are also pertinent to the final decision, and whether it denotes a disequilibrating force (maintaining a mismatch of resources to need) or an equilibrating force (tending towards a rematching of resources to need).

### 8.5.4   Example 4: Bottom right quadrant (See Exhibit 8.9)

This quadrant is labelled 'Review and evaluate', but as above it could equally well be labelled 'Why aren't we doing it?' This quadrant indicates a high need but, in terms of the dimensions we have chosen for the *y*-axis, low provision and low elected member concern. Again, any examples are likely to be controversial, and more so in this case than in the previous example. Nevertheless, there are existing examples to

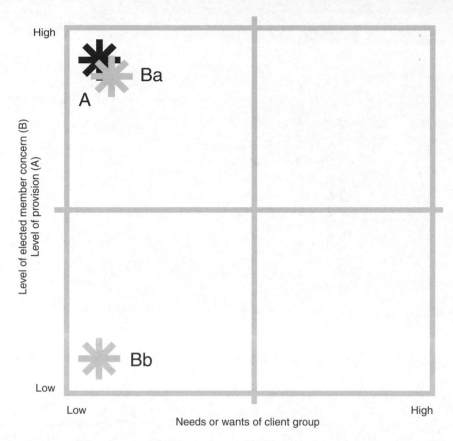

Exhibit 8.8  *Municipal golf courses. The need for municipal golf courses is low, but provision high. The plot therefore shows disequilibrium. Whether the situation can be resolved in this (simple) analysis depends on levels of elected member concern, and what the levels of concern mean. If they are high, but in favour of retaining the golf courses (Ba), the situation is clearly disequilibriated. If, however, they are high but in favour of abolition (Bb), then the combined plot shows both equilibrium and disequilibrium*

hand. By statute, local authority environmental health departments are required to undertake inspections under the provision of the Health and Safety at Work Act (high need). But, for a variety of reasons, much of the work of environmental health departments concerns food safety inspection – an entirely different duty (Prince et al., 1997). Thus there is a mismatch, and a fundamental disequilibrium, between level of provision and level of need. From the point of view of local politicians food safety has a higher priority than health and safety inspection, and this tends to maintain the disequilibrium. *Logic* would suggest a rematching so that provision is increased, but the

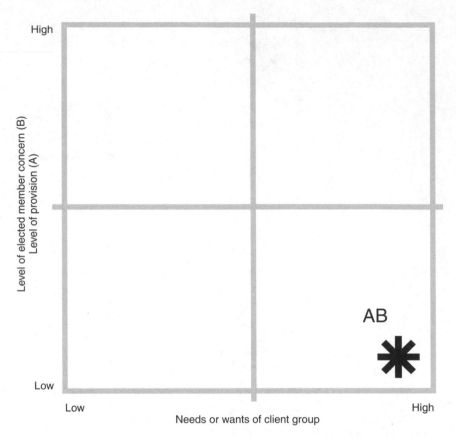

*Exhibit 8.9    Health and safety at work. The need for local inspection under the Health and Safety at Work Act is high under law, but often for local reasons provision is transferred to Food Safety Inspection, a separate requirement, and therefore provision is low. This demonstrates a disequilibriated state, but one not easily resolved*

situation is such that there are forces beyond immediate control that cannot easily be overcome.

In both examples along the line of disequilibrium there are forces tending to maintain the status quo that may be outside the control of the decision makers. In such cases all that may be possible is to sit tight and wait until the time is right for change, or to mount a campaign aimed at changing some of these forces. In either case the decision is a political one, not a purely technical one. What is certain, however, is that where such an analysis is produced, it should be a matter of concern to the agency, and the subject of careful future planning.

## 8.6  Concluding remarks

Although originally developed as a 'public sector' riposte to the Boston Matrix, for use as a marketing tool where profit is not the primary goal, the MMDM has, in use, shown itself to have far broader application as a general tool to aid strategic decision making. We are, of course, aware that there are many unanswered questions relating to the MMDM and its application to such elevated activities. In particular, it would be useful, if not essential, to assess its usefulness by systematic empirical study in relation to a broad spectrum of strategic decisions. Nevertheless, experience of using the MMDM in real situations has persuaded us of its fundamental power as a tool that really does help decision makers clarify their own thoughts and the situation around (sometimes very tricky) strategic decisions in the public sector. We also believe that it could also have similar application in the private sector.

Of course no tool, regardless of its power and scope, can ever guarantee perfect and foolproof decisions – the world is simply too complex to make any such claim more than overblown rhetoric. Nevertheless, it is our view that systematic approaches such as the MMDM can give *substantial* help to decision makers in avoiding *really stupid* decisions.

## References

Allison, G.T. (1971) *The Essence of Decision: Explaining the Cuban Missile Crisis*, Boston: Little Brown.

Cohen, M.D., March, J.G. and Olsen, P.J. (1972) 'A garbage can model of organisational choice', *Administrative Science Quarterly*, **17**, 1–25.

Damasio, A. (1994) 'Descartes's error and the future of human life', *Scientific American*, October, 116.

Damasio, A. (1995) *Descartes's Error: Emotion, reason and the human brain*, London: Macmillan.

Eisenberg, D.J. (1984) 'How senior managers think', *Harvard Business Review*, **62** (Nov–Dec), 80–90.

Hickson, D.J., Butler, R.J., Cray, D., Mallory, G.R. and Wilson, D.C. (1986) *Top Decisions: Strategic Decision Making in Organisations*, Oxford: Basil Blackwell.

Hosking, D.-M. and Morley, I.E. (1991) *A Social Psychology of Organising*, New York: Harvester Wheatsheaf.

Huff, D. (1973) *How to Lie with Statistics*, Harmondsworth: Penguin.

Janis, I.L. (1972) *Victims of Groupthink*, Boston: Houghton Mifflin.

Janis, I.L. (1982) *Groupthink: Psychological studies of foreign policy decisions and fiascoes*, Boston: Houghton Mifflin.

Janis, I.L. (1989) *Crucial Decisions: Leadership in policy making and crisis management*, New York: Free Press.

Janis, I.L. and Mann, L. (1977) *Decision Making: A psychological analysis of conflict, choice and commitment*, New York: Free Press.

Johnson, G. and Scholes, K. (1999) *Exploring Corporate Strategy,* 5th edn, New York: Prentice Hall.

Lee, R. and Lawrence, P. (1985) *Organisational Behaviour: Politics at Work*, London: Hutchinson.

Lee, R. and Lawrence, P. (1991) *Politics at Work*, Cheltenham: Stanley Thornes.

Lindblom, C.E. (1952) 'The science of "muddling through"', *Public Administration Review*, **19** (2), 78–88.

Lipshitz, R. (1993) 'Converging themes in the study of decision making in realistic settings', in G.A. Klein, J. Orasanu, C.E. Calderwood and C.E. Zsambok (eds), *Decision Making in Action: Models and Methods*, New Jersey: Ablex.

March, J.G. and Simon, H.A. (1958) *Organisations*, New York: Wiley.

Moore, P.G. (1980) *Reason by Numbers*, Harmondsworth: Penguin.

Morley, I.E. (1996) 'Negotiation and bargaining', in O. Hargie (ed.), *Handbook of Communication Skills*, London: Routledge.

Orasanu, J. and Connolly, T. (1993) 'The reinvention of decision making', in G.A. Klein, J. Orasanu, C.E. Calderwood and C.E. Zsambok (eds), *Decision Making in Action: Models and Methods*, New Jersey: Ablex.

Prince, L., Campbell, A. and Nanton, P. (1997) *Training for Health and Safety Enforcement*, Health and Safety Executive: Contract Research Report 155/1997, London: HSE Books.

Puffitt, R. (1993) *Business Planning and Marketing: A guide for the local government cost centre manager*, London: Longman.

Richardson, B. and Richardson, R. (1989) *Business Planning: An approach to strategic management*, London: Pitman.

Simon, H.A. (1960) *The New Science of Management Decision*, New York: Harper & Row.

Steinbruner, J. (1974) *The Cybernetic Theory of Decision*, Princeton, NJ: Princeton University Press.

Waddington, C.H. (1977) *Tools for Thought*, St. Albans: Paladin.

Walsh, K. (1989) *Marketing in Local Government*, London: Pitman.

Weick, K. (1979) 'Educational organisations as loosely coupled systems', *Administrative Science Quarterly*, **21** (1), 1–19.

# 9

# *Stakeholder mapping: A practical tool for public sector managers*[1]

## *By Kevan Scholes*

### *Editor's introduction*

Chapter 5 of *Exploring Corporate Strategy* makes it clear that the processes of formulating and implementing strategies in organisations have a strong political dimension. This is especially true in public sector organisations. The central tool for analysing this political dimension, presented in Section 5.3 of *Exploring Corporate Strategy*, is stakeholder mapping. There also are strong links to the importance of the political dimension in strategic choice (Chapter 8) and managing change (Chapter 11). This chapter extends these discussions from *Exploring Corporate Strategy* by providing further practical advice on how to create useful stakeholder maps and how maps can guide political priorities for successful implementation. The chapter concludes with the importance of ethical considerations – particularly the *obligations* which public sector managers have to their various stakeholders.

## 9.1 *Introduction*

The concept of organisational stakeholders is now long established and the implications to strategic management are well understood. In particular, it reminds managers of the following:

- Different stakeholders may have commonality of purpose at a very general level (e.g. 'providing quality services' or 'improving the quality of life for the community') but at more detailed levels they would wish to impose different purposes and priorities on an organisation.
- Therefore, purposes and priorities emerge from the *political* interplay between different stakeholder groups.
- Both politicians and strategic managers must understand this political context *in detail* and be able to develop and implement strategies which are politically viable as well as 'rational'. Indeed public sector

## Strategy in action

### Illustration 1

#### Stakeholder mapping to describe the changing political environment

*A repositioning of a major stakeholder will trigger a realignment of other stakeholders as priorities and strategies are changed.*

The late 1980s in the UK was a major period of local government as the Conservative central government attempted to exert more control and accountability over local authorities, many of which were Labour controlled. Between 1985 and 1990 this produced a significant shift in strategy at local authority level from what had been described as *policy-led* to *finance-led*. In other words, the need to define and deliver strategy within strict financial limits became the dominant consideration for those running local authorities. This change in emphasis caused – and required – some important repositioning to occur among stakeholders, as shown on the stakeholder map, which illustrates some of the more important shifts which occurred in Sheffield during this period:

A. Central government decided to be more proactive as discussed above.

B. The private sector was actively encouraged to play a greater role in the local economy directly (B1), through new agencies such as the Sheffield Development Corporation (B2) and the Training and Enterprise Council (TEC) (B3)

C. The trade unions became less influential (C) in line with the national trend.

managers are usually more attuned to this aspect of strategic management than their private sector counterparts.

Stakeholder mapping is one tool to assist managers in understanding this political context and if undertaken properly can be of considerable help in developing strategies which are likely to work in practice.

This paper extends the coverage of stakeholder mapping in the fifth edition of *Exploring Corporate Strategy* (Chapter 5, Section 5.3).

### 9.2　The power/interest matrix

Exhibit 9.1 is a reminder of the basic 'tool' of stakeholder mapping – the power/interest matrix. It is a template on which the 'orientation' of different stakeholder groups can be mapped and through which political priorities can be established. The broad approaches to stakeholder mapping are as follows:

• Mapping can be used simply to describe some of the major trends in the political environment. It can be particularly helpful in showing how shifts in one stakeholder group can trigger off changes elsewhere, as shown in Illustration 1.

*Illustration 1 continued*

D. A more executive style of leadership emerged (D1), reducing the power of the Labour group as a whole (D2)

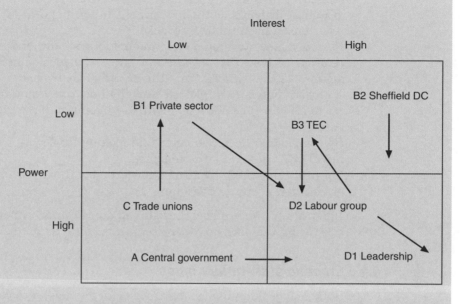

(*Source*: John Darwin, MBA project, Sheffield Business School. First published in *Exploring Corporate Strategy*, 3rd edn, 1993.)

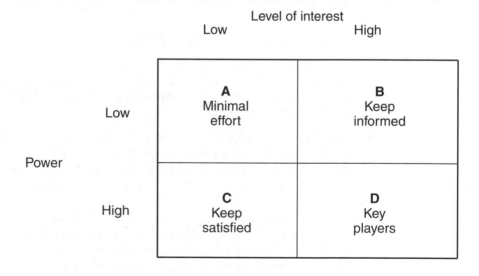

Exhibit 9.1   *Stakeholder mapping: the power/interest matrix (source: adapted from A. Mendelow. Proceedings of 2nd International Conference, on Information Systems, Cambridge, MA, 1991).*

- The more common use of mapping (on which this chapter concentrates) is *in relation to a particular strategic development* (such as the launch or withdrawal of a service, the development into new geographical districts or the investment in (or disposal of) a major asset – perhaps a hospital or a school).
- For this new development stakeholders should first be plotted in relation to how they *would line up* – the level and nature (for or against) of their *interest* and the extent of their *power*.
- A second map is then plotted showing how you would *need stakeholders to line up* if the development were going to have a good chance of success.
- By comparing these two maps and looking for the *mismatches* the political priorities can be established.
- Political priorities may also be concerned with *maintaining* stakeholders in their current positioning.

Illustration 2 shows how these broad steps can be undertaken in practice (using the pathology service in a hospital as an example).

### 9.3    *Creating stakeholder maps*

Stakeholder mapping can be a powerful and useful tool of analysis but managers using it for the first time often find it a little more difficult than they expected. This section provides advice on how some of these difficulties can be overcome.

#### 9.3.1    *Deciding which stakeholders to plot*

Like most practical tools of analysis, stakeholder mapping is most useful if it strikes a sensible balance between being too simplistic/generic and so detailed that it is difficult to interpret. The following guidelines should be helpful:

- Avoid plotting long lists of stakeholders who 'in principle' or 'potentially' could have an influence on the strategy. This is a particularly important guideline in relation to powerful groups such as 'the Ministry', 'the unions', and so on. Remember that the mapping is done in relation to specific strategies so a judgement must be made as to whether these groups are likely to exercise their power in relation to this particular strategy. This is clearly a matter of judgement of their level of interest – this is discussed below. Groups that certainly will remain indifferent to the strategy probably could be excluded from the analysis.

- Remember that stakeholder groups may need to be subdivided if there are significant differences of 'stance' within the group. This often applies to 'clients' (as in Illustration 2) or between different groups of employees. For example, the 're-engineering' of some aspects of public services by the use of IT and staff from different professional groups has clearly been viewed differently by each group. The development of *NHS Direct* ('online' diagnostic service provided by nurses) will progressively have an impact on the role and workload of family doctors (GPs).

### 9.3.2 Assessing power

Exhibit 9.2 shows the general list of sources of power. Illustration 3 uses this list for the example in Illustration 2.

Again some practical advice on using these assessments when deciding where to plot stakeholders on a map is important:

- There is a tendency to plot too many stakeholders in the bottom half of the map (i.e. to conclude that they have more power than is actually the case).

*Exhibit 9.2*   *Sources and indicators of power*

---

SOURCES OF POWER

**(a) Within organisations**
- Hierarchy (formal power), e.g. autocratic decision making
- Influence (informal power), e.g. charismatic leadership
- Control of strategic resources, e.g. strategic products
- Possession of knowledge and skills, e.g. computer specialists
- Control of the environment, e.g. negotiating skills
- Involvement in strategy implementation, e.g. by exercising discretion

**(b) For external stakeholders**
- Control of strategic resources, e.g. materials, labour, money
- Involvement in strategy implementation, e.g. distribution outlets, agents
- Possession of knowledge (skills), e.g. subcontractors
- Through internal links, e.g. informal influence

INDICATORS OF POWER

**(a) Within organisations**
- Status
- Claim on resources
- Representation
- Symbols

**(b) For external stakeholders**
- Status
- Resource dependence
- Negotiating arrangements
- Symbols

---

From: Gerry Johnson and Kevan Scholes, *Exploring Corporate Strategy*, 5th edn, 1999, p. 222

# *Strategy in action*

*Illustration 2*

### *Computer Services at Moreton University[2]*

In 1998 the Computer Services department of a major UK university (Moreton) was seeking to maintain its position as the virtual 'monopoly' provider of computing services to the academic schools and other departments of the university. However, the Director of Computer Services faced some difficult political problems. Together with his deputy he had drawn two stakeholder maps to assess the extent to which this 'monopolist' strategy could be maintained and made politically robust.

Map A relates to the situation at the time of the analysis – confirming the belief that the strategy was under severe threat. This unfavourable political situation had emerged over a period of five years or more as a series of events. The trigger had been the introduction of the concepts of the *internal market* and *outsourcing* into many parts of the public sector in the UK . This was most visible in the National Health Service as devices for improving value for money by creating *purchaser–provider* relationships between the different 'parties' involved in healthcare (Health Authorities, hospitals and GPs) and within large organisations such as hospitals. In higher education similar (market-type) arrangements had been introduced between the Funding Body and the individual universities. A number of universities had also adopted some type of internal market within the organisation to 'sharpen up' the concept of service and value for money, particularly between the academic schools (who taught students and undertook research) and the departments that supported them (including computer services, library, human resources, etc.).

However, little had changed at Moreton until the appointment, in 1996, of

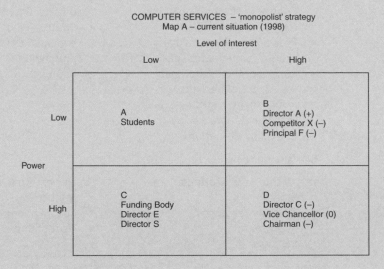

COMPUTER SERVICES – 'monopolist' strategy
Map A – current situation (1998)

*Illustration 2 continued*

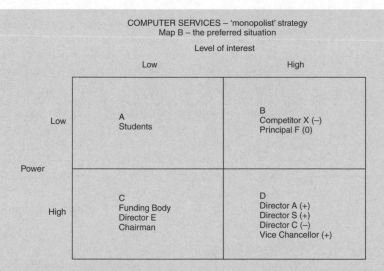

COMPUTER SERVICES – 'monopolist' strategy
Map B – the preferred situation

Level of interest

| | Low | High |
|---|---|---|
| **Low** | A<br>Students | B<br>Competitor X (–)<br>Principal F (0) |
| **High** | C<br>Funding Body<br>Director E<br>Chairman | D<br>Director A (+)<br>Director S (+)<br>Director C (–)<br>Vice Chancellor (+) |

Power

a new Director of the (academic) School of Computing and IT (this school ran programmes and undertook research in Computing Science and Information Technology and accounted for about 28 per cent of the university's students and 36 per cent of the revenue). The school also accounted for some 40 per cent of the Computer Services Department's workload. The new School Director (Director C) had come from another university where the internal market and outsourcing were well established and where her school had saved considerable sums of money by outsourcing their routine hardware and software purchasing and maintenance to a private sector service company. More specialist work, such as developing specialist information systems, remained in-house.

Shortly after her arrival she started to lobby the members of the Governing Body to allow her similar freedom at Moreton. As a result the Chairman eventually asked the Vice-Chancellor[3] for a position statement paper on outsourcing of support services. Privately the Vice-Chancellor was ambivalent both about outsourcing and about an internal market within Moreton. He feared that the result might be considerable use of management time for little financial gain. Some School Directors (particularly the Director of the School of Art and Design – Director A) who used Computer Service less frequently but for more specialist purposes (e.g. design related) were more concerned with the quality (tailoring) of support and the speed of response (for example when software applications developed 'bugs'). They were aware of private sector service providers (e.g. Competitor X) but were less concerned with cost. The Directors of the Engineering and Science Schools (Directors E and S), who together accounted for about 20 per cent of Computer Services work, both regarded outsourcing as a low priority issue for the university and were resistant to any suggestions of using outside suppliers.

*Illustration 2 continued*

Although the Higher Education Funding Council (HEFCE) – in general – was concerned with improving value for money in university computing services, the issue was not at the top of their priorities either. An interesting 'player' was the Principal of the largest Further Education College (Principal F) in the district, which delivered some of the university's courses on a franchise basis. He was openly critical of the second-rate service he claimed to get from the Computing Service at Moreton, which was creating vast amounts of costly work (for example student records) and creating delays with their students. He claimed that the Computer Services Department prioritised internal work over that from partner colleges. Because he was a member of the Governing Body of the university he was well networked with the senior managers and academics throughout the university.

A comparison of maps A and B shows key political priorities if the 'monopolist' strategy was to continue:

- It was acknowledged that Director C was unlikely to change her 'stance' or de-prioritise this issue. Therefore, her influence needed to be 'diluted'.

- Directors E and S were lobbied to give the issue more priority – the latter was persuaded that it was important to his School that Computer Services remained of sufficient size within Moreton.

- School Directors (as a group) were represented on the Governing Body by two of their number 'in rotation'. By good fortune Director A was just about to start her term on the Governing Body.

- The Chairman's zeal for outsourcing of services was diminished somewhat after he attended a conference for Chairmen of University Governing Bodies and heard some worrying stories from other universities. The Director of Computer Services (kindly!) provided him with press cuttings to further reinforce the message.

- Defensive (maintenance) activities were also needed. Attempts by Director C to get a student angle on the issue (cost reduction and hence more machines) were easily counter-balanced by arguments of tailoring of services. At a tactical level the service to partner colleges was considerably improved – silencing College Principal F (indeed it was observed by some in the university that this 'side-payment' was probably his motive for getting involved in the first place – he had no principled attachment to outsourcing).

- Eventually the Vice-Chancellor came off the fence and openly defended the monopolist position of the Computer Services Department at a Governors' meeting.

So, like most political strategies it proved to be a messy mixture of proactive and defensive moves and some good luck!

## Strategy in action

**Illustration 3**

**Assessment of power**
**Internal stakeholders**

| Indicators of power | DIRECTOR A | DIRECTOR C | DIRECTOR S | CHAIRMAN |
|---|---|---|---|---|
| **Status** | | | | |
| Position in hierarchy (closeness of board) | M | M | M | H |
| Salary of top manager | H | H | H | M |
| Average grade of staff | H | H | H | N/A |
| **Claim of resources** | | | | |
| Number of staff | L | H | M | N/A |
| Size of similar school | L | H | M | N/A |
| Budget as % total | L | H | M | N/A |
| **Representation** | | | | |
| Number of governors | 1 | 0 | 0 | 1 |
| Most influential governors | M | 0 | 0 | H |
| **Symbols** | | | | |
| Quality of accommodation | M | H | M | H |
| Support services | M | H | M | N/A |

**External stakeholders**

| Indicators of power | FUNDING BODY | PRINCIPAL F | STUDENTS |
|---|---|---|---|
| Status | H | M | L |
| Resource dependence | H | L | M |
| Negotiating arrangements | H | L | L |
| Symbols | H | M | L |

H = high    M = medium    L = low

- It is therefore important to revisit the initial mapping with a 'test' question such as:

  *If I were to pursue this strategy with disregard to the views of this particular stakeholder, could/would they stop me?*

  This question sharpens up the political assessment in several important respects:

  - It is a reminder that the analysis relates to a particular strategy – not a generalised view of the power of the stakeholder.

- The implementation of some strategies may be entirely within the approved discretion of a department or division. For example, the required investments may not need 'central' approval. As many public sector organisations move to more devolved structures this is becoming more common. In these circumstances plotting the Chief Executive or a central department as powerful would be incorrect.
- Even if a stakeholder could block the strategy they may choose not to exercise that power. This may be because of lack of interest (see below) but it may be because of the wider political context. For example, major service providers such as Royal Mail may 'tolerate' activities of small competitors (some of which may, in fact, be illegal such as breaching the £1 (shortly to become 50p) monopoly of Royal Mail) on the grounds that in the early twenty-first century the government or the regulator or public opinion is largely unimpressed by defensive behaviour amongst near-monopoly providers.

- So sharp political instinct is important in stakeholder mapping as well as 'objective' assessment of power.

### 9.3.3   Assessing interest

This is probably more difficult than the assessment of power. Certainly many managers have learnt the hard way that public expressions of interest (support) often cannot be relied upon. Even worse, some stakeholders will express support but, in fact, work quietly to oppose or, at least, delay the implementation of a strategy.

So it is important to assess the likely *actions* of stakeholders rather than just their words. Practical guidelines are as follows:

- Ensure that a *variety* of sources of information about stakeholder interest are used (in the same way as when assessing power). It is particularly important to use both *formal* (surveys, reports, etc.) and *informal* assessments (e.g. stories) of interest.
- Interest should be categorised as *for* (+), *against* (−) or *neutral* (0) in relation to the particular strategy.
- As with the assessment of power, it is useful to revisit the initial mapping with a 'test' question regarding level of interest such as:

  *How high is this strategy on their priorities – are they likely to **actively** support or oppose this strategy? Or will their interest be short-lived?*

This sharpens up the analysis in a number of ways:

- Many potentially powerful supporters/opponents of a strategy will *in the event* not act to support or oppose the strategy. If this is the case they should be plotted on the left-hand side of the map.

- Sometimes the level of interest of a stakeholder group is very dependent on the personal zeal of an individual (a manager, a politician, etc.). So the judgement of interest becomes, in fact, *very personal* to that individual. If they move position or responsibilities the map may not be valid. It is important to make this additional 'test' in relation to some individuals. For example, 'if this particular minister or chief executive changed how would the political landscape change?'
- This is a reminder that the political priorities which emerge from stakeholder mapping must be robust in relation to potential changes in the future (particularly prior to implementation of a strategy).

## 9.4    *Establishing political priorities*

Mapping stakeholders into the four boxes and undertaking the process of identifying 'mismatches' between how stakeholders are *likely to line up* and *would need to line up* (see above) can help in establishing the broad political priorities. This section looks in more detail at the implications of an analysis for the management of stakeholder relationships and also presents a series of commonly occurring maps (situations) and the typical political priorities and actions they would require.

### 9.4.1    *Managing stakeholder relationships*

A useful link can be made between the four boxes in the power/interest matrix and styles for managing change (see Exhibit 9.3) as described in Section 11.4 of *Exploring Corporate Strategy*. The following practical conclusions/ advice can be drawn:

- It will probably be both necessary and desirable to adopt differing 'styles' to different stakeholder groups even for the same strategy.
- *Key players* (box D in Exhibit 9.1) are both powerful and interested in the particular strategy. This could mean that a style of *participation* would be appropriate for stakeholders who are supportive of the strategy. This could be important in gaining and maintaining their ownership of the strategy. Opponents of the strategy are more problematic – although their *participation* could be important too. Often this would need to be preceded by *education / communication* as a means of gaining their support. In some circumstances the priority could be to 'reposition' opponents to box C (or box B). This is discussed in Section 9.4.2 below.
- *Stakeholders in box C* in Exhibit 9.1 are potentially powerful supporters or opponents of the strategy but are not very interested. Assuming that the priority is to keep them in box C, the most appropriate style is often *intervention* where the 'change agent' drives and controls the strategy whilst the threshold requirements of the stakeholder are met

Exhibit 9.3    *Styles of managing strategic change*

| STYLE | MEANS/ CONTEXT | BENEFITS | PROBLEMS | CIRCUMSTANCES OF EFFECTIVENESS |
|---|---|---|---|---|
| *Education and communication* | Group briefings assume internalisation of strategic logic and trust of top management | Overcoming lack of (or mis) information | Time consuming Direction or progress maybe unclear | Incremental change of long-time horizontal transformational change |
| *Collaboration/ participation* | Involvement in setting the strategy agenda and/or resolving strategic issues by taskforces or groups | Increasing ownership of a decision or process May improve quality of decisions | Time consuming Solutions/ outcome within existing paradigm | |
| *Intervention* | Change agent retains co-ordination/control: delegates elements of change | Process is guided/ controlled but involvement takes place | Risk of perceived manipulation | Incremental or non-crisis transformational change |
| *Direction* | Use of authority to set direction and means of change | Clarity and speed | Risk of lack of acceptance and ill-conceived strategy | Transformational change |
| *Coercion/edict* | Explicit use of power through edict | May be successful in crises or state of confusion | Least successful unless crisis | Crisis, rapid transformational change or change in established autocratic cultures |

From: Gerry Johnson and Kevan Scholes, *Exploring Corporate Strategy*, 5th edn, 1999, p. 511

– i.e. they are *kept satisfied*. An example would be the need to gain all proper approvals from an appropriate committee and to ensure that proper procedures are followed.

- *Stakeholders in box B* in Exhibit 9.1 are very interested in supporting or opposing the strategy but have little direct power. Nonetheless, the way in which they are managed is important. For supporters of the strategy a style of *education/communication* is usually appropriate. This makes sense not only in terms of the expectations of these stakeholders but also because well-informed supporters may gather wider support for the strategy through their actions. For example, they may *lobby* stakeholders in boxes C or D.

Opponents of the strategy may be responsive to persuasion by good quality communication. However, determined opponents may need to be bypassed through a style of *direction*. There are dangers in this – namely unfavourable lobbying of stakeholders in boxes C and D.

- *Stakeholders in box A* in Exhibit 9.1 are both disinterested and have little power. So, in general, the appropriate style is *direction*. Again care needs to be taken that this process is handled appropriately to avoid the dangers of unfavourable lobbying by disaffected stakeholders. This is less of a problem in box A than box B.

Clearly these general 'prescriptions' need to be treated with some caution in two particular respects:

- The above must not become a 'creed'. A judgement must be made about the most successful style in relation to the specific stakeholder group, the particular circumstances and the specific strategy.
- Political priorities are often concerned with repositioning of stakeholders. So the appropriate style usually relates to the box you would wish/need the stakeholder to be in – not the one they are currently in. For example, a powerful stakeholder who is currently disinterested in the strategy (box C) is only likely to reposition to become a key player (box D) thorough a process of *education/communication* (to raise their interest) possibly followed by *participation* to increase their ownership of the strategy.

### 9.4.2   Typical maps and how to respond

The general advice in Section 9.4.1 can be developed further by looking at commonly occurring situations/maps and the political priorities and dangers involved. Nine typical maps are shown in Exhibit 9.4 and the priorities and dangers are listed in Exhibit 9.5 together with the political mechanisms which might be most appropriate in these circumstances (these are taken from Exhibit 11.8 in *Exploring Corporate Strategy* – reproduced here as Exhibit 9.6). This section will briefly summarise each of these nine typical maps. Care needs to be taken when using these *stereotype* maps. They are drawn up to show where the *dominant 'weight'* of stakeholder influence lies. For clarity other boxes are left empty although, of course, there may well be other stakeholders located in these boxes. It is also likely that in some circumstances there may be a hybrid of these stereotypes in existence

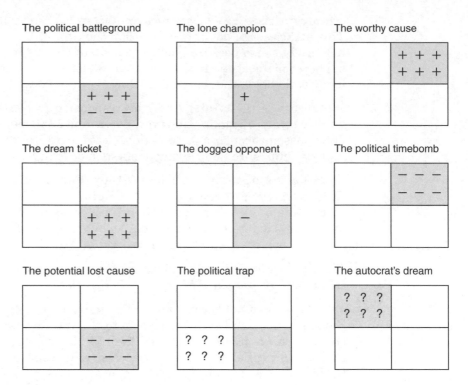

*Exhibit 9.4    Nine typical maps*

(quite often the *worthy cause* and the *political trap* would coincide). So, these maps are to be used only to point up the broad type of situation you have found in your mapping and, hence, provide a bridge into political priorities and actions as indicated below.

### The political battleground

Here there are many key players – divided in their support for and opposition to the strategy. There are clear dangers that this highly politicised situation freezes commitments and decisions and the strategy is left in limbo. To avoid this situation change agents could proceed in several ways:

- facilitating the dominance of the supporters – perhaps by assisting in building their resource base;
- overcoming the resistance of opponents by communication, or reducing their interest (e.g. through higher priority projects);
- creating a stalemate within which the strategy could proceed.

Exhibit 9.5   *Nine typical maps: features, dangers, priorities and political mechanisms*

| Typical map | Key features of the map | Dangers | Political priorities | Political mechanisms |
|---|---|---|---|---|
| 1. The political battleground | Both strong supporters and opponents of the strategy | 'Limbo' | Reduce political risk by: (a) supporter dominates (b) opponents retreat (c) stalemate | Building resource base; overcoming resistance; 'divide-and-rule' |
| 2. The dream ticket | Several champions of strategy; no powerful opponents | Complacency | Keep stakeholders both informed and satisfied | Alliance building and maintenance |
| 3. The potential lost cause | Several powerful opponents of strategy | Progress impossible; other strategies damaged | Change orientation at least of some stakeholders or abandon/ modify strategy | Overcoming resistance |
| 4. The lone champion | One powerful champion | Champion is lost | Keep on board; broaden base of support | Maintain participation and/ or communication; foster interest and momentum for change of other stakeholders |
| 5. The dogged opponent | One powerful opponent | Opponent prevails | Change orientation; reduce interest; reduce power; find champion | Overcome resistance; side-payments, new priorities; associate strategy with élite; participation/ communication |
| 6. The political trap | Apparent low interest amongst powerful players | Stakeholder 'repositions' and blocks strategy at a late stage | Maintain stakeholders in current position; seek a champion | Keep satisfied; raise their interest through participation/ communication |
| 7. The worthy cause | Supportive stakeholders – all with little power; no key players | No levers for adoption | Find a champion from box B | Empower stakeholders: – help them organise – alliance building – communication (for lobbying) |

*Exhibit 9.5  (continued)*

| Typical map | Key features of the map | Dangers | Political priorities | Political mechanisms |
|---|---|---|---|---|
| | | | Find a champion from box C | Raise their interest through participation/ communcation |
| 8. The political timebomb | Opponents – all with little power | Arrogance incites action/ lobbying | Maintain in box B | Keep informed; achieve compliance |
| 9. The autocrat's dream | No powerful or interested stakeholders | Complacency | Proceed to implementation | Direction/edict; keep monitoring stakeholder activities |

### The dream ticket

This is a situation which occurs infrequently. There are several power-ful and interested supporters and no powerful opponents. There is an obvious danger of *complacency* and it is important that these key players are properly participating or at least being kept informed and satisfied. The key political mechanism is alliance building and main-tenance.

### The potential lost cause

This is a difficult situation where ultimately the strategy may need to be abandoned or considerably modified. There is a wider danger that inappropriate handling of these stakeholders may create political dif-ficulties wider than the particular strategy – the change agent may 'foul their patch'. The priority is clearly to change the 'orientation' of at least some stakeholders. This is concerned with overcoming resist-ance – perhaps through the involvement of a respected outsider (e.g. a consultant or member of an external 'reference group' such as a pro-fessional body).

### The lone champion

There are many strategies which succeed through the zealous support of a single powerful champion – such as the minister of a department. But there are real political dangers too in these circumstances as many managers have found to their cost. The problem is the potential

*Exhibit 9.6    Political mechanisms in organisations*

| ACTIVITY AREAS | MECHANISMS | | | | KEY PROBLEMS |
| --- | --- | --- | --- | --- | --- |
| | RESOURCES | ÉLITES | SUBSYSTEMS | SYMBOLIC | |
| *Building the power base* | Control of resources Acquisition of/ identification with expertise Acquisition of additional resources | Sponsorship by an élite Association with an élite | Alliance building Team building | Building on legitimation | Time required for building Perceived duality of ideals Perceived as threat by existing élites |
| *Overcoming resistance* | Withdrawal of resources Use of 'counter-intelligence' | Breakdown or division of élites Association with change agent Association with respected outsider | Foster momentum for change Sponsorship/ reward of change agents | Attack or remove legitimation Foster confusion, conflict and questioning | Striking from too low a power base Potentially distructive: need for rapid rebuilding |
| *Achieving compliance* | Giving resources | Removal of resistant élites Need for visible 'change hero' | Partial implementation and collaboration Implantation of 'disciples' Support for 'Young Turks' | Applause/ reward Reassurance Symbolic confirmation | Converting the body of the organisation Slipping back |

From: Gerry Johnson and Kevan Scholes, *Exploring Corporate Strategy*, 5th edn, 1999, p. 522

loss of the champion – either because their interest declines (other priorities take over) or their power is lost – for example the minister is 'reshuffled' to another department.

In the former case it important to keep a continuing participation and/or communication. The latter risk can be lessened by broadening the base of support by fostering the interest of other stakeholders (from box C), or building the power-base of supporters (from box B).

## The dogged opponent

The general advice about managing powerful opponents has already been given (*The potential lost cause*). With a single dogged opponent this advice would stand – change their orientation by reducing their resistance. However, in these circumstances there are other possibilities too. It may be possible to reduce their interest (through 'side-payments' or other priorities). Their power could be diminished by association of the strategy with an élite (e.g. a powerful committee) or, even better, finding a more powerful champion.

### The political trap

This is a situation of apparent low interest amongst all powerful stakeholders which may tempt managers to conclude that they can simply proceed with the strategy (i.e. a style of *direction*). Some managers will be familiar with the political dangers of this approach – a powerful stakeholder intervenes and blocks the strategy at a key decision point – even late in the implementation process. Political priorities are designed to avoid this outcome by maintaining stakeholders in their current position through a style of *intervention* – keeping them satisfied. Alternatively it may be politically safer to attempt to create a map more like *The lone champion* by participation of one stakeholder as the champion of the strategy.

### The worthy cause

Many managers of community-based services will be all too familiar with this situation: the frustrating combination of high levels of interest from stakeholders who have little power to assist the strategy. This is often described as the Cinderella strategy. The priority is to find a champion (key player) either from box B or from box C.

Supporters from box B may be empowered in several ways:

- help them to build, organise and/or create alliances;
- provide information which they could use to lobby stakeholders in box C.

For stakeholders in box C it is again an issue of raising their interest through *participation*.

### The political timebomb

Here, there are several opponents of the strategy – all of whom have little power. The danger is that these stakeholders are disregarded in such a way that they are incited to gain power either by building alliances or by adverse lobbying of stakeholders in box C. The political priorities are usually to maintain the stakeholders in box B. The mechanism might be to keep them informed or to achieve compliance in any of the ways shown in Exhibit 9.6.

### The autocrat's dream

The final map is one with stakeholders only in box A. So managers proceed with strategy implementation through direction/edict, although there may be ethical considerations with such a stance (see below). It is essential to avoid complacency by continual monitoring of stakeholder reactions.

## 9.5   *Ethical considerations*

Stakeholder mapping can be a useful tool for managers. However, the 'mechanics' of undertaking the analysis as described in this chapter can often result in managers (accidentally) coming to the view that it is their role to manipulate all other stakeholders in Machiavellian ways to ensure the best possible chances of successful implementation of a strategy.

This is not an ethically sustainable position in most circumstances since managers are meant to be much closer to 'the honest broker' who is able to understand the conflicting expectations of stakeholders and plot an 'acceptable' path through the political landscape. This is rather easier to say than to do and this is a reminder and an encouragement to managers to consider their analysis and actions against this ethical 'test' too.

One way of doing this is to plot 'ought to be' maps as well as the 'need to be' maps discussed above. This helps sharpen up the obligations that public sector managers (and politicians) have to the various stakeholders. It could be argued that this is particularly important in public sector strategies. Indeed in the UK the government's Best Value proposals of 1998 were keen to emphasise this aspect of obligation and 'duty'. So the extent to which an 'ought to be' map differs from the 'needs to be' map could raise some very important questions such as:

- whether minimal effort is a satisfactory stance in relation to stakeholders in box A. These may well be disadvantaged or disaffected groups in society for whom, it could be argued, managers – and certainly politicians – have some responsibility in terms of improving their interest and involvement.
- more widely, that promoting the interests of those most affected by a strategy – whether or not they have interest or power – could be regarded as part of the 'honest broker' role of a manager as described above, even if it makes the implementation of a strategy more difficult or even impossible. So managers have a responsibility for the means as well as the ends. These are difficult, but important, issues for managers.

### 9.6   Conclusions

Stakeholder mapping is a useful tool for analysing the political context in which strategies are developed; for assessing the political viability of a proposed strategy; and for developing the strategy in a way which improves the chances of successful implementation. The power/interest matrix has been used as the analytical tool to look at these three important ingredients of any strategy which relate to Chapters 5, 8 and 11 respectively in *Exploring Corporate Strategy*.

### Notes

1    This is a revised and adapted version of a chapter first published in V. Ambrosini (with G. Johnson and K. Scholes), *Exploring Techniques of Analysis and Evaluation in Strategic Management*, Harlow: Prentice Hall, 1998, Chapter 10.

2    The university is fictitious. The illustration represents the issues facing several similar organisations at the time.

3    In universities the Vice-Chancellor is the equivalent of the CEO.

# 10

# Implications of ownership for strategy: The example of commercial semi-state bodies in Ireland

*By Eleanor Doyle*

## Editor's introduction

The past 20 years have been characterised by governments concerning themselves with issues of ownership and control of public sector organisations. These general issues of ownership are discussed in Chapter 6 of *Exploring Corporate Strategy*. In this chapter Eleanor Doyle looks at the Irish experience of establishing and improving the performance of some sectors of the public service through the creation of 'semi-state bodies'. These are publicly-owned enterprises with 'commercial freedom', so the issues are whether and why this intermediate form of ownership is better than, on the one hand, old-style public sector bodies or, on the other hand, full privatisation.

## 10.1  Introduction

In Ireland commercial 'semi-state' organisations are enterprises wholly owned by the Irish government that operate in commercial markets. The term is often used to distinguish such enterprises from the rest of the 'public service' that provides non-commercial products or services. Currently, both the Irish semi-state and public sectors are undergoing significant changes as they attempt to meet the challenges posed by a new competitive environment. Yet it is only recently, within the context of the Irish government's Strategic Management Initiative (SMI) (launched in 1994), that the need to perceive public and semi-state organisations differently has been addressed. The Public Service Management Act (1997) added impetus to the SMI by establishing legal requirements that all government departments and bodies must produce a Statement of Strategy setting out key goals, the strategies to achieve them, and indicators of output and outcome against which performance is assessed.

External pressures in the form of European-wide directives for increased competition have required a fundamental reassessment for many of the semi-state organisations of their goals and how they should try to achieve them with moves towards increased deregulation of utilities, for example (see Flynn and Strehl, 1996). This has further encouraged a focus on the purpose and role of the semi-state organisations. Because of their past structure and behaviour, change has not been easy for the semi-state organisations and the adoption of more commercially driven agendas has substantially altered the relations with the owner of the organisations. Consequently, their question of the potential for privatisation has been introduced into Irish public debate.

This chapter considers the implications of alternative types of ownership, i.e. 'traditional' public sector, semi-state and private organisations, for the strategic management of such organisations. Examples of the Irish experience, how ownership has influenced organisational development and how recent changes have altered the ownership role are examined. These issues are raised in Chapter 6 (Section 6.2) of Johnson and Scholes (1999). The implications of government ownership for strategy are explored in Section 10.2. In order to understand the semi-state sector in Ireland, the reasons for its emergence are explained in Section 10.2.1 while Section 10.2.2 focuses on the impact of monopoly structures for performance. Examples of the transformation in the Irish semi-state sector are presented in Section 10.3, which deals with both examples of difficulties faced and success stories. A relative assessment of issues for the strategy and ownership relationship for public, semi-state and newly privatised organisations is considered in Section 10.4. Concluding remarks are presented in Section 10.5.

It is worth noting that the performance of semi-state and public enterprises is an extremely important feature of modern economies because of their prevalence and their linkages to other enterprises, both private and public. Irish semi-state companies provide a significant proportion of the national infrastructure, including sectors such as energy (electricity, gas), steel, air and rail transport, banking, timber and health insurance; in the recent past this list also included telecommunications, sugar and shipping. The public sector plus semi-state sector wage bill accounts for approximately half of total current government expenditure, indicating the size and importance of such organisations in Irish economic life. Thus, the performance of these companies has considerable implications for the overall competitiveness of the economy and is particularly worthy of analysis.

## 10.2   *Government ownership and performance*

The three organisational forms of public sector, semi-state and private sector differ in terms of their attention to market forces, the latter being the closest to market driven. The context of public sector organisations is predominantly politically driven since they are owned by government and focus (albeit not solely) on satisfying political demands (see Alford, this volume). Semi-state organisations are caught between the two extremes since they are enterprises with commercial targets reliant on the market environment for their commercial goals but yet are also wholly owned by and accountable to the government. In the Irish experience until very recently, the semi-state sector was treated similarly to the rest of the public sector, with no true account taken of its market focus. While this makes a discussion of the semi-states' management needs difficult to assess, recent directions indicated by the Strategic Management Initiative and developments in Irish industrial policy and regulation are indicative of how their treatment has been separated.

The main structural difference between the traditional public sector and semi-state organisations is the appointment of a Board of directors to the semi-state organisations so that public control is exercised via the Board, the relevant Minister and in certain cases by the government. The Minister is responsible for preparing basic policy, securing parliamentary acceptance thereof and communicating it to the Board. Interestingly, the manner of the appointment of Board members provides a signal of how the management of the semi-state organisations was viewed by government. In the past, appointments to the Boards of semi-state organisations have been used as 'a kind of Honours System for party hacks distinguished chiefly for their loyalty' (*Business and Finance*, 2 May 1985), rather than being based on individuals' qualifications for or suitability to the posts. This contributed to create tension between the Chief Executives of some semi-state enterprises and the government. Excessive government involvement in operational matters was identified as a feature of semi-state organisations in the *Industrial Policy Review Group Report* (1992), which suggests that the scope of management was not clearly set out, thus distancing management from decisions taken and the risks involved.

These features provide support for the view that while private organisations were managed, public (and semi-state) enterprises were administered (Farnham and Horton, 1996). The management function is concerned with making the best use of resources, while the focus of administration is on establishing procedures designed to link policy with practice, ensuring consistency and facilitating control. The administrative processes were considered to dominate public and semi-state enterprise. The emphasis on administration can be understood in the context of the emergence of the public (or semi-state) organisation as supporting political policy and law makers – with no allowance made for the different types of activities carried out by public as opposed to commercial semi-state bodies. Bureaucratic administrative structures characterised public (or semi-state) organisations where responsibilities were usually precisely defined and limited delegation existed. The structure generated a culture of caution where problems were referred upwards. Long hierarchical structures appear to have developed due to the size of public bodies, their national dispersion and requirements for uniform standards of practice. These characteristics implied that neither top management nor employees perceived themselves as 'owning' decisions and contributed to their lack of participation in risks based on choices made, where those choices were largely driven by politics rather than commercial or organisational goals. Recent developments in the public and semi-state sectors have clearly been implemented in a concerted attempt to address these problems.

To be fair to top management in the semi-state sector, the Irish Management Institute in 1985 (*Business and Finance*, 2 May) was of the view that, given the anti-market policies and rigid pay controls with which they were faced, their continued commitment and performance made them the 'corporate saints of Ireland'. Indeed, the earnings issue had become increasingly important because of the difficulty in attracting and retaining qualified top managers from the private sector due to limits on pay set by the Gleeson Report on public sector pay (later succeeded by the less limiting Buckley Report).

Another indication of how the government influenced performance in the semi-state sector is provided by its approach to proposed investments by a semi-state organisation. While government departments are involved in monitoring major investments, they would rarely have had the required expertise to appraise a programme in detail and would, therefore, rely on the information provided by the organisation concerned. Given the political context of the organisations and their often vague objectives, political interests and expediency would (in some cases) have been allowed to overshadow economic and efficiency arguments such that perceived politically palatable investment appraisals were provided. A potentially corrective measure against such behaviour is performance-related pay because individuals' incentives would not be driven by the political motive. Alternatively, a reduction in the political emphasis of the organisation would go some way to addressing the problem, and this appears to be the preferred route adopted by the Irish government.

The decision makers within semi-state organisations quite often lacked clear, consistent objectives. This arose because politicians were faced with trying to satisfy many different interests which they attempted to integrate into policies pursued by public organisations. Consequently, general goals often emerged because public appeal was wider the more generally stated the goals. Such difficulties were obviously compounded by variations in goals induced by new political pressures or new political leadership. Thus, no practical guidance as to how the organisations should be run was provided from the ultimate owners of the organisations. The situation of delegated choice created by the government – where decision makers in the semi-state organisations made choices on the government's behalf, in the government's 'best interest' – works if, and only if, both parties are clear as to the goals and objectives of the organisation. Even then, a system of control incorporating clear rules and procedures is necessary to achieve consistency between decisions and 'best interest'.

Lane (1995) mentions a range of possible government policy objectives that commercial semi-state organisations may have to play a role in implementing. These could include the generation of full employment, equality, economic growth and price and trade stability. Even where objectives were set, such as the commercial targets of semi-state companies, some objectives appeared to be in conflict with others. This was recognised in the Irish context by the *Report of the Industrial Policy Review Group* (1992: 75), which considered that

> these companies ... have been placed in an increasingly difficult position, with the Government calling for increased profitability while insisting on the maintenance of what is often an ill-defined social objective.

A relevant example is the provision of transport services to rural areas where losses are incurred. While a policy of income redistribution might be used to finance the losses (where travellers on more profitable routes pay higher prices), this is in conflict with a profit objective. Staying with transport, it can be argued that unprofitable public transport systems are justified based on reduced traffic congestion and time savings for travellers – profitability and economic efficiency being in conflict in this case (here the benefits to society outweigh the costs).

From the perspective of the CEO in the semi-state enterprise the only way to ensure that multiple objectives could be met would be to have reasonable estimates of the trade-offs between alternative courses of action, these being communicated by the relevant government Minister. In practice, however, this did not occur and Ministers did not always make explicit their desired objectives for semi-state companies. This may have been because it did not make political sense to state the aims publicly, or because the aims may not have been known to the Minister. Rees (1989: 14) points out that Ministers may be incapable of communicating the objectives as *they can recognise the decision they prefer when confronted with the alternatives, but cannot state in an abstract way the general aims they wish to see pursued.*

Furthermore, public organisations involve highly elaborate structures with complex systems of interdepartmental committees and multiple consultative and communication channels. This meant that further complications arose where the semi-state organisation received objectives from more than one ministry or committee.

The managerial implications are that with a range of sometimes vague objectives to meet, semi-state management found it difficult to define clearly the role of their organisation or its strategic intent, i.e. the future desired state and position of the organisation. In other words, unclear or mixed objectives contributed to unclear strategies. These difficulties were a direct result of the impact of government ownership on how the organisations were structured and managed, i.e. similar to the 'traditional' public sector approach. It was difficult (if not impossible) for employees to generate enthusiasm or motivation when goals and objectives did not permeate clearly from top management and resulted in different members or sections of the organisations pulling simultaneously in different directions. In the case of all of the Irish semi-state companies until the mid-1990s, no mission statements were expressed, so that neither the primary purposes of the organisations nor how they would be achieved were set out.

Therefore, while political goals and the political context are crucial elements of both public and semi-state enterprises, in the case of the latter the increased uncertainty introduced by the political dimension increased the difficulty of dealing with and achieving commercial organisational goals. For example, attempts to meet the government's objective of full employment led to the expansion of employment in Irish semi-state organisations in the 1970s, a policy which was not driven by the strategic requirements of the organisations themselves. A case in point is the Electricity Supply Board, which, in a parliamentary report, was considered to be overmanned by approximately two thousand people in 1986.

### 10.2.1   *The birth of the Irish semi-state organisation*

To consider how the semi-state organisation developed in Ireland, it is useful to consider its establishment from a historical perspective. When private individuals do not perceive an incentive to provide particular goods or services within the prevailing economic system, governments often intervene in the provision of desirable goods and services. This was the case in Ireland, where

*public enterprise was used as an arm of Government policy to make up for the lack of entrepreneurial drive among the existing business and property-owning classes ... to fill a gap in the provision of vital goods and services which was not being catered for by the private sector. (Hastings, 1994: 30)*

Hence, historically, most network monopolies were owned and run by the government, e.g. telephones, electricity, air, bus and rail transport, gas, and today, over one hundred state-owned enterprises still exist in Ireland.

Some commentators pointed out that the government of 1930s Ireland, when the first semi-state enterprises were established, was not ideologically predisposed to active intervention to achieve economic development (Hastings, 1994: Haughton, 1995). However, in the context of wishing to 'jump start' economic development in sectors where entrepreneurs in free markets did not intervene, alternatives to government ownership would have been available in the form of public subsidies, regulation or some combination of the two, yet these options were not chosen. The reasons behind direct ownership may relate to the facts that European governments appeared to favour government ownership of utilities and that capital markets were underdeveloped, hindering entrepreneurs from establishing private firms. With hindsight, it is easy to argue that an alternative approach may have been preferable since the performance of the semi-state sector is considered to have been poor.

The sluggishness of the Irish government's reorientation towards deregulation and/or privatisation of the commercial semi-state organisations may be indicative of a more deeply rooted political value placed on such organisations, perceived as vital components of the national infrastructure. Such a move would have been logical as the reasons for the establishment of the semi-state sector, i.e. a lack of entrepreneurship and the limited availability of capital, had disappeared. In addition, Ireland's nearest neighbour, the UK, has turned to privatisation and introduced market-type mechanisms for the control of many of its public services. However, an alternative hypothesis relating to the inertia of the government to such structural changes may be just as plausible and may also lie behind the sluggish performance of the semi-state sector itself.

### 10.2.2 *Monopoly power and performance*

It is possible that the performance of some public and semi-state enterprises arises from their monopoly position rather than their ownership structure. It is generally true that monopoly enterprises can generate welfare costs compared to more competitive forms of enterprise, if they are not properly managed and/or regulated.[1] If the monopolist produces intermediate products, higher prices have knock-on effects for downstream firms that will charge higher prices to cover their higher costs and so consumers lose out. Lobbying is another potential monopoly cost where companies lobby government to retain or alter legislation to maintain barriers to other entrants. An example is the introduction of competition to the Dublin–London air route in 1986 where lobbyists for Aer Lingus (the national state-owned airline) argued that the high price of flights on the route was due to the costs and the high quality of service provided. Yet competition led to a dramatic drop in prices with no appreciable loss in service quality.

Furthermore, workers in monopoly organisations where profits are made can possess significant bargaining power in wage demands as their unions negotiate for what is often perceived as their 'share of the profits' due to the threat of strike action which would interrupt profit flows. Such power can, however, be exercised by any organised group of employees, in private or public enterprises, when their expertise is not widely available.

Inefficient activities that can occur under public or semi-state monopolies represent the redistribution of income from taxpayers to employees in the state-owned organisation, as taxes fund their existence. Public or semi-state monopolies may have been even less efficient because the government could fund losses via borrowing or taxation. Hence, neither management nor employees were actually faced with the need to control costs tightly, produce efficiently or realise a profit. This is especially true since neither management earnings nor tenure has been directly related to performance for Irish state-owned organisations. Government sensitivity to the problem of unemployment has meant that it has, in the past, supported trade unions opposed to the implementation of new working practices because although such practices might serve to improve efficiency, job losses would result. Hence, even when management might wish to engage in improving efficiency, confrontation with government and unions can occur.

It is clear that the Irish government was unhappy with the commercial performance of the semi-state sector in the early 1980s.

> *State companies have not, on the whole, distinguished themselves commercially. ... They have been criticised for being over-staffed, over-paid and for offering poor service. Many of them are in a poor financial state. (Minister for Finance, 1984)[2]*

The government's impetus for analysis of the performance of the commercial semi-state sector was the spiralling of the Irish national debt to over 20 per cent of GNP in 1981. Underlying the initial establishment of the semi-state organisations was the aspiration that they would eventually pay their own way and finance their expansion through funds generated. This had not happened by the mid-1980s.

The government perceived that the semi-state companies needed to improve their commercial performance. Interestingly, the proposition that their monopoly position underlay the semi-state sector's disappointing performance was refuted by a report by the National Planning Board (1984) which indicates the contributory factors to poor semi-state performance as:

- lack of clarity regarding financial targets;
- virtual absence of penalties for failure;
- absence of decision makers' participation in risks attendant on their choices;
- undertaking investments on scales disproportionate to company size;
- subsequent over-exposure and inability to deal with economic recession.

Significantly, none of these issues are the result of a monopoly structure, but instead relate to the structures of the organisations and how they were run, with limited management freedom for decision making in the context of political constraints.

## 10.3 Implementing change in Irish semi-state companies

Irish state-owned enterprises have been subjected to exceptional changes in recent years as illustrated by the first public flotation of a semi-state company (the national telephone company Eircom) in July 1999. The government has also announced its intention to float the national airline, Aer Lingus. The zealous privatisation policy implemented in the United Kingdom was not followed in Ireland, although three other semi-state companies passed into private hands in the 1990s (Irish Life in the finance/insurance sector, Irish Sugar/Greencore and the B&I Line sea transport company). The recent changes have been largely driven by external pressures as the application of the rules of the Treaty of Rome via competition policy have led to EU-wide measures aiming to ensure increased international competition in traditionally protected sectors such as public utilities and transport.

The shield of political control, if not ownership, is being stripped away from the semi-state organisations, requiring a reorientation and even reinvention of the structures and strategies of the organisations affected. Commercial pressures matter like never before and within the semi-state organisations an over-the-shoulder government focus is being – or has been – replaced by a forward-looking customer focus.

The changes in the semi-state sector and the broader public sector are also due to pressure imposed by the Irish government through its Strategic Management Initiative, launched in 1994, the main foci of which were:

- the contribution of the public service to national development;
- the provision of excellent services to the public; and
- the more effective use of resources.

The purpose of the SMI is to put in place suitable organisational structures and management processes to ensure that the public service is capable of meeting the challenges that it is currently facing and likely to face over the next few years. A more specific programme of change for the 'traditional' public sector – the civil service – was outlined in the report *Delivering Better Government* in 1996, which represents a clear recognition of the need to treat the broader public sector differently to the semi-state sector. Considered in the light of the government's recent approach to semi-state organisations, particularly since the position adopted regarding the Aer Lingus crisis of 1993, it is possible to identify a fundamental shift in how the government approaches the semi-state sector and perceives it differently to the traditional public sector.

### 10.3.1    The context of implementing change

The introduction of new and improved management practices in the private sector spurred the belief that such practices should be introduced in the public and semi-state sectors also. In the context of developments in EU competition policy significant change was imperative for the semi-state sector. The resulting desire for rationalisation evoked strong responses from the trade unions, which have traditionally been very strong in Irish semi-state companies. Relations between unions and management were adversarial as a result of the companies' structures, where the unions and workers were able to capitalise on their position within monopoly organisations. Such adversarial relations were evident across all of the major crises within semi-state organisations in the 1990s.[3]

The entrenched cultures within the organisations contributed to the crises which were all the result of top-down management-driven programmes for change. These emerged as the organisations had to deal with the government's implementation of recommendations of the 'Culliton Report' – *Report of the Industrial Policy Review Group* (1992) – and the 'Moriarty Report' – *Employment Through Enterprise – the Response of the Government to the Moriarty Task Force on the Implementation of the Culliton Report* (1993). Private enterprises in Ireland had also faced such dramatic rationalisation programmes in the 1980s, with similar crises and difficulties for Ford, Semperit and Waterford Glass, for example. The fact that semi-state enterprise followed the difficult path of private companies to restructure in the face of severe international recession is indicative of the Irish government's desire to redefine its relationship with its semi-state companies by explicitly expressing a policy agenda for more market- and customer-focused companies. The signal for change was clearly provided by the government during the discussions for the Programme for Competitiveness and Work[4] in 1994:

> *Given the historical operating environment of many of our semi-state companies, one in which there has been no exposure to the competitive need for responsiveness to the market, a fundamental shift in the style of their operation is called for. What was considered appropriate in the past is no longer acceptable to the recipients of State services and to me. (Brian Cowen, Minister for Transport, Energy and Communications, Parliamentary Report, 4 March 1994)*

This new approach was a direct result of the Culliton and Moriarty reports. The Culliton Report, commissioned by the Irish government to review industrial policy and performance, recommended a broader approach to the formulation and evaluation of Irish industrial policy. Problem areas were identified as taxation, infrastructure, education and training. The report also signalled a change in how semi-state enterprises were perceived and treated by the government.

> *Provided that the commercial State enterprises are indeed allowed to operate in a fully commercial manner, their contribution to the economy could become as significant as it once was. (p. 75)*

It was agreed that each enterprise, in consultation with its sponsoring department, should draw up a clear *commercial* mission statement to be published in its annual accounts. In itself, this marked a culture change for the organisations concerned. Furthermore, benchmarking of the prices and charges of the semi-state companies was introduced. In Eircom (then known as Telecom Eireann) and the ESB benchmarking of work practices and output per worker were also introduced. The success of Eircom's restructuring strategy, which involved significant job-shedding, can be judged by the demand for shares in the company when it was publicly floated. Similar reductions in employment were required in the ESB as part of its attempts to improve efficiency prior to the introduction of competitors into its market.

### 10.3.2 The Aer Lingus crisis – a watershed for semi-state sector management

The change in approach to semi-state companies was not simply cosmetic, as the Aer Lingus crisis proved. For the five years to 1992, the airline made losses in its air transport division, leading the Transport Minister to declare that changes were required 'at the top'. A Corporate Recovery Plan was to be published in late 1992; only two years earlier, a previous rescue plan had been implemented without the desired consequences. Delayed publication of the plan was blamed on an election and a change of Minister; however, it became apparent that the government was not satisfied with the proposals which eventually emerged in February 1993 (Aer Lingus, 1993). The departure of chief executives followed, a new executive chairman was appointed and the 'final' plan emerged in July, resulting in the walk-out of 1,000 staff as the repercussions for the (highly unionised) workforce became apparent. Although the company was willing to negotiate on how to achieve cost savings, it was clear that the level of savings required to save the company was not negotiable.

More difficult than the agreement with the Aer Lingus workforce, however, were the dealings with the expert air maintenance subsidiary – TEAM – which dragged on for 12 months and

> *exposed a facet of an industrial relations culture which many observers believed had disappeared 15 years earlier. (Hastings, 1995: 20)*

The protracted nature of the discussions was ultimately blamed on the conditions under which TEAM had been created, essentially a recipe for disaster. Political intervention where the government pushed for a high-profile jobs project for the North Dublin area led to its establishment. TEAM emerged from the Mechanical and Engineering section of Aer Lingus, which had a relatively inflexible culture. The union leadership, as 'crafts' workers, considered that what was happening at TEAM had wider implications representing an effort to undermine the principle of the craft in all semi-state companies. An interim examiner was appointed to TEAM as the workforce balloted and rejected proposals, which they later accepted. The examiner considered that both the management style within the company and the trade unions structure would have to change for the successful implementation of the agreement.

The traditional tripartite relationship between government, semi-state management and trade unions was irrevocably shaken and an important feature of this rupture was the realisation that attempts to involve politicians in the ultimate commercial decisions were fruitless. Despite the politically unpalatable facts that significant job losses and work practice changes were required, and that the government had lost the support of two members of the Irish parliament (whose constituencies included North Dublin) in a crucial vote on the crisis, the government was willing to follow through on its rationalisation and commercialisation strategy for the semi-state companies.

Changes are also apparent in relation to the roles of management and unions across the semi-state sector generally. Traditionally top management of semi-state organisations have 'come through the ranks' of the organisations themselves such that while managers are *au fait* with the business, they are apt to be overly internally directed in their thinking and ingrained in the established culture: not traits that enable or facilitate organisational change. For these reasons, current government policy on the appointment of chief executives favours 'outsiders' from the private sector.

Within the context of monopoly firms, employees and their trade unions have been aware of the power they can exert when they bargain with management or attempt to negotiate with or appeal directly to the government. This is especially true when negotiating on behalf of workers with essentially irreplaceable expertise (a relevant case in point was the ESB strike of 1991). The Irish Congress of Trades Unions established a review group to consider various unions' management of change in view of the changing environment within which they must operate. Some shop stewards and union officials are themselves speaking a language of leading change in co-operation, not conflict, with management. Of course unions are also faced with similar problems to management in that union leadership often emerges from the industry that they oversee, so that an external perspective may be difficult to establish.

### 10.3.3 Success stories

The picture of semi-state restructuring is certainly not entirely bleak, as other semi-state companies seem to have been capable of successful reorientation. They include the gas company Bord Gais (see Case Study in *Exploring Corporate Strategy*), the turf company Bord na Mona and the Agricultural Credit Corporation Bank.

For Bord Gais, new competitors are set to enter its gas-provision market as a result of the deregulation of the European gas industry. To meet the challenge, a process-based structure was implemented to replace the traditional functional approach of the organisation. The role of information technology was viewed as a vital ingredient in transforming the company from an 'engineering company' with the sole gas supply for Ireland to a customer-orientated gas provider capable of successfully competing with other providers. Standardisation of procedures replaced *ad hoc* practices conducted across the various regional offices of the organisation as the increased importance of the commercial mandate was translated into a transformation and reorganisation of the company. Information technology was perceived strategically as a mechanism for operational and procedural changes as well as an enabler providing the systems required to achieve the company's new mission and goals.

The reduction in the intervention of government in the operations of the organisation coupled with an internal reorganisation have changed the competitive environment of Bord Gais. The increased management freedom afforded to the organisation should lead to a superior clarity of purpose for its management and employees, hence its performance can be expected to improve. However, its ability to deal with competition may turn out to be an even more important determinant of its future success. It is important to note that without such an increase in management freedom the likelihood of being able to deal with competition would be reduced. Hence, both an appropriate organisational architecture and the possession of appropriate resources to meet market needs are necessary ingredients for ensuring success for an organisation, yet individually they are insufficient to bring about this outcome. More generally, where commercial objectives are clear for semi-state firms, the removal of undue government intervention represents an improvement in their ability to deal with their competitive environment.

### 10.4   *Organisational forms: Semi-state, public and private sector*

The application of the traditional public sector form of organisation to the semi-state sector in Ireland did not serve to promote efficient organisations as political intervention appeared to override the commercial mandate, a mandate which was easier to deal with in the context of domestic monopoly. The present requirement for semi-state organisations to develop clear commercial strategies and adopt customer-focused cultures is best achieved with the removal of the layer of political interference. With increasing customer sophistication, satisfying their needs and meeting their rising expectations are imperatives facing semi-state organisations. The establishment of valuable relationships with customers could provide the commercial semi-state organisations with unique competitive advantages that competitors would find difficult to replicate. Organisations within the semi-state sector are better positioned to achieve their goals when management freedom to do so is clearly assigned. Hence, the new semi-state organisational form represents an improvement on the more traditional public sector approach, and also raises new challenges for management and employees. Ownership remains the same; the difference arises in terms of how the owners attempt to exert influence on both organisational strategy and operations.

Within the broader public sector the programme for Delivering Better Government aims to create a more customer-focused public service that is efficient, effective and internationally competitive, where appropriate, while at the same time providing a more satisfying and rewarding place to work (Tuohy, 1997). Significantly, the venture has received all-party political support. The difficulties associated with this cultural upheaval should not be underestimated and the problems incurred across many of the semi-state companies trying to instigate change should indicate the potential for problems that exist. The old-style model of public sector organisation, therefore, was clearly insufficient to support the requirements of the semi-state and broader public sector organisations as they seek to face up to the organisational changes required to operate closer to customers with increased decision-making authority and responsibility.

The ongoing reorientation of the semi-state and public sectors raises important issues regarding their privatisation because privatisation provides an alternative organisational form open to government. The need to increase competition and efficiency has provided one of the driving forces behind the transformation of the public and semi-state sectors and arguments for privatisation are often based on similar reasoning. However, the divergence of international government's approaches to this issue is indicative of the complex interdependent roles played by national political, economic and societal factors in determining the type and extent of government activity. Semi-state activities are followed by some countries in some sectors, but not in others.

Even within a particular sector, no policy convergence emerges. For example in the rail sector, France's SNCF, Germany's Deutsche Bundesbahn and Ireland's Iarnrod Eireann are examples of organisations that remain as public monopolies. New Zealand and Sweden have privatised on a vertically integrated basis where joint ownership of rail operations and track lies in private hands. In the UK the structure of the rail industry was replaced with a franchising process, thereby splitting the natural monopoly asset of the track from the non-natural monopoly of the rail operations. No clear evidence exists to indicate that any one form of ownership structure leads to better performance than other forms.

Privatisation offers a channel through which increased investment can be attracted into former government-owned sectors that lacked funds for modernisation. This argument was often cited in the context of UK arguments for privatisation. In Ireland, the privatisation debate is still at a relatively early stage and the government has adopted a hesitant approach to the issue. EU directives appear to be a more important determinant of market deregulation and privatisation (as in the Eircom flotation and proposed flotation of Aer Rianta) than a shortage of funds for necessary investment.

As the privatisation of British Rail indicates, however, skewed incentives can generate perverse outcomes. While expansion was implicitly built into the privatisation, the system does not reward Railtrack (the owner of the track and stations) for building new track. Two-thirds of Railtrack's announced investment of £27 billion in 1999 was for routine maintenance. Furthermore, while Railtrack has a duty to add services for the train operators, no financial incentive exists to encourage this activity – 97 per cent of Railtrack's train access income is independent of the number of trains running (*The Economist*, 3 July 1999: 70). Clearly little advantage is gained from such privatisations, despite their proposed benefits, without the devotion of sufficient resources to identify the incentives required to induce desired outcomes. The Irish government would benefit from such investment as it considers divesting itself of its semi-state companies.

## 10.5   *Conclusions: Options for government*

Irish semi-state organisations retain considerable national significance given their contribution to national infrastructure in areas such as the transport, communications and energy sectors. In the Irish experience the performance of both the semi-state sector and the broader public sector was perceived to be below satisfactory levels, hence the requirements for restructuring both that are currently under way.

Arising from analysis of the failure of the semi-state companies to deliver, their inadequate performance was not attributed to the monopoly structures within which they operated but rather to a lack of management freedom that allowed cultures to evolve where performance issues were not high on the organisations' agendas. Deregulation of markets to meet increasing competition requires the management freedom to develop and implement appropriate and successful strategies, which was not afforded in the past. Thus, the current semi-state structure represents a significant improvement on the former structure and is more appropriate for the achievement of commercial goals where decisions regarding product or service provision benefit from occurring as near to the recipient as possible.

The Irish government, along with its international counterparts, faces the prospect of examining the privatisation option for some semi-state organisations and must consider the potential costs and benefits of both organisational forms. Given the Irish experience, government ownership and its effects on the managerial function appear to have contributed significantly to under-performance in the semi-state sector. This implies that the choice between semi-state and private organisation is largely irrelevant from a performance perspective for commercial organisations once the problems created by government ownership can be redressed. More important than the ownership question are the requirements to reduce undue government interference and increase competition – vital ingredients for increasing efficiency, the desire for which is at the heart of attempts to restructure the broad public and semi-state sectors nationally and internationally.

Increased efficiency of the semi-state sector generates considerable benefits throughout economies. The government benefits if competitive enterprises that are capable of meeting national and international competitors are developed and generate profits, taxes and increased income. Top management's position is improved as it can focus on defining its missions and implementing necessary measures to achieve them without undue interference from the government, yet in the knowledge that it is increasingly accountable for the organisation's performance. Employees stand to benefit if clearer objectives (coupled with incentive systems) are developed; and if moves towards less adversarial relations between unions and management are successful, the working environment is enhanced through the increased cohesion of the organisation. Taxpayers also benefit if the competitive mandate translates into a more efficient use of organisational resources. Society as a whole stands to benefit once the competitive agenda ensures the provision of desirable goods and services, *especially* when such provision is not always profitable.

To provide such desirable goods and services the choice between semi-state and private provision must be made, and where the private option is preferred, regulation can be used to ensure adequate quality and quantity of outputs. Where the decision to change ownership is taken, governments can choose to retain the monopoly structure and use regulation to ensure that consumers are not exploited via higher prices or reduced services, or change the structure of the industry to stimulate increased competition (Duff, 1997). In the latter case, separate companies would be formed to deliver particular goods or services and payments might be made to the natural monopoly company or using an infrastructure (e.g. the UK rail system). This would require a regulatory body to ensure that payments to the monopoly company were set at a fair level and were cost related.

The privatisation choice outlined is not, however, without substantial costs. Industry restructuring, franchising and regulation generate a set of transaction costs that must be met to achieve the privatisation goal. An extensive cost–benefit analysis on an industry-by-industry basis would be one means of assessing the relative merits of semi-state versus private organisation – efficiency gains will not automatically be greater than the sum of the transaction costs. From an economics perspective, only where the benefits outweigh the costs should the privatisation form of organisation be followed.

It may be impossible for some semi-state organisations with deeply rooted cultures to reorientate themselves to deal with competition and customer-focused strategies, in which case the privatisation route may be advisable as the only route towards efficiency gains. The fact that Bord Gais was established later than other semi-state organisations (in 1975) may explain some of its ability to restructure in the face of international competition, allowing it greater flexibility and openness to meet its challenges proactively. Management at Bord Gais appeared to thrive on the challenges they face and have developed an organisational culture where pride is taken in the company's ability to generate profits for the Irish government. Here the decision to privatise is more complex and may depend on the government's overall ideological approach to the issue.

The implication is that governments must decide the extent to which they wish to be involved in market activities, if at all. They must also take into account the costs and benefits associated with privatisation on a case-by-case basis in order to use all available information in deciding whether the privatisation option satisfies their overall goals.

## References

Aer Lingus (1993) *Strategy for the Future: The Cahill Rescue Plan for Aer Lingus*, Dublin: Aer Lingus.

Duff, L. (1997) *The Economics of Governments and Markets: New Directions in European Public Policy*, New York: Longman.

Farnham, D. and Horton, S. (1996) *Managing the New Public Services*, 2nd edn, Basingstoke: Macmillan Press Ltd.

Flynn, N. and Strehl, F. (1996) *Public Sector Management in Europe*, London: Prentice Hall.

Hastings, T. (1994) *Semi-states in Crisis*, Dublin: Oak Tree Press.

Haughton, J. (1995) 'The historical background', in J.W. O'Hagan (ed.), *The Economy of Ireland: Policy and Performance of a Small European Country*, Dublin: Gill & Macmillan Ltd.

Johnson, G. and Scholes, K. (1999) *Exploring Corporate Strategy*, 5th edn, London: Prentice Hall.

Lane, P.R. (1995) Government intervention, in J.W. O'Hagan (ed.), *The Economy of Ireland: Policy and Performance of a Small European Country*, Dublin: Gill & Macmillan Ltd.

Rees, R. (1989) *Public Enterprise Economics*, 2nd edn, LSE Handbooks in Economics, Oxford: Philip Allan Publishers.

Tuohy, B. (1997) *Re-shaping the Public Service in the Information Age*, Dublin: Department of Public Enterprise (http:www.irlgov.ie:80/tec/ publications/reshapein.htm).

## Notes

1   Of course 'natural' monopolies exist where the most efficient provision of a good or service is by a sole producer. With recent developments in technology and capital markets, traditional networks (of railways, electricity, telephone cables, etc.) can today be established and run efficiently by private operators, hence the European deregulation of such markets.

2   Address to the Institute of Bankers in Ireland, 16 November 1984.

3   These include the Electricity Supply Board (ESB), the postal service (An Post), the national broadcasting station (RTE), Irish Rail (Iarnroid Eireann) and the national airline (Aer Lingus).

4   This programme involved the agreement between the government and various social partners, including trade unions, which focused on developing policies to secure economic growth, which included measures to encourage wage moderation.

# 11

# *Formation and control of public–private partnerships: A stakeholder approach*

## *By Richard Butler and Jaz Gill*

### *Editor's introduction*

If competition was the watchword of public sector reform in the 1980s, then collaboration and partnership have come centre-stage in more recent times. The advantages and difficulties of the various types of strategic alliances are discussed in Chapter 7 of *Exploring Corporate Strategy*. This chapter by Richard Butler and Jaz Gill looks at public–private partnerships against a conceptual framework developed for private–private partnerships. The chapter looks particularly at partnership formation, accountability and control. The next chapter, by Sandra Hill, considers two other types of partnership commonly found in the public sector, public–voluntary sector partnerships and inter-agency working within the public sector.

Public–private partnerships (P3s) are becoming increasingly important in the delivery of a range of public services and public projects. A major issue in these partnership is the question of who controls them and, more generally, what their accountability is to a wider public. This chapter develops a stakeholder approach to the study of public–private partnerships which is derived from the authors' work on private sector joint-ventures. The essence of the stakeholder approach is that it uses a methodology, developed from earlier studies of organisational decision making, for measuring the influence of various interests of a range of decisions. While influence over decision making forms the key set of dependent variables, the independent variables cover the legal/constitutional make up of a P3, the tangible resource dependencies, intangible resource dependencies, networks of interpersonal relationships, and managerial structures. The framework developed would enable an extensive study of P3s to be made using a sampling frame covering a full range of P3s including public–private joint-venture, public finance initiative projects and contracting. The framework could also be used to develop intensive case studies, or a combination of extensive and intensive methods, which is suggested as the preferable way forward to further understanding of P3s.

## 11.1 *Introduction*

The search by government for a third way between state-run nationalised industries and privatisation has put the issue of public–private partnerships firmly on the political agenda. What is perhaps somewhat surprising is that the issue does not seem to have fully entered the agenda of academic researchers in management, especially in view of the growth in research concerning strategic alliances, joint-ventures and other forms of partnership in the private sector. As joint-ventures in the private sector in industrialising countries seem destined to disappoint (Beamish, 1984) it would also be appropriate to understand why this is so and to see what lessons can be learned by the public sector.

This chapter considers, in general, the nature of public–private partnerships (P3s) by focusing upon the question of partnership formation, accountability and control. The process by which partnership are formed brings into view questions about the rationale for organisations wanting to form partnership and the kinds of factors they take into account when making a choice. Associated questions include the initial expectations of possible future outcomes from the partnership, the problems of control, and the broader question of public accountability.

We start, however, with a discussion of partnership from the viewpoint of the expanding organisational theory literature on the subject, looking at the resource dependence and interpersonal factors in partnership formation and management, including the key role of trust (Gill and Butler, 1996). Examination of what is different about partnerships in the public sector is made as we proceed. One initial obvious answer to this question is that the public sector, when compared to the private sector, introduces a political dimension and the question of public accountability not apparent in private sector partnerships. We will also come to realise, as the chapter proceeds, that the distinction between what is public and what is private is becoming increasingly blurred.

## 11.2 *Partnering as a co-operative strategy*

From a resource dependence view of organisations we see that the main problem faced by an organisation in its environmental relationships is how to gain power over key dependencies (Pfeffer and Salancik, 1978). Three broad types of strategy can be identified, namely, direct ownership, competition and co-operation, each with its own particular logic of growth.

Growth through direct ownership involves reinvestment of earnings. It can also involve merging or buying, which still requires the availability of earned resources, such as when a firm buys a supplier company (vertical integration) or when it purchases a company whose product range gives an opportunity for diversification. A merger implies a more equal power distribution than a buy-out. Internalising inter-organisational relationships in this way, in a sense, removes the formal boundary between organisation and environment and therefore, once achieved, is no longer a means of managing the environment. The various elements of the newly owned organisation are now under a single authority system.

To some extent what is considered inside and outside the organisation is arbitrary but in discussing the matter of partnerships it is a useful distinction, especially when discussing P3s. Comparison between direct ownership and competition also provides the basis for the long-held distinction between the market and the firm (Coase, 1937). There are, of course, an immense diversity of competitive strategies. For example, Miles and Snow (1978) identify the defender strategy involving price competition and internal efficiency maximisation, and the prospector strategy involving innovation and adaptability to try to stay ahead of known competitors. Whatever type or mix of types of competitive strategies is pursued, the underlying logic for gaining power over the environment is that of alternative maintenance (Thompson, 1967: 32), that is, the firm operating in a competitive environment is well advised to ensure that it has multiple suppliers and a pool of customers to select from.

The co-operative strategy provides a 'third way' in comparison with both the competitive and the direct ownership strategies. Co-operation has the underlying logic of gaining power over key dependencies through the exchange of commitments and obligations in order to reduce the potential uncertainty of a relationship and in order to try to ensure continuance of that relationship (Buckley and Casson, 1988; Thompson, 1967: 35).

We see a partnership as belonging to a generic category of co-operative inter-organisational relationships involving the negotiation of mutual commitments and obligations. These commitments can, however, be a double-edged sword. The commitments made may reduce uncertainty but they may also restrict autonomy.

## 11.3   *Types of partnership*

Direct ownership and competition provide useful referents against which to compare partnerships. Many types of partnership are possible, ranging from informal to highly formal arrangements, as given below.

- *Informal partnerships* may cover tacit agreements made between the senior management of organisations. An example would be an agreement between two local shops covering opening hours, items to sell, pricing, and the like, with the aim of controlling competition. An informal agreement to share information or premises may precede a more formal joint-venture, sometimes covered by a letter of understanding. Such an agreement will involve a high degree of trust (Parkhe, 1993).
- *Co-optation* is the absorbing of outside elements into the management of an organisation (Butler 1991: 132). Overlapping directorships, advisory boards, and the like, are ways of gaining support from the environment, sharing information in anticipation of some future benefit.
- *Non-equity joint-ventures (NEJVs)* involve a more formal agreement to carry out a definite project. Consideration of the NEJV is difficult to divorce from the *equity joint-venture (EJV)*, which involves a formal contract and definition of the share of ownership by each partner. A joint-venture usually involves the creation of a separate joint-venture company, with a management structure of its own, which can come to take on a quite separate identity (Butler and Sohod, 1995).
- *Contracting* involves a formal agreement between two or more organisations whereby each undertakes to fulfil certain mutual obligations. An example is an agreement whereby a manufacturer agrees to supply a specific type and quality by specific times in exchange for an assured order book (Butler 1991: 131). More complex contracting arrangements are found in civil engineering for large-scale projects where many contractors come together to complete a project. A central feature of contracting is the contract document and the obligations that imposes, with the possibility of recourse to law if agreements are broken.

### 11.3.1   Types of public–private partnership

We adapt this list of types of partnership to the public sector through the use of a framework bounded by two dimensions, namely, whether investment comes from private or public sources or whether the service provider is public or private (PSPRU, 1998). The schema is given in Exhibit 11.1 and shows in-between categories of mixed public–private modes on each of the two dimensions to give nine conditions or cells.

Direct service organisations are found where both service provider and source of investment are public (cell 1). Opposite to this (cell 9) are public limited companies (PLCs) and charities, where investment and service provision is private. Both cells 1 and 9 are outside the domain of P3s but all other seven calls can be seen, in some way, to involve a form of public–private joint action even if they are

*Service provision*

| | | Public | Public/Private | Private |
|---|---|---|---|---|
| | Public | Direct services  1 | 2 | Contracting, Vouchers  3 |
| Investment Source | Public/ Private | Partial charging  4 | Joint-ventures  5 | Private Finance Initiatives (PFIs)  6 |
| | Private | Full charging PFIs  7 | Regulated industries, Privatised utilities, Public corporations  8 | PLCs Charities  9 |

*Exhibit 11.1    Types of public and private partnerships*

not always conventionally seen as P3s. For instance, regulated industries (cell 8), such as the British water companies, seen as public utilities prior to privatisation, could be considered joint public–private service providers even though capital is owned by shareholders.

Many public services are partially supported by partial charging for services (e.g. leisure centres, cell 4). As the proportion of investment from charging increases, a shift to cell 7 is made and we may hypothesise that such a shift could be a prelude to privatisation. Joint-ventures between public and private bodies whereby service provision and capital provision are of the mixed public–private type occupy the central cell 5 of Exhibit 11.1. Private finance initiatives (PFIs), whereby financial institutions (such as banks) provide capital for building roads or prisons and form operating companies to run these ventures through Design, Build, Finance and Operate agreements (DBFOs), are in cell 6. However, a PFI may also be in cell 7 if operating the project, such as in the case where private finance has been put forward for building a National Health Service hospital, remains in the public sector.

Private service provision combined with public investment (cell 3) may be seen in cases such as contracting out of certain activities by local authorities and vouchers given to the public to 'spend' on services. British wartime rationing was effectively a voucher system and peacetime examples can be found in the UK and US. This does, of course, give rise to the familiar problem of people selling on their vouchers for cash in a black market, but then each of the nine conditions described will have its own particular failures. This issue leads on to the broader question of accountability, to be discussed below.

As with any typology, which cell a particular examples falls into is somewhat arbitrary and open to change. However, this approach does give us a way to understand the range of types and also how they might change from one condition to another.

## 11.4 *The propensity to partner*

Reference has been made above as to why organisations may seek to form partnerships. We now look more closely as to why an organisation might pursue a co-operative strategy towards its environment rather than direct ownership or competition by considering two groups of factors. These are contextual factors and interpersonal factors. The discussion proceeds initially through a synthesis of the findings from private sector joint-ventures and then discusses how the public sector may differ from the private sector.

### 11.4.1 *Contextual factors*

Contextual factors refer essentially to resource-dependent relationships in the environment covering variables such as scarcity, interdependence, number, ambiguity, strategic-fit, regulation and experience.

- *Scarcity* refers to a shortage of resources and is seen to lead to an increased propensity to partner. Scarcity may be the result of crowding within a field of activity in that a number of organisational actors may be chasing a static or diminishing pool of customers and other resources. A partnership becomes a way of reducing competition through exchange of obligations.
- *Interdependence* refers to the extent to which the workflow of an organisation is mutually dependent upon the workflow of other organisations in a field. An example of high interdependence is when one organisation passes its product to a second organisation, which, after further processing, passes it on to a third, so that after yet further processing the final product is sold to customers. Interdependence is likely to increase the propensity to partner (Pfeffer and Salancik, 1978).
- *Ambiguity* refers to lack of knowledge about a particular area of activity that an organisation may wish to move into. We see joint-ventures formed around research and development agreements whereby two organisations agree to share knowledge in a particular field of activity.
- *The number* of partnerships an organisation has in existence could

mean that there are knowledge and procedures in existence to cope with partnering. Numbers combined with *favourable experience* of these partnerships would increase the propensity to partner.

- *Strategic-fit* refers to the extent to which the notion of partnering fits with other strategies an organisation may be pursuing in other parts of its domain. A high strategic-fit for a particular partnership would be exhibited if a partner was not competing with the organisation in question in any other part of the field, that is, there is no *endogenous competition* within the partnership. Further, if the partnering organisations came to understand that they had a common competitor there would be *exogenous competition*. Hence lack of endogenous competition, but the presence of exogenous competition, would increase the propensity to partner. Conversely, the presence of endogenous competition and the absence of exogenous competition would decrease the propensity to partner (Pfeffer and Salancik, 1978; Gill and Butler, 1996).
- *Regulatory imperatives* may require an organisation to form a partnership, a factor that can be expected to be particularly important in the public sector. An example of this is the formation of the mobile telephone company as a joint-venture between BT and Securicor. The terms of BT's privatisation in the 1980s required such a venture.

### 11.4.2   Interpersonal factors

Research is increasingly emphasising the importance of interpersonal factors in the formation and the success of partnership. *Trust* in particular has been pointed to as a necessary ingredient of a successful partnership (Gill and Butler, 1996; Schann and Beamish, 1988). A number of other interpersonal factors are also suggested. For example, *knowledge* of, and availability of, a suitable partner is a prerequisite for partnership formation. However, a key factor in knowledge about suitable partners can be membership of social networks.

*Compatibility*, in the sense of sharing a common set of norms, or culture, is also a factors that will directly increase the propensity to partner but also increase trust. These factors presented above are summarised in Exhibit 11.2.

### 11.4.3   Control of partnerships

Who controls a partnership is a vexed question which is seen most clearly in the case of joint-ventures where there is a three-way tension between two (or more) parent organisations and a separate joint venture unit with its own management structure (Harrigan and Newman, 1990). Butler and Sohod (1995) analysed the influence of the parents and managements of 57 British joint-ventures across a range of decision issues within the joint-venture company. They found that the

*Exhibit 11.2*   *The propensity to partner*

| **Contextual factors** | **Partnership type** |
|---|---|
| Scarcity (+) | Informal |
| Interdependence (+) | Co-operation |
| Ambiguity (+) | NEJV |
| Number (+) | EJV |
| Favourable experience (+) | Contracting |
| Strategic-fit (+) | |
| exogenous competition (+) | |
| endogenous competition (−) | |
| Regulatory imperative (+) | |

**Interpersonal factors**
Availability (+)
Networking (+)
Trust (+)
Compatibility (+)

(+) or (−) denotes likely direction of relationship between a factor and the propensity to form a partnership.

joint-ventures had generally high autonomy over marketing decisions and a range of general operating and personnel decisions while parents had high influence over strategic decisions.

More in-depth studies show a complex interplay between the various stakeholders in joint-ventures. Often, joint ventures have not lived up to initial expectations of performance (Butler and Gill, 1999) owing to a breakdown in trust or if the partners' original objectives begin to diverge. Suspicion between partners can arise owing to the perception that one partner is gaining undue advantage or taking the opportunity to compete on the side.

## 11.5   *Public accountability of P3s*

The question of who controls partnerships leads on to the issue of public accountability when considering the public sector. The term 'public' implies a degree of public interest in the activities of certain organisational actors that is wider than in the case of 'private' organisations. Direct service organisations are one way in which the state can respond to try to accommodate this wider public interest. The assumption, under this model, is that elected representatives at national and local levels can reflect public choices sufficiently accurately within the decisions made by these organisations. Downs (1957) and other public choice theorists (e.g. Buchanan and Tullock, 1962) have pointed to the separation between the elected representatives and the officials of the various agencies, drawing a comparison with the separation between shareholders of private companies (i.e. of PLCs) and the managers of those companies. The problem in both cases is that the officers/managers tend to have goals other than those of the electors/shareholders.

Cells 2 to 8 in Exhibit 11.1, therefore, represent various means of trying to accommodate the strengths and weaknesses of each of the two opposing methods given in cells 1 and 9. What these two opposites mean, in practice, can be illustrated by considering how organisations in each of two conditions would tend to grow.

Growth of organisations in the private investment and private services cell would tend to occur, as mentioned above, through retained income. This logic, therefore, gives a propensity to efficiency since the rewards to management come through the ability to accumulate capital. With public investment and public services, growth tends to occur through demonstrating to elected representatives the case for a larger budget which, in turn, leads to a propensity to expand services. This efficiency–expansionary tension will, therefore, to differing degrees, tend to pervade the mixed modes represented in the other cells 2 to 8 in Exhibit 11.1.

### 11.5.1   *Mechanisms for accountability*

A number of specific mechanisms to try to reflect public choices within the various conditions of Exhibit 11.1 can be identified.

- *Market management* refers to mechanisms that maintain competition through reducing barriers to entry and that maintain property rights and a sound currency. These approaches are related to a reasonably efficient marketplace (cell 9). Price is the means by which messages about supply and demand are transmitted to providers and the user can 'exit' (Hirschman, 1970) to an alternative supplier if dissatisfied.
- *Political planning* refers to mechanisms that reflect the choices of an electorate and attempt to turn these choices into specific plans for implementation by various agencies. The kinds of structures we see here are assemblies who approve budgets and targets, election of representatives to those assemblies, planning bureaucracies and direct providing agencies (cell 1).
- *Public Inquiries* are used to represent public interests in the construction of airports, roads and other large projects which may involve mixed public–private investment and/or services.
- *Appointed or Elected Boards* of governors or trustees are used to widen the representation beyond that of officers. Members of such boards may be appointed by officials in a higher agency, by elected representatives or by a wider constituency. The terms of appointment will generally be set by a higher agency or by an assembly.

- *Bidding Rules* refers to a range of regulations that attempt to control the way in which contracts are awarded. These may include competitive tendering, franchising or use of comparators.

The purpose of these mechanisms is to provide, at least, an appearance of accountability to the public. The extent to which real accountability happens, and what this means anyway, will vary with the context and interpersonal conditions in a partnership.

## 11.6   *A stakeholder approach to the study of P3s*

The above discussion has indicated that the general framework already developed for the study of joint-ventures in the private sector can be adapted to the study of public–private partnerships. The main adaptation concerns the need to include the issue of public accountability in the overall framework. It is for this reason that we suggest a more explicit stakeholder approach which can examine the processes whereby different interests come to exert control over a range of decision issues.

The unit of analysis in a study of P3s would be a public–private project as defined in Exhibit 11.1. Although the discussion proceeds mainly upon the supposition of a joint-venture (which occupies a central position in Exhibit 11.2), in any extensive study a sample could be drawn from across the types outlined.

The main dependent variable is control and this could be operationalised by means of the degree of influence of interested parties over a range of decision topics. The methodology for this is well defined and has proved quite reliable (Hickson et al., 1986; Butler and Sohod, 1995). The interested parties in a study of P3s will include the direct partnering organisations, suppliers, customers and clients, and representatives of the public, who may be directly elected or appointed along the lines discussed above under mechanisms for accountability. In addition, the internal management of the partnership is also part of the stakeholding domain and a significant part of any investigation would be any crossover of influence between, say, founding partners and the internal management of a partnership. Such a crossover, especially if the accountability mechanisms set up at partnership formation begin to decay, would have major implications for public accountability.

One set of independent variables will include the legal structure and formal aims and objectives of the partnership, while a second set of independent variables concerns the resource context as outlined above, including factors such as the distribution of ownership, arrangements for repayment of loans and the like (Butler and Sohod, 1995). The obvious hypothesis here is that control over decision making follows ownership. A third set of independent variables include less tangible factors such as the flow of expertise and information, which provide the rather more interesting hypothesis that influence is related to the ability of key stakeholders to control information. Further, as Butler and Sohod (1995) found, there can also be, especially as the partnership progresses, a reverse dependence in the sense that the original partners can come to depend upon their creation.

A fourth set of independent variables will include interpersonal relationships as described above, while a fifth set of variables concern the management structures involved in the partnership. The composition of the board of directors (or its equivalent), appointment of key executives or the type of planning procedures will also be significant factors.

## 11.7   *Conclusion*

So much of the debate concerning the public sector has, over the decades, involved an ideological battle between proponents of public versus private provision of goods and services. Heald (1983) has argued for a more balanced approach and consideration of P3s enables us to move in this direction. This chapter has proposed a stakeholder approach to the study of public–private partnerships based upon established research into private sector joint-ventures and upon a methodology, developed from earlier studies of organisational decision making, for measuring the influence of various interests over a range of decisions (Hickson et al., 1986). While influence over decision making forms the key set of dependent variables, the independent variables include the legal/constitutional make up of a P3, the tangible resource dependencies, intangible resource dependencies, networks of interpersonal relationships and managerial structures.

It has been argued that P3s are becoming increasingly important in the delivery of a range of public services and public projects but that a major issue concerns the locus of control and how they can be made accountable to a wider public. A typology of P3s has been outlined using the two dimensions of whether a service is provided by a public or private organisation, or whether the investment comes from the private or public sector. This framework could, it is suggested, enable us to develop an understanding of different types of P3s using extensive survey or intensive case study approaches, or a combination of both, to develop an improved understanding of P3s.

## *References*

Beamish, J. (1984) 'Learning and the accumulation of industrial technological capacity in developing countries', in M. Fransman and K. King (eds), *Technological Capability in the Third World*, London: Macmillan.

Buchanan, J.M. and Tullock, G. (1962) *The Calculus of Consent*, Ann Arbor: University of Michigan Press.

Buckley, P.J. and Casson, M. (1988) 'A theory of co-operation in international business', in F. Contractor and P. Lorange (eds), *Co-operative Strategies in International Business*, Lexington, MA: D.C. Heath and Co.

Butler, R.J. (1991) *Designing Organisations: A Decision-Making Perspective*, London: Routledge.

Butler, R.J. and Gill, J. (1999) 'Trust and the dynamics of Japanese joint ventures in Malaysia', in K.S. Jomo and G. Felker (eds), *Industrial Technology Developments in Malaysia*, London: Routledge.

Butler, R.J. and Sohod, S. (1995) 'Joint-venture autonomy', *Scandinavian Journal of Management Studies*, **11** (2), 159–175.

Coase, R.H. (1937) 'The nature of the firm', *Economica N.S.*, **4**, 386–405.

Downs, A. (1957) *An Economic Theory of Democracy*, New York: Harper and Row.

Gill, J. and Butler, R.J. (1996) 'Cycles of trust and distrust in joint ventures', *European Management Journal*, **14** (1), 81–89.

Harrigan, K.R. and Newman, W.H. (1990) 'Bases of inter-organisation co-operation: propensity, power, persistence', *Journal of Management Studies*, **27**, July, 417–434.

Heald, D. (1983) *Public Expenditure: Its Defence and Reform*, Oxford: Basil Blackwell.

Hickson, D.J., Butler, R.J., Cray, D., Mallory G. and Wilson, D.C. (1986) *Top Decisions: Strategic Decision Making in Organisations*, San Francisco: Jossey Bass/Oxford: Basil Blackwell.

Hirschman, A.O. (1970) *Exit, Voice and Loyalty: Responses to Decline in Firms, Organisations and States*, Cambridge, MA: Harvard University Press.

Miles, R.E. and Snow, C.C. (1978) *Organisational Strategy, Structure and process*, New York: McGraw Hill.

Parkhe, A. (1993) ' "Messy" research, methodological predispositions, and theory development in international joint-ventures', *Academy of Management Journal*, **18** (2), 227–268.

Pfeffer, J. and Salancik, G. (1978) *The External Control of Organisations: A Resource Dependence Perspective*, New York: Harper and Row.

PSPRU (1998) 'Alternative models of public–private partnership', Public Services Privatisation Research Unit, written by D. Hall, J. Hallam, M. Jaffe and C. Meech, published by CCSU/UNISON/TGWU, 1 Mabledon Place, London WC1H 9AJ.

Schaan, J.L. and Beamish, J. (1988) 'Joint venture general managers in LDC's', in F. Contractor and P. Lorange (eds), *Co-operative Strategies in International Business*, Lexington, MA: D.C. Heath and Co.

Thompson, J.D. (1967) *Organisations in Action*, New York: McGraw Hill.

# 12

# *Public sector partnerships and public/voluntary sector partnerships: The Scottish experience*

*By Sandra Hill*

### *Editor's introduction*

Chapter 11, by Richard Butler and Jaz Gill, looked at the issues concerned with public–private partnerships. These relate to the general issues of Strategic Alliances discussed in Chapter 7 of *Exploring Corporate Strategy*. This chapter by Sandra Hill considers two other types of partnership commonly found in the public sector, public–voluntary sector partnerships and inter-agency working within the public sector. She concludes that these partnerships are particularly dependent on the development of mutual respect, understanding and sharing of strategic objectives and values and the establishment of trust.

 Managing the cultural differences which occur within and between the sectors is perhaps the most challenging aspect of the public sector manager's task and requires different management styles to be adopted if joint working arrangements are to be successful.

## 12.1 *Introduction*

The past few years have seen an increasing interest in the notion of partnership in the delivery of public sector services. After a period of government policy in which competition and market forces had been viewed as essential factors in the efficient and effective use of public funds and the delivery of services, a new approach was introduced by the Labour government elected in 1997.

 Accountability in terms of governance, ethics and definition of purpose have all been reinforced through a series of policy documents which strengthen the notion of partnerships not only between the private and public sector but with the public and voluntary sector in an attempt to make the social inclusion agenda become a reality for the

Scottish community. However, the relevance of stakeholders, their relative power and interest and the cultural contexts in which they operate introduce major challenges in terms of turning the policy into action when partnership is at the heart of service delivery.

## 12.2   Development of partnerships

The effective delivery of public services is increasingly dependent on partnerships between the private, public and voluntary sectors.

Partnerships in various forms have been a successful means of development for organisations in the private sector operating for many years. The contracting out of a range of services traditionally provided by the public sector became common in the 1980s through initiatives such as Compulsory Competitive Tendering (CCT). Later, the Private Finance Initiative (PFI) gave birth to a range of infrastructure programmes designed to achieve better value for money for public services and to offer new market opportunities for the private sector. A range of urban regeneration programmes was also in place to bring various sectors together to benefit disadvantaged groups and communities (Bolger and Pease, 1998). The further development of partnerships came with the strengthening of the voluntary or Third Sector in the equation in terms of the provision of social care and housing, where small providers of services were given more scope to compete within the larger public arena and public sector organisations were no longer monopolistic providers of public services. Other approaches towards partnerships in the public and voluntary sectors have been given a higher profile, become more formalised and expanded with the introduction of a range of government-supported partnership programmes, including Social Inclusion Partnerships (Scottish Office, 1999a), Local Care Partnership Schemes (Scottish Executive Health Department, 1997), A Partnership for Employment and New Deal (Scottish Office, 1999b), the Scottish Partnership Forum (Scottish Executive Health Department, 1999), Scottish Rural Partnerships (Scottish Office, 1998) and Local Learning Partnerships (Scottish Office, 1997).

## 12.3   Types of partnerships

The public/voluntary sector has extensive experience of partnership arrangements extending from joint developments, formal partnerships and service level agreements to more loosely defined networking. In their article 'Formation and control of public–private partnerships', Butler and Gill (1999) describe a range of partnerships from highly formal to informal. Whilst their typology of partnership is concerned with private/public partnerships, the classifications they outline are applicable in public/public and public/voluntary sector arrangements. For example, the *informal partnership* described by Butler and Gill, where tacit agreements are made between the senior managers of organisations, would be applicable in the case where agreements are made between local authority housing managers and health service managers regarding priority allocation of housing for patients being discharged from long-term care. *Co-option* as a type of partnership is also commonly in use, with overlapping of directorships and advisory boards being common practice within the public sector and between the public and voluntary sectors. An example of this would be the appointment of a health trust chief executive to the board of a local charity. *Non-equity joint ventures* and *equity joint ventures* are becoming more common practice within these sectors, with formal agreements being reached with their own identity and management structure commonly to be found in client-focused services such as housing for special needs and finally *contracting* as a partnership as typified by CCT.

The increasing complexity of the public sector and its continual striving for best value has led, over the years, to the sector recognising that working in partnership is the only sensible way to design and deliver services. That, coupled with demands for greater public involvement and the need to identify and satisfy an extensive range of stakeholders' needs, has accelerated a range of partnership arrangements.

*Joint developments,* as described in *Exploring Corporate Strategy*, Section 7.3.3, are commonly pursued by a range of public and voluntary organisations for specific client groups; for example, social work, health authorities and the voluntary organisation Alzheimer's Scotland contribute jointly to provide a range of day and home-based care for people suffering from the disease and for their carers.

*Networks* (*Exploring Corporate Strategy*, p. 341) exist throughout the public/voluntary sector offering a range of benefits to the professions involved in the delivery of services and the recipients of the services by offering opportunities for information sharing, learning from each other and exploring the potential for further development as a result of the networks.

The success or failure of such arrangements are dependent on a number of factors, not least the ability of those involved in the partnership to understand each other's values, cultures and operating systems.

## 12.4   *The propensity to partnerships*

Butler and Gill explore the propensity to partnership. Whilst the development of public/public and public/voluntary partnerships need to adopt a *co-operative* partnership, there are a number of factors which would explain their inclination to pursue this approach. Contextual factors such as *scarcity of resources* and *interdependence* are key issues in these sectors. The sharing of resources, including experience, skills and knowledge, is clearly of benefit to the development of strategies. Research and development jointly undertaken by a range of organisations is common practice now, with many funding sources insisting on bids for public research funds to be submitted only by partnership consortia.

## 12.5 Characteristics of successful partnerships

Partnerships require a different set of managerial skills to those traditionally used in the public sector in the delivery of policy and strategic objectives (Bolger and Pease, 1998). Also important is the *strategic fit* described by Butler and Gill. When considering partnerships it is crucial that organisations address the extent to which the partnership will enhance the environment, the achievement of the organisation's purpose and their capability to achieve objectives. The need to demonstrate the added value in terms of service delivery and best value has to be transparent if the partnership is to be viewed as successful by the sponsors, the organisations involved and the end users in meeting the objectives of the policy being implemented. *Compatibility and control* issues are often contentious matters for public/public and public/voluntary partnerships. (See Illustration 2.) The ability to share values, respect and work with cultural differences and agree mechanisms of control, reporting and performance measurements is dependent on the partners' ability to trust.

The involvement of the voluntary sector in partnerships calls for a deliberate approach to be taken. It has to be recognised that there may be significant cultural differences between organisations. The motivation, values and styles of management in the voluntary sector will often be significantly different from that of the public sector. Even within different parts of the public sector there are likely to be major cultural differences, values and priorities. Understanding, respect and the ability to find ways of joint working are crucial. Collaboration in partnership is dependent on sharing information and developing open communication systems.

The interpersonal factors described by Butler and Gill are expanded upon by Mariotti (1996) in his book *The Power of Partnerships*. Whilst Mariotti is concerned with private sector partnerships, the attributes he describes are equally applicable in the public and voluntary sectors. The added challenge for these sectors is that many of the partnerships that evolve do so because of the need to access funding as a first priority rather than the identification of added value by working in partnership. In order for public and voluntary organisations to develop successful partnerships they need to clearly identify ways of acquiring the attributes Mariotti believes to be fundamental to success. (These factors are demonstrated in Illustrations 1 and 2.)

- *Character – the combination of qualities that distinguish one group from another*. This is of particular importance in partnerships between the public sector and with the public/voluntary sector. The strong professional identities of staff groups working in each sector, their values, attitudes and priorities and the traditional organisational cultures that exist in these sectors may lead to significant challenges in the creation of successful partnerships.
- *Integrity – adherence to a moral or ethical code*. Many of the professional groups involved in the public sector and indeed within voluntary groups will be governed by a professional code of ethics. These codes of ethics will affect their behaviour and are likely to influence their values and attitudes. Groups within the voluntary sector are most often created to achieve one particular purpose. Members of the group may have strong allegiance to the cause, whether their prime interest is research and development, expansion of services or the need to raise the public's awareness of the cause. The priorities may be in conflict with those of their potential partners in the public sector where the agencies involved have a much wider community remit.
- *Honesty – displaying integrity*. It could be assumed that all involved in these sectors display integrity. However, as previously stated, professional codes of conduct are important in the interpretation of this characteristic.
- *Trust – reliance on the integrity, ability or character of others*. For any partnership to be successful trust needs to be established and maintained. Given the cultural differences within and between agencies this may not be automatic even though strategic aims have been agreed. (See Illustration 1.)
- *Open communication – free exchange between all parties*. Trust and open communication are interrelated. Lack of trust between parties can be related to fear over sources of power, professional jealousy or lack of a common language between professional groups.
- *Fairness – free of favouritism, or bias*. In the public/voluntary context the wide-ranging demands and the power of various stakeholders, particularly in highly politicised situations, will raise the question of fairness for many partnerships.
- *Self-interest of all partners – 'something in it'*. Partnerships need to be able to demonstrate the value they add to the recipient of the service

# Strategy in action

*Illustration 1*

### *Public/public partnership in action: Community planning in Lanarkshire*

Partnerships between parts of the public sector are not new. Under the new Labour government many of the previous arrangements for partnership working which existed within the public sector have become more formalised. This has presented opportunities for different parts of the public sector to work together to improve services to their communities. However, cultural differences, a tradition of competition for resources and, in some cases, lack of understanding of respective roles and responsibilities have presented many challenges for public sector managers to overcome. Tom Divers, on taking up his appointment as the General Manager of Lanarkshire Health Board in 1996, found this to be the case when seeking to implement Community Care Planning within Lanarkshire.

The National Health Service in Scotland is organised on an area health board basis with each health board's principal role being described in *Designed to Care* (Stationery Office, 1997) as the 'protection and improvement for the health of their residents'. The Health Improvement Programmes devised by each board are in turn delivered primarily by local Health Trusts. In Scotland two types of Trust were created as a result of *Designed to Care*, acute hospital trusts responsible for a defined set of acute hospital services within a health board area and primary care trusts providing primary and community care services, including mental health and learning disabilities, within the geographical boundary of the health board. Social Work departments are the responsibility of local authorities and, whilst they are also provided on a defined geographical area basis, the areas covered are not coterminous with that of health board areas. In the Lanarkshire area, one health board covers two local authority areas, North and South Lanarkshire. The structures and management of the organisations are significantly different in that the health board is headed by a non-executive chairman, appointed by the Secretary of State, whilst the local authority has elected members as the non-executive arm of the organisation.

Tom Divers is responsible for the commissioning of healthcare for a population of 560,000 with an annual budget in excess of £400m

One of his first priorities on taking up post was to start to implement the Community Care Planning agenda. He was aware that despite the emphasis that had been placed on community care, which was based on the need to move people into appropriately supported community accommodation and out of traditional hospital institutions, over the preceding years, not one single continuing care bed in the Lanarkshire Health Board area had been closed. It was generally thought that in Lanarkshire there were around 35 per cent more health service continuing care beds than there needed to be if the balance of community care was to be redressed.

The **contextual** factors as described by Butler and Gill can be clearly illustrated. The successful implementation of community care planning was

*Illustration 1 continued*

*interdependent* on other organisations, primarily social work and housing. Scarcity of resources is always an issue to be considered in the public sector and the lack of vision and knowledge about the potential for new service delivery clearly illustrates the *ambiguity* referred to and the need to share knowledge and experience. The **interpersonal** factors of *compatibility and control* were to be the most important issues to be tackled. (See Exhibit 12.1.)

*Exhibit 12.1*    *Community Care Planning within Lanarkshire: Contextual and interpersonal factors*

---

**Contextual factors**
**Scarcity (+)**
The need to use scare resources effectively and efficiently
**Interdependence (+)**
The range of agencies involved in the allocation and use of resources and the range of professional expertise for services
**Ambiguity (+)**
The need to share ideas between agencies and the uncertainty about the future direction of developments
**Number (+)**
The synergy that could be created if all parties were to share knowledge and experience
**Strategic fit (+)**
All agencies aiming for the most appropriate level and efficient and effective means of delivering services
**Regulatory imperative (+)**
Central government initiatives for joint funding/working arrangements

**Interpersonal factors**
**Availability (+)**
Of a range of organisations contributing to the community care agenda
**Knowledge/Networking (+)**
Of clients' needs and options for design of services
**Trust (–)**
The lack of trust exhibited by contributing agencies as a result of past experiences, particularly over budgets
**Compatibility (–)**
The different cultures, values and priorities for developments displayed

---

Adapted from Butler and Gill (1999)

Just before his appointment, two new local authority Social Work Directors had been appointed and so a new senior team, responsible for the implementation of community care planning, had major issues to tackle.

Tom Divers described the first signals about partnership being the setting up of regular meetings between himself as the Health Board General

Manager, and the two Directors of Social Work for the area. At a later stage the Primary Care Trust Chief Executive also became involved in these meetings. He states: '*What was evident on the ground was a huge amount of distrust between the organisations and battles over budgets. Better working relationships had to be developed and these were encouraged through Community Care Planning. The way in which the whole strategy for Mental Health Services was put together was radically different from what had gone before. There was evidence of lack of trust; radically different cultures existed not only between organisations but also within organisations. There was a need to break down barriers and change the way in which the joint planning arrangements worked.'* The Directors of Social Work, the Trust Chief Executive and the Health Board General Manager became personally involved in the joint planning group to demonstrate to staff throughout their respective organisations that working arrangements had to change. A powerful indication of change occurred in 1998 when the health board was able to invest around £800,000 of non-recurring monies to support implementation of Community Care Planning. Rather than the control of this resource being retained by either of the statutory bodies it was routed through community housing organisations to look for solutions for people with learning disabilities to be discharged from long-term hospital care and be settled within the heart of the community. Tom Divers believes '*that act of faith shown by the Health Board by putting the money into the development of this initiative was a very powerful signal to the local authority that the Health Board was prepared to find resources and put them into an area which might not be viewed as really being the health service's responsibility*'. This decision was viewed as extremely risky by some and at the time Tom Divers was asked by colleagues from other areas if he was confident that it was within his powers to transfer money in such a way. However, with the publication of *Modernising Community Care: An action plan* (Stationery Office, 1998), such action is exactly what the policy makers require if partnerships are to become a reality.

Using Butler and Gill's Framework of Propensity to Partner, Community Care Planning within Lanarkshire at this time can be illustrated as shown in Exhibit 12.1.

In order to continue to support the partnership approach, a number of seminars were organised for elected members of the two councils. This was an opportunity to discuss issues from past joint working arrangements and to begin to identify solutions for the future. Again the Health Board offered a substantial amount of money to put towards joint community care plans if social work and their colleagues from housing would work together with them on commissioning the Community Care Plans. This relocation of resources again demonstrated commitment to the principles of partnership and within the year the commissioning initiative project was complete.

Tom Divers believes that the need to develop trust and demonstrate that trust by the joint commitment of funds is crucial to the success of partnerships.

An extension of this type of joint working can be seen in the Community Planning exercises being established in the locality. An initiative in Lanarkshire, led by the local authority, involves all key partner agencies such as health, the local development agency, local employment agencies, Scottish Homes and the police, and the group's remit is to improve the services to the local population. Increasingly the involvement and engagement of the communities being served drive the initiatives. Therefore, instead of planning being thrust on communities from statutory organisations, the first priority is to community development and its investment in developing the capacity of communities to engage in partnership working of this type. This example of community planning may be viewed as the ultimate articulation of inter-agency planning.

Source: interview with Tom Divers, Lanarkshire Health Board General Manager

and in the working relationships of the partners. The issue of control, both of resources and of ethos and values, may be an area of contention. (See Illustration 2.)

- *Balance of rewards vs. risks and/or resources required*. The partnership cannot be seen to be too lopsided or some partners may feel loss of power and question the value that the partnership adds to their agency and may seek to end the partnership or look for other organisations to enter into partnerships with. (See Illustration 2.)

## 12.6  *Adding value through partnerships*

Creating the conditions for success of partnerships is dependent on each partner being able to recognise the synergy of the relationship created through joint working.

Illustration 1 shows the development of partnership working and highlights the difficulties in bringing together different agencies within the public sector. It clearly illustrates that while agreement on partnership working can be reached between agencies, consideration has to be given to the differences in cultures which exist. It is the *interpersonal factors* which are often most challenging and difficult to resolve. In order to facilitate the development of trust, public sector managers need to demonstrate their willingness to change management styles and approaches and share knowledge and information for inter-agency partnerships to operate successfully.

## 12.7  *Stakeholder relationships in partnerships*

The analysis of success in partnerships in the public/public, public/voluntary sector may be difficult to determine. The ability of the partner-

# Strategy in action

**Illustration 2**

### Partnership in action: Public/voluntary sector partnerships

## Terminal One – Blantyre Youth Development Team

Terminal One is a youth group located in Blantyre in Scotland. It was formed in 1984, supported by the local council and initially run by local authority educational development officers. Initially the group focused on being a pressure group campaigning for youth rights. In the late 1980s they successfully campaigned against the closure of the local Job Centre. Building on this success, the group fought for better facilities for the young people in the local community and by 1991, to the surprise of much of the local community, the youth development team took possession of premises from the local council. Terminal One was born.

Terminal One is a unique community resource because of its commitment to youth empowerment. This is reflected in its management structure. From the outset Blantyre Youth Development Team had young people on its management board with only those in the age group 14 to 25 being eligible to vote. All other members of the management committee, including local authority representatives, attended meetings only in an advisory capacity.

Throughout its history the group has remained committed to its principles of youth empowerment, retaining the management committee structure that it was set up with. Those involved in the project are proud of its success and believe the attention the project has attracted, nationally and internationally, confirms this success.

Funding for the group initially came from successful Urban Aid grant applications. In 1998/99 Terminal One received a grant of over £111,000 from Urban Aid. By this time, in addition to organising a range of social and educational events for local young people, from concerts and discos to local fêtes and fun days, the group also provided a range of educational and development resources accessible to the young members of the local community.

A total of 35,169 attendances were recorded at the centre over the year 1998/99 and over 9,000 hours of volunteers' time was given to support the activities of the group.

At this time Terminal One employed a total of 13 employees, including a project manager and an assistant.

The present Chairman is 18-year-old Ewan Anderson with 19-year-old Lianne Grieve as Vice Chair.

Terminal One states as its Core Purpose:

*To focus on the personal development of young people. The objectives are to provide a high standard of skilled staff and modern facilities, which young people can access for social and vocational purposes; and to create an environment in which young people can perform to their fullest potential; and to be recognised for their efforts. (Source: Annual Report)*

*Illustration 2 continued*

The achievement of this purpose is attained through the group's commit-ment to youth empowerment and the responsibility for the development of the service and control of the resources being held by the management team and the young people themselves. They view these values as integral to the project and believe that they have developed a valuable community resource without 'outside interference' from public bodies.

When the Scottish Office announced the end of Urban Aid funding in 1999, Terminal One was faced with major difficulties. The Social Inclusion Partnership (SIP) initiative (Scottish Executive Health Department, 1997) replaced the exist-ing funding mechanism and the local authority became the agents for SIP funding. This shift brought about dilemmas for the management team of Terminal One and they feared that the control over their future would be lessened as the regulations for access to SIP funding challenged the structure and values of the organisation. In order to access funding a new partnership had to be formed with the local auth-ority, who were operating different guidelines from those of Urban Aid funding.

The Project Manager, herself a previous youth team member, talks of partnership in the Annual Report, stating:

*Undoubtedly forging effective links with other agencies is the key to any organ-isational success. We are proud to acknowledge that we recognise that this as one of our particular strengths. This year has brought about significant part-nership working for the project. With the introduction of the government's initiative on Social Inclusion Partnership (SIP) Terminal One has played a key role in conjunction with ten other partners in helping secure additional funds of £3.5 million for Blantyre and North Hamilton. In addition, along with New Routes and Independence in the Community we are driving forward a local community initiative in the form of a Community Forum.*

*Perhaps our most important partnership under way at the moment is the potential to work more closely with South Lanarkshire Council as our present funders. The opportunity exists for our expertise in working with young people to be used to deliver Universal Connections services within Blantyre.*

Universal Connections is the name of local authority-established youth groups set up throughout the local area. The Council encouraged Terminal One to become a Universal Connection in order to meet the new funding cri-teria. However, the management committee of Terminal One thought that the structure, philosophy and management style of Universal Connections was too bureaucratic and centrally controlled by the local authority. They feared that if they became part of this larger, council-run group they would lose their unique approach to youth empowerment. They believed that becoming a Universal Connection would compromise the values and management philosophy upon which Terminal One had been built. When faced with the dilemma of becoming a Universal Connection and retaining funding, or

*Illustration 2 continued*

resisting the change and facing potential closure because they did not meet the criteria laid down by the council for SIP funding, real difficulties in reaching a partnership agreement were encountered. Closure of Terminal One would not only mean the loss of a community resource but the 13 members of staff employed by the management committee would lose their jobs. One member of the Committee commented: '*You have to think hard ... you have all these people employed who have mortgages, it is people's careers you have in your hands.... You don't want to close the project but you have these principles ... it is tough.*'

The chairman commented: '*at the meeting with the council, relationships were strained because of the decision to be taken. You then have to go back to the staff and feed back the situation we are faced with. You have to believe that what you are doing is right. You take it for granted that what you are doing is right because you have such belief about youth empowerment. In most other projects empowerment is on paper only. It is real for us. We don't want to give it up.*'

Terminal One firmly believed that it was and should be answerable and accountable to the users first and foremost. By entering a partnership with the local council their lines of accountability would change. It was their view that the council was only interested in accountability in terms of costs and had little interest in the quality or appropriateness of the provision. The terms of funding meant that Terminal One would be required to sign service level agreements for a predetermined set of activities, prescribed by the council, which would then be provided by them on behalf of the council. This would result in the closure of some of the activities and resources that Terminal One was involved in and valued.

A committee member described the dilemma to be faced over these agreements: '*We need to agree this service-level agreement. We need the money. We want to do a good job and share knowledge with others but we cannot be in a partnership if we do not share knowledge but are just told what we will have to do if we want to survive. We are becoming defensive and wary of the knowledge that we are sharing; we get little back in return. Partnership is about open communication. An open dialogue needs to work both ways.*'

A final comment from the Chairman: '*They [the council] do not seem to understand that the services we provide are determined by the young people using the facilities. They are not decided upon by the management committee or by external experts. The young people are the experts. The success of this project is dependent on retaining that involvement.*'

What does the future hold for Terminal One?

ship to demonstrate how it creates value in the eye of the customer may be particularly challenging, as in many instances there may be differing views over who the customer is. As can be seen in Chapter 9 of this book, the mapping of various stakeholders will assist managers to assess the power and interest that stakeholders are likely to have in given situations and the effect that this is likely to have on the effectiveness of partnerships. In some cases, the customer or user of the service, as a stakeholder, may traditionally have had very low interest and low power. However, the need to engage communities in the development of their public services and the ethos behind Social Inclusion could change this significantly.

The levels of power and interest shift significantly when communities become active partners with statutory bodies participating in the design and delivery of future services. If, however, control of resources remains with the traditional sources of power then the shift in interest may be evident but the level of power remains the same.

The relocation of resources to community housing associations as described in Illustration 1 represents a real transfer of power from statutory bodies to voluntary bodies in housing with the potential to increase the levels of interests of the stakeholders they represent, i.e. in this case people with learning disabilities.

The need to manage stakeholders' relationships is crucial. Firstly, there is a need for partners *to share strategic aims and objectives.* This is dependent upon the ability of executives to be able to define clear, specific and feasible objectives in the first place and for these objectives to be communicated and supported throughout the organisations.

An example of this at the macro community level in Scotland is the development of local alliances made up of senior management representatives from local authorities, development agencies, health boards and other public bodies who meet to discuss issues which impact on the ability of local communities to develop and deliver the strategic objectives which have key significance for the community such as transport infrastructure, economic regeneration and the local development needed to support government strategies.

The success of partnerships set up around money depend on who benefits from the money spent. Where one partner is driven by values and the other driven by the allocation of financial resources, conflict is inevitable. Cultural differences between voluntary groups and the public sector are likely. This has significant implications for public sector managers who are entering into partnership arrangements with voluntary bodies. As previously mentioned, there are real challenges for managers in developing the skills required to assess cultural differences, establish values and then reach agreement on these values in order for the strategic aims and objectives of the partnership to be achieved. Management styles and approaches may need to be altered in order that trust between stakeholders is established and effective communication happens. Public sector managers may find that organisational structures are not compatible with the less formal structures which may be found within the voluntary sector, and that when communities themselves start to play a part in the partnership, the traditional bureaucracy of public sector organisations becomes a barrier to effective partnership working. Difficulties between stakeholders in partnerships can arise because of lack of trust, as shown in Illustration 1, where the key factors which managers needed to address were the interpersonal factors described by Butler and Gill. Illustration 2 demonstrates the importance of addressing the contextual factors where the *regulatory imperative* drives the propensity to partnership. *Scarcity of resources* and the *interdependence* of agencies involved in the partnership are recognised but the *strategic fit* of stakeholders and the *ambiguity* over achieving strategic aims and objectives creates conflict.

Illustration 2 shows the **contextual** and **interpersonal** factors described by Butler and Gill. The key issue about partnerships such as this is the *interdependence* of each party and the extent to which they can ensure that they can achieve *strategic fit* (see *Exploring Corporate Strategy*, p. 23). Terminal One needs the local authority to support the venture in terms of funding. The local authority recognises the valuable contribution made by the group to local young people. As in the first illustration, *trust* needs to be developed between the stakeholders before the true sharing of knowledge and expertise can occur. In this case, the key stakeholders are not only managers from both organisations but the users of the facility, who are experienced in planning and delivering their services and have become used to having considerable influence over the use and control of resources. Public sector managers need to consider the attributes described by Mariotti in situations such as this. If such a partnership is going to achieve its objectives and satisfy its key stakeholders then the different characteristics displayed by the parties involved, the influence of professional backgrounds and experience, trust, open communication and fairness will all need to be considered. Particularly in this case the self-interest of all parties has to be examined. These attributes will be achieved through efforts of the partners to *understand the values of each group and demonstrate respect* for these values. *Compatibility* will only be achieved when information and experience is shared and *open communication systems* allow discussion regarding matters of resource allocation and control to happen. The *balance of rewards and risks* needs to be addressed to satisfy stakeholders' expectations.

## 12.8   Summary

- Partnerships in the public/public and public/voluntary sectors depend on the development of mutual respect, understanding of and sharing strategic objectives and values, the establishment of trust and the ability to develop acceptable ways of joint working.
- Managing the cultural differences which occur within and between the sectors is perhaps the most challenging aspect of the public sector manager's task and requires different management styles to be adopted if joint working arrangements are to be successful. New behaviours, such as the ability to work collaboratively, sharing knowledge and skills with a wide range of agencies and professional groups and devising acceptable ways of joint working, in many cases in non-hierarchical teams, need to be developed.
- The traditional bureaucracy of the public sector does not sit well with the devolved structure required in partnerships. New structures need to be devised which allow for flexibility, are non-hierarchical and encourage open communication between stakeholders.
- Partnerships set up around funding arrangements should be driven by the needs of those on whom the money will be spent. Where one partner is driven by values and the other's prime concern is the allocation of resources, conflict is inevitable. This can only be overcome by open communication and trust.

## References

Bolger, D. and Pease, C. (1998) *Reinventing Management*. The findings of a study on the potential impact of the Scottish Parliament on the role and function of public sector managers, Nov.

Butler, R. and Gill, J. (1999) 'Formation and control of public private partnerships: a stakeholder approach'.

Mariotti, J.L. (1996) *The Power of Partnerships – The Next Step*, Oxford: Blackwell.

Scottish Executive Health Department (1995) *Local Partnership Agreements NHS MEL (1999) 59*, Scottish Executive Health Department.

Scottish Executive Health Department (1997) *Local Care Partnerships Scheme NHS MEL (1997) 57*, Scottish Executive Health Department.

Scottish Office (1997) *Lifelong Learning: The Way Forward*, Scottish Office.

Scottish Office (1998) *Towards a Development Strategy for Rural Scotland, Part III Partnership*, Scottish Office.

Scottish Office (1999a) *Social Inclusion – Opening the Door to a Better Scotland*, Scottish Office.

Scottish Office (1999b) 'A partnership for employment', Press Release, Sept.

Stationery Office (1997) *Designed to Care: Renewing the National Health Service in Scotland*, Stationery Office.

Stationery Office (1998) *Modernising Community Care: An Action Plan*, Stationery Office.

# 13

# *Strategy and structures in the public sector*

## *By Kevan Scholes*

### *Editor's introduction*

The relationship between structure and strategy is a major theme in *Exploring Corporate Strategy* and is discussed at three levels. In Chapter 6 the focus is on explaining how the corporate purposes of organisations are determined and put in place. The structural issue here is how the strategic agenda at the corporate centre of organisations relates to the strategies of strategic business units (SBUs). The role of the corporate parent needs to be understood.

In Chapter 9 this broad agenda is pursued in more detail by considering how the structure and design of an organisation can help or hinder the successful implementation of strategy. The first strand of this discussion is the 'centralisation/devolution' debate – requiring decisions on how strategic management is split between the corporate centre and the parts (such as departments or divisions). Chapter 9 also looks at a further level of detail – at the way in which the building blocks and co-ordinating mechanisms create different configurations (using Mintzberg's stereotypes – such as the machine bureaucracy or adhocracy) as they adapt to the circumstances in which they are operating. Also, there are connections to issues of management control as discussed in Section 10.4 of Chapter 10.

This chapter by Kevan Scholes takes these general principles and models and applies them to public sector organisations in order to identify the key structural issues for public sector managers and to provide some guidance on best practice.

## 13.1 Introduction

The history of the public sector in many different parts of the world is one of hierarchical bureaucracies that grew in size and scope considerably up until the 1980s. Then the 'new agenda' for the public services challenged both the effectiveness and efficiency of these traditional bureaucracies. However, the extreme antithesis of highly devolved, flexible structures not only proved difficult to put in place and run smoothly, it also proved to be inappropriate in most situations. Out of this experience has come a more balanced view of the virtues of a 'middle way' between these extremes together with an understanding that different circumstances and strategies require different structural arrangements. These may need to live alongside each other in the same organisation. So the practical debate has now settled down to three key issues, each of which is discussed in *Exploring Corporate Strategy*, namely:

- What is the role of the corporate centre?
- How will the corporate centre relate to the parts (divisions and departments) of the organisation? In particular, what brand of centralisation or devolution will best suit the organisation?
- Choices of detailed configuration (of building blocks and co-ordinating mechanisms).

## 13.2   *Managing a portfolio of services*

Most public sector organisations consist of a range of separate services – whether these are provided by the organisation itself or by third parties within the control of the organisation. Indeed, given that many organisations in the public sector are large and relatively diverse, the concept of a portfolio of services may exist at more than one level of aggregation, as the example of Exhibit 13.1 shows. At the level of the whole organisation there are key decisions about the *arenas* in which the authority will be involved (such as Education and Social Services). Much of this is determined at a higher level (through legislation) but some is discretionary. Within each arena there are decisions about the

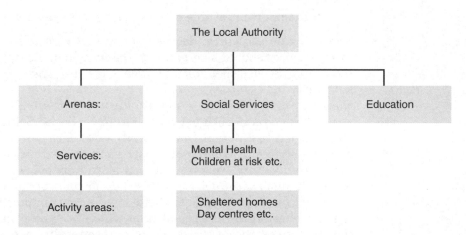

*Exhibit 13.1   Corporate centres at different levels – the Local Authority*

mix of *services* to be provided and who should undertake the provision. Within each service are more detailed choices as to the *activities* that should make up the service. At each of these levels there are two key strategic issues:

- Which arenas, services or activities should be within the portfolio.
- How the *corporate centre* should interact with each arena, service or activity within the portfolio in order to add value to the work of these separate parts.

### 13.2.1    Who is the corporate centre?

To avoid confusion in later discussions, it is important to be clear about terminology and exactly what is meant by the *corporate centre* – since it is a concept which will be used extensively in this chapter. In general terms the corporate centre is anything that sits above the level of the strategic business units (SBUs)[1] of the organisation. Although Exhibit 13.1 is not an organisation chart as such (since the arenas, services and activities may not be structured in the neat way depicted there), it can be used to illustrate this issue. In large organisations, such as the local authority shown in the exhibit, there are many levels. Each level constitutes a collection of SBUs managed by the corporate centre at the level(s) above. Each corporate centre should concern itself with different strategic issues. For example, the corporate centre of the whole organisation is crucially concerned with questions about the scope of the local authority and the broad arenas in which the authority should operate; within the social services SBU the key issues for the corporate centre are about the scope of social services provision and how it should be organised ... and so on through the levels.

It is important at this stage to make some observations:

- Strategic and structural decisions at the lower levels – such as how social services should be organised – cannot be made independently of the higher-level issues about how arenas are organised within the authority.
- Nonetheless it is possible – and usually sensible – to allow diversity of structures and approach between arenas. So Social Services may have a sub-structure different from Education. This raises issues about the role and style of the corporate centre and the extent to which it can cope with diversity. This is discussed more fully below.
- Although much of the debate in this chapter concentrates on structural issues *within* organisations, there are usually important corporate centres external to the organisation which both determine and limit the freedom of the organisation to determine its own strategies, as already acknowledged. So, the government department and/or funding

agency will have a sector-wide brief and be considering strategic questions like 'How many local authorities (police forces, universities, hospitals, etc.) should there be and how should they relate to each other?'

### 13.2.2 The role of the corporate centre

An important theme of this chapter is that the corporate centre must add value to the work of the SBUs (in providing best value services) if it is to justify its existence (remembering that there are many levels where this justification must be made). The next two sections of the chapter will look at two different 'schools of thought' on how value can be added and the role of the corporate centre and apply this to the public sector context. It is important to note at this stage that recent trends in large, diverse, private sector organisations have consistently been in the direction of breaking up 'the empire' and allowing separate, smaller, more focused businesses to face their funders (shareholders/investors) and customers independently. The challenge to the public services should be clear – are corporate centres really adding more value than their cost?

## 13.3 The synergy school

Exhibit 13.2 is a schematic representation of how the corporate centre might add value to the SBUs by creating *synergy* through the way in which the separate services are organised and interconnected. Synergy is defined in *Exploring Corporate Strategy* as follows:

> *Synergy can occur in situations where two or more activities or processes complement each other to the extent that their combined effect is greater than the sums of the parts. (Johnson and Scholes, 1999, p. 331)*

For example, synergy in public services could be secured by the corporate centre in two main ways:

- through *sharing* resources, infrastructure or activities between services (e.g. sports facilitates for schools and community recreation);
- *transferring skills* from one SBU to another (hence preventing 'reinventing the wheel'), e.g. customer care or service development processes.

Synergies of this type are most likely to occur in *related* arenas, services or activities, and there have been many debates as to what exactly 'related' means in this context. This is clearly an important question for public service managers expecting to gain the benefits of synergy. The evidence from other organisations is that it is important to consider three different types of relatedness when looking for opportunities to create synergy:

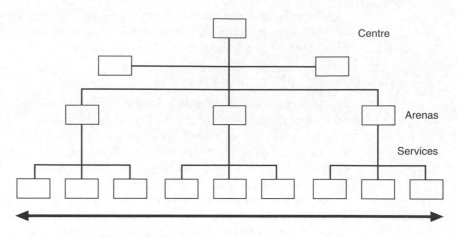

*Exhibit 13.2    Adding value through synergy*

- *Related products/services*. This has been a traditional basis on which many public services have structured their provision on the grounds that synergy will occur through the 'glue' of a common technical and professional expertise in the design and running of similar services. Local authorities have predominantly grouped services in this way in both their management and political structures. So both departments and committees have been built around areas of professional expertise (social services, education, etc.).
- *Related customers/clients*. This has been an important basis of structuring in the private sector – for example through sector-focused teams. Many public services are now grouping services or activities by client group – whether that be by age (such as paediatrics in hospitals) or by geography (neighbourhood services) in an attempt to build real expertise about the special needs of each client group.
- *Related by competence*. Whereas technical or professional competences have been the rationale for creating portfolios of related products/services (see above), other forms of competence may also be a source of synergy. The critical one examined in this chapter will be *parenting skills* – the ability (or otherwise) to add value to particular types of services/activities (but not others). This could result in the grouping of services which might look odd from either a product or client group perspective but might make sense if all the activities require and are amenable to a particular parenting formula. For example, they may all be *centres of excellence* within their own arena but liable to be 'steam-rollered' by the parenting formula for mainstream services. Many organisations in the public service have this dilemma and some choose structural solutions to address it. For example, many universities now have graduate schools within which sit the graduate programmes for

all their academic schools. This is a home that protects them from the steamroller of the mass-market, high-volume, undergraduate provision.

The essence of the synergy school is that *added value occurs through the management of linkages between SBUs and/or by the creation of new SBUs which cut across the formal structure.*

### 13.4 *The parenting school*

The essence of the parenting school is that *value is created through core competences found at the corporate centre, which are properly matched to the types of SBUs in the portfolio (and vice versa).* Corporate parenting will now be discussed more fully and applied to the public sector.

#### 13.4.1 *The corporate parent as 'middleman'*

It has already been seen that there are many levels in and beyond the organisation all of which must add value to the work of the SBUs below. Indeed the 'next level above' will be an important judge of whether sufficient value is being added since they may have the option of 'skipping a level' and dealing directly with the SBUs below (see Exhibit 13.3). So, for example, the question might arise as to whether the Department for Education and Employment (DfEE) (a central government department) should deal with local authorities through their corporate centres or directly with their education department. Or if the argument is pushed further, why not deal with schools and colleges *directly* since they provide the service to the clients? Of course

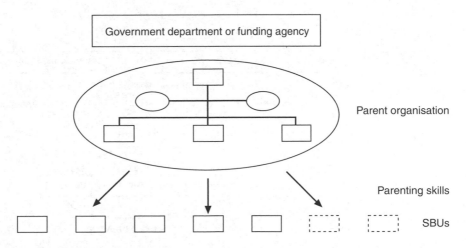

*Exhibit 13.3    Corporate parent as middleman*

this has been a big policy issue in the UK over several years, particularly on issues of curriculum, standards, testing and funding. It is now fairly common for central departments and agencies to deal with providing organisations at more than one level, hence raising the question as to *which issues should be handled at which level.*

These questions of the value added by 'middlemen' are not only of concern to funders, they are of importance to clients too. This is exemplified in the recent concerns that public services should improve the client's experience through making their services more 'seamless' rather than the highly fragmented jungle of separate services as perceived by most clients. The catchphrase *joined-up government* has been used by politicians to describe their aspirations to improve the clients' experience of public services. The discussion in *Exploring Corporate Strategy* (Section 9.2.7) illustrates three different ways in which the paths for client access to services could be smoothed (Exhibit 13.4). The key issues for public sector managers when thinking through these structural issues are as follows:

- Both *one-stop* and *one-start* shops provide a single entry point through which the client accesses the full services of the organisation. So if this entry point is to add value to the clients' experience it must have the competence to:
  - diagnose the client's need;
  - identify the services that fit the needs ('pigeon-holing');
  - provide some services directly.
  It must also have the *authority to refer on* to the appropriate delivery

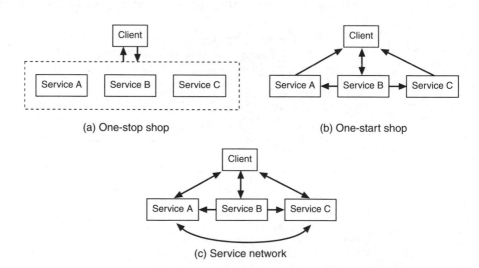

(a) One-stop shop          (b) One-start shop

(c) Service network

*Exhibit 13.4   Linking services – three approaches*

point within the service. The GP's role in healthcare is a good example of the one-start shop.

- The *service network* is a more ambitious way of smoothing the clients' path. It removes the single entry point (such as the GP as middleman) by creating the competences listed above (diagnosis, pigeonholing, etc.) *in all of the separate services*. Although, in principle, this would be a better deal for clients, not only does it require much higher levels of competence in all SBUs but also the linkages between these SBUs must run smoothly. They are not orchestrated by a middleman but rather rely on personal contact and trust between managers and professionals in the separate services. This is a tough agenda to maintain in large organisations.

### 13.4.2 The parenting matrix

The parenting school argues that three conditions must be fulfilled if the corporate centre is to add value:

- There must be a *parenting opportunity*, i.e. some SBUs must not be fulfilling their potential.
- The corporate centre managers must have *sufficient feel/understanding* of the SBUs to avoid destroying value.
- The corporate centre must have the appropriate *parenting skills* to add value to the SBUs.

Exhibit 13.5 is the Ashridge Parenting Matrix, which is discussed in Section 6.4.4 of *Exploring Corporate Strategy*. It is a device whereby the key three parenting criteria can be applied to categorise SBUs within a portfolio as follows:

- *Heartland SBUs* are those that satisfy all three parenting criteria. The parent can add value without danger of doing harm. These would normally be regarded as core services within a public service organisation. The mainstream clinical specialisms in a hospital would be in this category.
- *Ballast SBUs* may also be core services and regarded as central to the purposes of the organisation or portfolio. Although the parent understands them well, there is not a parenting opportunity to add value. These could be candidates for increased devolution within the corporate structure. Otherwise they are subjected to the costs of 'corporate help' (overhead) which is not adding value. The increased local management of schools in several countries is a good example.
- *Value-trap SBUs* are a real concern in many parts of the public sector and need to be spotted. This is where the SBUs are under-performing (there is a parenting opportunity) but the corporate parent does not have the competence to deal with it and is likely to do more harm than good. Two examples in the public sector might be:

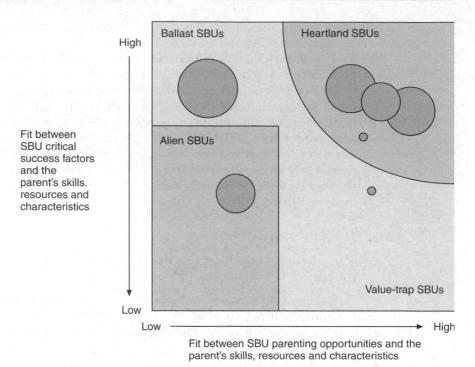

High

Ballast SBUs

Heartland SBUs

Fit between
SBU critical
success factors
and the
parent's skills.
resources and
characteristics

Alien SBUs

Value-trap SBUs

Low

Low ——————————————————————————→ High

Fit between SBU parenting opportunities and the
parent's skills, resources and characteristics

*Exhibit 13.5    The parenting matrix: the Ashridge Portfolio Display*

- services which are located in the *wrong portfolio* and subjected to an inappropriate parenting formula (the graduate school example from Section 13.3 above);
- services which should be *outsourced* and provided by more experienced and competent outsiders (IT services might be a candidate).

- *Alien SBUs* satisfy none of the criteria. They are misfits, which offer little opportunity to add value and fit awkwardly with the parent's parenting style. So unless the organisation is mandated to continue providing the service, they should be divested or moved to another portfolio. The progressive removal of Higher and Further Education from local authority control in the UK from 1989 onwards was an example.

## 13.5  *Centralisation and devolution*

Section 9.4 of *Exploring Corporate Strategy* revisits the issues about the role of the corporate centre(s) at a more detailed level by using Goold and Campbell's (1987) three stereotype 'strategic styles' of *Strategic Planning*, *Financial Control* and *Strategic Control* to describe the full spectrum of arrangements from highly centralised to highly devolved. The purpose is to provide some guiding principles whereby managers can decide how, within the broad principles discussed above, strategic responsibilities should be *divided* between the corporate centre and the 'parts' of the organisation. The detailed implications for the structures and management controls within the organisation which 'tie' the centre to the parts and the parts to each other are described in these stereotypes. Clearly in highly centralised regimes these ties are many and detailed. In highly devolved regimes they are fewer and simpler. But in all cases these structural arrangements must result in a situation where the corporate centre(s) as middlemen demonstrably add more value than cost.

### 13.5.1 The role of the centre

Exhibit 13.6 is the checklist from Section 9.4 of *Exploring Corporate Strategy* about how a corporate centre might add value to the work of the SBUs. It is not intended to repeat the discussion here but rather to make some summary points for consideration by public sector managers:

- There is not one right way to structure an organisation. The degree of devolution should be matched to choice of strategies. So, for example, a highly centralised regime (a well-functioning bureaucracy) may be well matched to the delivery of a *no-frills cost-efficient* service.
- In centralised regimes the corporate centre clearly is expected to add value in many of the ways itemised in Exhibit 13.6 – but not necessarily all. In devolved regimes the corporate centre mainly adds value through its parenting skills (the final two items in Exhibit 13.6) and/or the ability to create synergy (the previous two items).
- There is a strong relationship between the structures and controls in organisations and the culture that they create over many years. So there is a need to consider how culture will need to be changed along-

---

**Increasing value for money through**
- Efficiency/leverage
- Expertise
- Investment and competence building
- Fostering innovation – coaching/leaning
- Mitigating risk
- Image/networks
- Collaboration/co-ordination/brokerage
- Standards/performance assessment
- Intervention (e.g. acquisition, disposal, change agency)

*Exhibit 13.6    The role of the centre*

side structural changes which are deemed necessary to support new strategies. This is why many public services have found it difficult to rise to the opportunities of a less regulated world.

### 13.5.2    Elements of good practice

There is now considerable experience of operating devolved regimes in the public sector (whether that is *strategic control* or *financial control*). This accumulated wisdom allows for a practical checklist of good practice against which managers can judge their own approach (see Exhibit 13.7). There are two sets of issues which need thinking through. First, the need to be clear about the type of devolution to be adopted (in line with the discussions above) and, therefore, the detailed 'rules' of how the regime will operate. In many cases insufficient time is spent on deciding and communicating this devolution philosophy within the organisation. Second, a series of quite practical considerations to ensure that managers design devolved regimes which are appropriate to the circumstances in which their organisation is operating.

### The devolution philosophy and rules

The following should be borne in mind:

- The most fundamental need is to be clear on which activities are to be devolved from the corporate centre (at each level) and which are not – using the checklist of Exhibit 13.6. This is sometimes referred to as the *tight/loose agenda*.
- Devolution cuts both ways – so managers of SBUs need to accept *accountability* alongside their strategic *responsibilities*. Most public sector organisations are tackling this. What often is not being tackled

---

*Devolution philosophy*
- *Clarity* on 'tight/loose' – responsible **and** accountable (SBUs and centre)
- *Visibility* (e.g. cross-subsidisation)
- Resource *outcomes* (not history or outputs)

*Practicalities*
- 'Unit' *size*
- *Simple* management processes
- Quality management *information*
- *Mitigation* during transition
- *Investment* must happen

---

*Exhibit 13.7    Devolved regimes – elements of good practice*

is making the corporate centre accountable for adding value through the activities which it undertakes.

- Devolved regimes also need increased openness and *visibility* in the organisation. So, for example, the corporate centre may wish to cross-subsidise developing services from established services. Indeed, this would be a common conclusion that would fall out of portfolio management principles. Managers of the established services are more likely to accept this if it is visible and part of an overall corporate strategy which is clearly articulated.

- Devolved regimes require a corporate centre to agree targets and measure the performance of the SBUs under their control. In undertaking these processes the first wave of public sector reforms attempted to move away from measuring and resourcing *inputs* (historical budgets, headcount, etc.) to resourcing against *outputs* (e.g. number of customers served). But this should only be seen as a step towards the resourcing of *outcomes* (e.g. whether a university's graduates get jobs or a hospital's patients' quality of life is improved). For some organisations this is easier said than done. It is clearly nonsense to resource a police force against its established headcount or its arrests or convictions – but at least these are measurable. Surely they should be resourced against 'providing a safer and less threatening community' – but how is that measured?

### Practicalities

- One of the most common failings is the creation of devolved units which are not of *critical mass*. So they are not robust enough to survive the new rules of devolved regimes. The primary school sector within education (5–11-year-olds) is in obvious danger of this error if the local management of schools is implemented in the same way as for the larger units found in secondary schools (12–18-year-olds) and colleges (16–19-year-olds).

- The benefits of devolution have often been lost through the immense complexity of the management processes they have spawned. The creation of internal markets and service-level agreements can easily degenerate into a complex mess. So keeping management processes *simple* should be a guiding principle.

- Devolved regimes are hungry for *management information*. This has proved very problematic for many public services – particularly with financial information (where the heritage is one of external reporting, not internal facilitation) and data about the quality of service (where the tradition has been 'the provider knows best – take it or leave it').

- One of the common pitfalls in any change in approach is that there will always be winners and losers. It is good practice to agree a regime of *mitigation*, which limits the (one-year) impact on the losers to give them time and incentive to adjust. This mitigation can then be reduced towards zero over, say, a three-year period.

- A significant worry about obsessively implemented devolution is that an early casualty is the organisation's investment in its own future. Many organisations have committed this sin and needed to change the regime to reverse the trend somewhat. A common example is training. In centralised regimes this is decided at the centre and funded by 'top-slicing' from the budget, and then provided as a 'free' service to SBUs. In devolved regimes the temptation is to do entirely the opposite. Training is decided at SBU level, paid for out of their own budget, and provided by internal or external people, as they feel fit. Internal trainers must survive within this market situation. Not surprisingly, training has often been a short-term casualty as SBU managers attempt to reduce their costs to meet their bottom-line targets. As a result of this, many corporate centres have reverted to top-slicing training budgets.

The general lesson from these examples is that the proof of any management philosophy (such as devolution) is to be found in the *behaviours* that it triggers and the impact on performance. Over-dogmatic implementation of management philosophies can be dangerous.

### 13.5.3   *Connecting the parts – the ubiquitous matrix*

The discussion in the previous sections has largely been focused on the vertical relationships within a structure – how the corporate centre relates to the parts. The synergy school also emphasised that value can be added through the way in which the parts are connected – for example through resource sharing or the transference of competences from one part to another. There are also the difficult dilemmas reported in Section 13.3 about the basis on which the parts should be created – whether departments/divisions should be built around professional field, client groups or organisational competences. Sometimes these may neatly 'align', allowing for a divisional structure based on a group of related professional skills required for the creation and delivery of services to a clearly defined client group. A chemistry department in a university may fit this bill. But in many cases this alignment is not so clear, leaving the organisation with the dilemma of how it reconciles in its structure these competing demands of professional field, product group and client group.

The most common solution to the dilemma is the matrix structure described in Section 9.2.5 of *Exploring Corporate Strategy*. Despite some of the difficulties of making matrix structures work, it is a common structural form in professional service organisations (both public and private sector) – either formally or informally – at one or more of the levels shown in Exhibit 13.1.

The reason for this is often the practicality of *critical mass* (cited as a key practicality in Exhibit 13.7). Again the local authority example in Exhibit 13.1 can illustrate the point. In the late 1990s it was fashionable to structure at the first level into *Directorates* which are large and fairly self-sufficient (one Directorate usually houses the traditional 'Corporate Services' of Corporate Finance, HR and (possibly) IT services). So even at this first level a matrix starts to emerge as, for example, IT development occurs both centrally and within the front-line Directorates. Often IT staff will be designated to the Central Services Directorate but be permanently seconded to a particular front-line Directorate. This story will then repeat itself *within* a Directorate where some functions are performed Directorate-wide and others confined to the separate Service Departments which make up the Directorate. At the third level the need for sharing at departmental level between sub-units which deliver small groups of services becomes more pressing as the unit size becomes smaller.

Given this common occurrence of matrix management in the public services (even if this descriptor is not used), the messages from *Exploring Corporate Strategy* are important:

- Decide on the 'lead arm' of the matrix. For example, tailoring services to the elderly would use 'client group' as the lead arm and ensure that mechanisms exist to draw on and co-ordinate the work of professionals from different professional groups – health, social services, housing, etc.
- The issues of *identification* and *ownership* by professional staff must be tackled. So secondment, project teams and other devices may be essential to make the matrix work.
- *Collaboration* between senior managers and senior professionals is a critically important behaviour in matrix structures and one which does not always come easily. The ability to tolerate *ambiguity* is also important.
- There should be a clear means of resolving *stalemate* – which is an ever-present danger in matrix structures.

## 13.6   *Organisational configurations*

The sections above have looked at the important questions of parenting and centralisation/devolution. But organisational design is also concerned with the detailed ways in which an organisation is configured – the building blocks and co-ordinating mechanisms as discussed in Section 9.5 of *Exploring Corporate Strategy*. Although, in practice, configurations tend to emerge over a period of time rather than being a carefully considered choice, the combination of these elements often 'produces' organisational configurations with features similar to one (or a combination of) Mintzberg's stereotypes as shown in Exhibit 13.8.

This section will try to answer three questions in the public service context:

- Which configurations have best suited public services (historically)?
- Is there a need for change?
- What are the implications of diversity of configuration?

### 13.6.1   Choice of configuration

It is valuable to reflect on the match between the situational factors for the public services (see Exhibit 13.8) and the extent to which the commonly found configurations are suited to these circumstances. The following factors would often describe the 'situation' of the public services historically:

- continuity in the environment (with some exceptions);
- a diverse environment in terms of the variety of demands;
- some services facing simple environments whilst others faced complexity;
- some services delivered by simple tasks and systems whilst others required high professional skill and judgement.

This tended to result over time in the dominance of the following configurations in the public services:

- divisionalisation (such as in local authorities and hospitals) as a key means of managing diversity and reducing complexity;
- *within* divisions, the adoption of either a professional bureaucracy (where tasks are complex) or a machine bureaucracy (where tasks are simple);
- small pockets of adhocracy – particularly in centres of professional excellence.

The key question is whether these inherited configurations are likely to be suited to the future challenges for the public services. The following issues could usefully be considered by public sector managers:

- To some extent the reshaping and slimming down of the public services has reduced diversity (in general) and within particular services.
- Deregulation has meant that many public services are likely to face increased diversity and change in their environment. Some parts of the organisation may continue to provide services as sole provider whilst others face open competition.
- Information technology is providing opportunities to deliver services in new ways, which again might lead to increased diversity. For example, IT can be used to routinise some services and deal with

Exhibit 13.8a    *Mintzberg's six organisational configurations*

| | Situational factors | | Design parameters | |
|---|---|---|---|---|
| Configuration | Environment | Internal | Key part of organisation | Key co-ordinating mechanism |
| **Simple structure** | Simple/dynamic Hostile | Small Young Simple task CEO control | Strategic apex | Direct supervision |
| **Machine bureaucracy** | Simple/static | Old Large Regulated tasks Technocrat control | Technostructure | Standard-isation of work |
| **Professional bureaucracy** | Complex/static | Simple systems Professional control | Operating core | Standard-isation of skills |

Source: H. Mintzberg, *The Structuring of Organisations*, Prentice Hall, 1979

Exhibit 13.8b    *Mintzberg's six organisational configurations*

| | Situational factors | | Design parameters | |
|---|---|---|---|---|
| Configuration | Environment | Internal | Key part of organisation | Key co-ordinating mechanism |
| **Divisionalised** | Simple/static Diversity | Old Very large Divisible tasks Middle-line control | Middle line | Standard-isation of outputs |
| **Adhocracy** | Complex/ dynamic | Often young Complex tasks Expert control | Operating core Support staff | Mutual adjustment |
| **Missionary** | Simple/static | Middle-aged Often 'enclaves' Simple systems Ideological control | Ideology | Standard-isation of norms |

Source: H. Mintzberg, *The Structuring of Organisations*, Prentice Hall, 1979

clients more remotely (through Web sites or call centres). However, other services might use IT to help 'educate' clients and communities – providing high-quality and accessible information about services, rights and entitlements, and so on. The professional contact will then move more towards advice to clients about their choices – which will be customised to each client. So at the same time some parts of the organisation may need to move towards the machine bureaucracy whilst the adhocracy as a configuration will better suit the customised services.

### 13.6.2 *Diversity of configuration*

These observations about the changing circumstances of public service organisations relate back to the earlier important issues of whether the corporate centre has the *parenting skills* to simultaneously manage a machine bureaucracy and several adhocracies within the same organisation. Or whether it would be better to split the organisation into separate independent entities – or even to divest some of the parts. Diversity of configuration also involves different approaches to management control – as discussed in Section 10.4 of *Exploring Corporate Strategy*. So top-down planning systems will be the dominant mechanism in machine bureaucracies whereas the adhocracy is more concerned with self-regulation and control by (professional) staff. An issue of growing importance is the extent to which this professional freedom should be regulated externally – for example through the imposition of quality standards or even through the corporate governance arrangements (clinical governance being an example of this debate – as discussed in Chapter 7 of this book).

## 13.7 **Summary**

This chapter has looked at some general principles of organisation structure and design and applied them to the public sector context at three levels of detail:

- the broad question of the role of the corporate centre(s) and the management of SBU performance;
- the more detailed issue of *centralisation* and *devolution* and the practicalities of making devolved regimes work in practice;
- the 'micro-level' issues of organisational *configurations* – the building blocks and co-ordinating mechanisms. These link to issues of management control.

There has been a considerable change in practice within the public sector on all of these issues – perhaps particularly the centralisation/devolution issues. This chapter has attempted to help managers think through the issues at a conceptual level and hence avoid the danger of being caught up in management fads.

## References

Campbell, A., Goold, M. and Alexander, M. (1995) 'Corporate strategy: the quest for parenting advantage', *Harvard Business Review*, **73**(3).

Goold, M. and Campbell, A. (1987) *Strategies and Styles*, Oxford: Blackwell.

Goold, M., Campbell, A. and Alexander, M. (1994) *Corporate-Level Strategy*, New York: Wiley.

Johnson, G. and Scholes, K. (1999) *Exploring Corporate Strategy*, 5th edn, New York: Prentice Hall.

Mintzberg, H. (1979) *The Structuring of Organisations*, New York: Prentice Hall.

Scholes, K. (1994) 'Making the most of devolution', Sheffield Business School Occasional Paper No.11.

## Note

1   A strategic business unit (SBU) is defined in *Exploring Corporate Strategy* as 'a part of the organisation for which there is a distinct client group'. So it usually relates to a collection of related activities or services – but may not be neatly reflected in the structure of the organisation.

# 14

# *The relationship between quality, approaches to management control, and the achievement of best value in public sector professional service organisations*

*By John McAuley*

## Editor's introduction

The need to improve service quality has been and remains a major pre-occupation for many public service organisations and those who fund their activities. This chapter by John McAuley looks at the issues of management control – as discussed in Chapter 10 of *Exploring Corporate Strategy* – in relation to this issue of service quality. It looks particularly at the different schools of thought about management control in professional service organisations – the so-called 'romantic' and 'classical' views, and explores how current management practice in the public sector is changing.

## 14.1  Introduction

This chapter is an exploration of different understandings of the nature of quality and the ways in which differences in perception of the relationship between approaches to quality and management control are reflections of opposed basic assumptions about the nature of organisational life. Dale et al. (1997: 2) suggest that 'there is no single accepted definition of quality ... [I]t is usually meant to distinguish one organization, institution, event, product, service, process, person, result, action or communication from another in relation to the ability to achieve both implicit and explicit requirements.' Pollitt (1993: 183) has commented that the use of the term 'by politicians and managers alike has become positively promiscuous ....' Lying beneath this apparent promiscuity there is, however, characteristically, purpose and direction in definitions of quality towards the achievement of particular political, economic, social and managerial control agendas.

This relationship is expressed as a dominant discourse underpinned by what has been termed managerialist and neo-managerialist philosophies (see, for example, Raine and Willson, 1997; McAuley et al., 2000; Alford, this volume) about the nature of quality in public sector organisations. External stakeholders and internal rhetorics drive agendas over the nature of quality. The chapter will begin with a discussion of the core dimensions of quality as a means of establishing control through an examination of the romantic and classical approaches (Pirsig, 1974) to quality. A key principle has been that by and large the interests of political stakeholders and their agents have been classical, the interests of professionals within the organisation have been characteristically romantic, and senior management of organisations have been in a crucial pivotal position in relation to these opposed interests and discourses. There will be an exploration of the ways in which the quality agenda is pursued within five different explanations of processes of strategic management (Johnson and Scholes, 1999: 27) in order to show how each of these approaches suggests different approaches to quality and managerial control (Johnson and Scholes, 1999: 446–447). It will be suggested that members of the organisation tend to have, as mental constructs, dominant approaches to strategy which encompass one or more of the models, and that this model will be reflected in approaches to quality and management control. The chapter concludes with a discussion of the ways in which clever combinations of these approaches create a relationship with the principles of 'best value' (Rose, 1997) as advocated in current government policies.

Examples will be cited with particular reference to the criminal justice system. This is a particularly useful example in that governments since 1979 have tended to understand criminal justice as pervaded by a culture that is alleged to be 'spendthrift, idiosyncratic and unaccountable. Accordingly, a three-pronged strategy was employed, cash limits and *emphasis on efficiency ... greater standardisation in policies and practices to curb the autonomy of the professionals* and reduce their idiosyncrasies; and reorganisation of the agencies into stronger hierarchies, *supported by target setting and performance monitoring ...*' (Raine and Willson, 1997: 82). The issues identified in italics relate directly to ways in which the dominating discourses about quality and control are used by political stakeholders in order to attempt to change the conditions of the service. Characteristically, within services these issues are vigorously contested. For example, within the Three-Year Plan of Centro[1] Probation Service it is asserted that 'contemporary rhetoric and public policy about crime and sentencing are driving attention and resourcing away from the community measures that are run by the Probation Service, measures that have demonstrated particular success in recent years' (1997).

## 14.2  *The classical and romantic traditions in quality*

Quality is political in both the macro and the micro senses. At the macro level, external stakeholders attempt to redefine organisational purpose through quality criteria and processes such as Quality Assurance, Performance Indicators and League Tables. Traditional claims to professional dominance (e.g. Becker, 1970; Larson, 1977; Macdonald, 1995) have shifted such that, in one view of the Probation Service, as a typical example of professional services, the 'imposition of particular quality concerns upon managers and staff that have not always been conducive to the tasks of the service or the performance levels of employees' (Kemshall, 1996: 1). It is micro in the sense that organisations reinterpret, within boundaries, macro concerns to develop particular stances in relation to quality.

Pirsig (1974) made the distinction between classical and romantic approaches to quality. He suggests that the Western world is one in which the classical definition pervades. Underpinning the classical gaze is a preoccupation with rationality, order, stability, accountability and system so that there can be the development of a world in which there is a set of universal rules that can be applied with equity to the members of the society. Philosophically, the classical approach is closely aligned to Utilitarianism (McAuley, 1996). The classical values the democratic but is essentially hierarchical because it is through hierarchy that order prevails (Jaques, 1990). Quality is defined by adherence to procedures and the assertion of quantification.

The romantic is underpinned by an understanding of the world that is idiosyncratic, imaginative, original, personal, with an emphasis on process. Quality is about trusting the ability to make a qualitative and subjective judgement about matters; quality comes from the heart: 'the passions, the emotions, the affective part of our consciousness, are a part of nature's order too. The Romantic can be elitist but does not value the official definition of the situation given by hierarchy' (Pirsig, 1974: 287). The divisions between the two are not absolute. For both the romantic and the classical, form and pattern are of great importance – although for the classicist, form will characteristically fit function, and for the romantic, form will be the discipline base for expression of the subjective.

### 14.2.1  *The classical tradition*

Within this tradition it is the prerequisite of senior management and key external stakeholders to 'allocate resources and control performance in line with the strategy' (Johnson and Scholes, 1999: 463) on the basis that these members, controversially (e.g. MacIntyre, 1981; Locke, 1996), make claims to be quintessentially rational (e.g. Hatch, 1997). Classicism is closely aligned with the doctrines of managerialism discussed by Alford in Chapter 1 of this volume. Pollitt (1993: 183) suggests that most contemporary definitions of quality stress 'the need continuously to meet and improve upon customer requirements. This in turn implies a systematic effort to ascertain what those requirements are.' This position is classical in two senses. The first is that it stresses the primacy of the external stakeholder and the requirement to meet their needs and wants. This links to the idea of modernism – that organisations become responsive to 'the rise of mass culture, and market society based on mass production' (Gephart, 1996: 26) and are therefore accountable to them. When the Chief Inspector of Probation stated that the UK service is 'the only one to have this obsession with Social Work values, and this has been part of the cause of the deterioration of our image. We should know that we are, always have been, in the PUNISHMENT [*sic*] business!' (Smith, 1997: 1), he is asserting an alignment with society at large as the customer. This definition is at odds with an 'underlying ambivalence about the role of probation officers as either punitive or preventative' (Webster et al., 1998: 49) found amongst practitioners.

The central inspectorate, as agent of the Home Office, uses Service Quality and Evaluation Inspections of individual services in order to shift practitioner perspectives. This is a classical form of social and cultural control which focuses on the 'standardisation of norms' (Johnson and Scholes, 1999: 471) throughout the service. Smith (1997: 4) suggests that the Inspectorate 'is as much a regulator as an Inspectorate and it is a promoter of good practice as well. ... The real revolution of the 80s and the 90s has been to devolve powers away from the centre, then to take it back through the regulators.' However, within the classical tradition it is entirely appropriate, because of the reciprocity between the external and the internal of accountability, that there should be negotiation between the quality agency and the organisation.

The second core element of classicism is that of quantification. This comes from the desire to establish, in a utilitarian sense, that issues of quality can 'in principle be determined by empirical calculation of consequences' (Williams, 1972: 100) so that, for example, performance indicators can be used as comparators between organisations (Middlehurst and Kennie, 1997: 59). Issues of quantification are inextricably intertwined with attempts to achieve control through performance targets (Johnson and Scholes, 1999: 467). A particular example from the USA might be used to illustrate this desire for quantification. Lattimore et al. (1998: 511) have developed 'a combined statistical model for probationer risk classification and ... resource allocation model for workload balancing' such that a relationship is created between the 'number of visits to probationers by type of visit and risk classification'.

There is a flaw in the classical approach around these issues. Those consequences that are amenable to meeting the immediate needs of external stakeholders and to quantification may be those which occur at the manifest level; the latent issues are hidden from calculation. Morgan (1997: 30) points to the ways in which quality controls may institutionalise deficiencies. Within the professional arena it can lead to satisficing or to emphasising that which is tangible in provision as opposed to that which is complex (McAuley, 1996). There is also the potential for the McDonaldisation of the professional milieu (Oldfield, 1994; Prichard and Willmott, 1997) with the concomitant emphasis on fragmentation of tasks in the interests of the logics of efficiency and productivity and the commodification of the professional (Harley, 1999). This issue may be illustrated by the preparation of Pre-Sentence Reports within the Probation Service. These are reports on offenders that are presented to the courts in order to help the court assess the level and type of punishment. Hicks (a Chief Probation Officer) points to the conflict that can occur between the logics of efficiency (the speed of production of the report) and the logics of effectiveness (the rigour of the report), where efficiency is taken to be the overriding feature. He argues that 'the higher level of aspiration is for improvements in *the total process* and for the service *to focus its concern on its best contributions*' (Hicks, 1995: 25). This emphasis on a holistic enskilled approach is reinforced by the assertion by Downing and Lynch (1997: 185) that quality assurance systems need to be developed in the local area in order to encourage good professional practice.

### 14.2.2    *The romantic view of quality*

The romantic view of quality has at its heart a concept that the individual and the group have responsibility for quality. It is associated with the idea that what professionals provide has integrity and that it meets professional standards. Quality is a social construct (Berger and Luckmann, 1967) shared between members in communities of practice (Lave and Wenger, 1991). It is something that members cherish as individual practitioners, and the sum of the contribution to quality becomes the ethos of the organisation (Harrison, 1993). From this perspective, issues of quality in the Probation Service would 'not be related to instrumental objectives but rather to the expressive good of fulfilling client needs, reducing harm to the individual and society and excellence in practice' (Downing and Lynch, 1997: 186). In terms of enactment, this philosophy is echoed in the Centro Three-Year Plan such that the 'planning imperatives which underpin this document reflect the (instrumental) expectations articulated in Home Office Plans ... but they are also informed by a *strong and clear vision for the future of the Service ... driven by a continuing pride in our mission'* (1997: 1) (author's parentheses and author's italics).

Shared understanding of the nature of quality in the treatment of the client group (and indeed the very construction of the nature of the client) is a pervasive form of personal, social and cultural control. The romantic milieu may be seen as a negotiated arena in which different segments or groupings engage in power struggles, in which their fates are intertwined and in which the members 'operate from positions of relative institutional power' (Strauss and Bucher, 1961: 245). They are 'a mix of organising practices which are historically located and variably resilient and resistant' to the more classical approaches to their management (Prichard and Willmott, 1997: 288). In this view quality 'is a dynamic concept, changing over time and according to the various perspectives of the various participants in the process'. Given this dynamism, Kemshall suggests that a key issue is 'rather than getting it right first time, [probation] officers may need to do it differently each time'. In this sense quality is concerned with the assessment of versatility in task and response (Kemshall, 1996: 7).

The romantic view is not unproblematic. A key feature is that between the competing rhetorics there can be the emergence of imperialising discourses. These are politically motivated rhetorics that assert the superiority of a particular approach to quality over others. Perhaps more dangerous, however, are situations in which members collude with each other as a regression from the anxieties of the work situation (Hirschorn, 1997) and lose sight of any externally verifiable understanding of quality, or where there is a collusion to protect the professionally incompetent (Goode, 1967).

## 14.3 *Quality and management control within organisations*

Classical and romantic approaches to quality give an overarching sense of the way in which quality can be used as a vehicle of control. Johnson and Scholes (1999: 463) mention that control can be manifested through administrative means, through social control and through self-control. The ways in which these approaches to control can be manifested in classical and romantic forms to varying degrees are embedded in different types of organisational ideology and in the relationship between senior management and external stakeholders. The term 'ideology' refers to the propositions that members hold as to the way in which the organisation 'ought' to conduct its affairs in order to preserve its integrity, its 'essential and enduring tenets', and in order to fulfil its core purposes (Collins and Porras, 1996: 73).

An important aspect of organisational ideology is the overall mindset with regard to strategy making (Whittington, 1992), with understandings of quality providing a significant leverage point in control and implementation. Organisational practice corresponds, informally or formally, implicitly or explicitly, approximately or exactly, to the more formal theories of strategy. In the following, there is a discussion of the five-fold categorisation suggested by Johnson and Scholes (1999: 27) which looks at approaches which stress Rational Planning, Crafting or Logical Incrementalism, Chaos/Complexity, Cultural or Institutional, and the Ecological or Natural Selection approach. Within the chosen example, the Probation Service, elements of all five exist, although there is a predominant approach.

### 14.3.1   Elements of the romantic and the classical in the Rational Planning approach to strategy, quality and control

Within this ideology, quality is used as a means of controlling behaviour in both romantic and classical ways. The Rational Planning approach can be found in two forms. The first is where the processes are initiated through the enactment of transformational leaders; the second is where the rational planning process is a shared activity amongst senior management (McAuley, 1996).

The ideology is associated with the idea of the transformational leader who through close identification with the vision creates a definition of the nature of quality as it relates to the growth and development of the organisation. This person then articulates the new vision to stakeholders (Gioia and Chittipeddi, 1994). A key indicator for success in this ideology is that the leader is seen to influence the political agendas and is able to put forward assertively the local agenda. Additionally there may well be strong quality structures set up which reinforce the level of personal control. The leader will characteristically identify priorities for the service and there will be different grades and levels of quality for different external stakeholders. This may be illustrated within Centro Probation Service. During the late 1980s the then new Chief Probation Officer carefully crafted, with senior colleagues, a mission and vision for the Service. Initially this statement was articulated clearly as the embodiment of the direction in which the CPO wanted to take the Service – it was personal. The mission statement stated that:

> *Probation in Centro works with others in the justice field to provide without discrimination the highest standards of service, to help courts make use of community penalties, to help offenders stop*

*offending, to help families in conflict, and to make a real contribution to public safety.*

The vision for the service included five elements, including such criteria as the development of an 'effective service', 'a quality service seen to be indispensable by courts and public alike', and a commitment to the development of clients, responsiveness and reliability. Initially the mission and values were regarded by some within the service with suspicion; the sharpness of focus within the statement was seen as a potential threat to the autonomy of the individual professional. It is perhaps of interest to contrast this essentially local customer focus with its essentially romantic claims with the more classical concerns of the transforming Home Secretary. The New Labour government has proposed that the service 'be brought under centralised control, that its name be changed to reflect its new purpose of public protection and that it be brought into closer structural alignment with the prison service' (Nellis, 1999: 302). It appears that probation officers will become 'community punishment officers' and the service (which will be restructured so that the regions fit in with the police regions) the 'community punishment and rehabilitation service'. The Home Secretary apparently believes that these names symbolise clarity 'on what the service does, nicely balances "tough" with the constructive tone of rehabilitation … without being too ambitious' (Travis, 1999: 8). The power of the symbol of the change of name and the restructuring may be seen, by opponents, as 'an authoritarian impulse which is deeply at odds with the Service's own local traditions' (Nellis, 1999: 302). It is perhaps worth noting that in New Zealand, which in the early 1990s embraced the managerialist agenda with enthusiasm (Boston et al., 1991), the Probation Service and the police were combined to form the 'Department of Corrections'.

In this sense the leader takes on the mantle of managerialism. For supporters, focus on the leader's identification with the rational plan and the vision of quality provides clarity; for those who feel discomfort with the quality criteria there is a 'real' person against whom their opposition can be pitched. It has the energy of resistance (Nevis, 1987) which can be part of the discourse rather than the emotion being diffused in apathy.

The charismatically romantic but classically rational transformational leader can, despite claims to rationality, be problematic in relation to issues of quality and control. The leader can gauge incorrectly because of lack of understanding of the context (Johnson and Scholes, 1999: 530), the appropriateness of the advocated patterns of quality and control. The dramatic and personalised nature of the agenda can militate against the sharpness of the vision. The imposition of control by the leader can be experienced as offensive by the followers, contradicting their sense of autonomy and self-control. The low level of devolution involves disrespect for members' local knowledge.

There is another take on Rational Planning such that strategic approaches to control and understandings of quality are the outcome of 'careful objective analyses and planning' (Johnson and Scholes, 1999: 26) by managers working collectively. At the core of the ideology is, as bureaucratic imperative, a belief that quality is the lynchpin of accountability; it is a quintessentially classical understanding of quality. Control is created through a strong regulatory framework with sets of rules and procedures that all can follow. There is a strong emphasis on order and the 'tight ship'. It gives an edge of competitiveness in that that this approach presents to the outside world a picture of a tidy place (Middlehurst and Kennie, 1997). Also, suggests Harrison (1993), this approach gives a sense of stability, of equity, efficiency and a standardised service. There is a great deal of emphasis on such matters as quality prescriptions, quality trails, audit processes, analysis of risk and monitoring (Pollitt, 1993). These processes are not neutral in the sense that they promote particular agendas.

From the point of view of the practitioner, this ideology gives strong boundaries with clear lines of accountability. As long as the professional undertakes what is required in terms of the quality documentation, there is a measure of protection. Overall, it is the quintessential model of strategic planning (Johnson and Scholes, 1999: 466) where the boundaries set by the transformational leader or senior management pervade the process. Thus bottom-up plans are essentially tightly corseted by the quality criteria determined by those who set the performance agenda. Power in the reconciliation process is unequivocally held by senior management, operationalisation is tightly controlled through the quality assurance processes, and communication is managed by the power brokers.

### 14.3.2 *The essential romanticism of crafting and logical incrementalism in understanding quality and control*

Johnson and Scholes (1999: 26) suggest that this ideology is one in which members develop strategies on the basis of managers' experience and learning with a tendency to be rather less formalised than in the rational planning process. Certainly within the Probation Service, and within other public sector professional organisations, this has been a favoured ideology, although the burden of paperwork and the insistence on detailed planning at the senior level have sometimes made it appear a particularly cumbersome form of Rational Planning.

Although there is understood to be a need for innovation and change in understanding the quality agenda, the general message is that this can be done without feelings of panic and emptiness. It can be achieved through development, through the long slow road (Kanter, 1983) and through devolved processes (Johnson and Scholes, 1999: 464). The approach to quality is crafted. Within the boundaries of the vision, the resourcing guidelines and the identification of core constraints, agreement about quality is consensual. The hierarchy operates effectively through claims of mutuality of professional respect. The leader is ideally understood to be a very senior practitioner who represents the very model of quality and who understands the issues that confront colleagues (Prichard and Willmott, 1997); there tends to be a palpable aversion to leadership from those who are not themselves members of the profession (McAuley et al., 2000). Control on behaviour is personal, affective and bound up in the preservation of professional integrity. The sort of data that is seen to count in monitoring is qualitative with profound irritation in relation to quantitative data (e.g. Praill and Baldwin, 1988; Kemshall, 1996).

There is, however, an ambiguity about where understanding of quality lies in this type of organisation. One view is that quality lies close to the client (whoever that is); the other is that it lies close to the advancement of the service. For some, the tensions between the requirements for meeting the quality criteria of diverse activities are irreconcilable; for others they represent just one of the many necessary challenges which are part of the lives of all professionals (e.g. Gibbons et al., 1994). For example, within the Centro Three-Year Plan it is suggested that reconciliation of diverse professional understandings of the nature of work rests in the development and promotion of the most effective forms of practice. It is stated that 'work plans must be seen to apply what is known about best effective practice in a rigorous professional way, and to be amenable to monitoring and testing' (Chief Probation Officer, Centro 1997).

Scholes looks at three key roles in Professional Service Organisations – finders, minders and grinders (terms used in the Sheffield cutlery industry). What he suggests is that value comes from the work of individual professionals (the grinders) who are at the front line delivering the organisation's services to clients. The finders and the minders must genuinely add value (Scholes, 1994). In this context the role of the finder – senior management – is negotiation with external stakeholders, assertively putting forward the local knowledge of the members, and mediating into the organization external requirements for quality and relating them to local knowledge. Davenport (1993) suggests that there are two critical roles for the minders – the middle manager – in relation to quality. The romantic aspects include responsibility for cross-functional understanding of quality issues so that managers not only focus on their own function or area of work but also take responsibility for specific quality issues across functions or areas of work. This helps to create integration and a shared understanding of quality issues. Secondly, the 'minder' has responsibility for the communication and development of understanding of the quality strategy and its implementation both upward and downwards in the organisation (Smith, 1997b).

In the Probation Service, Smith (1997b) refers to the development of the Senior Probation Officer (a quintessential minder) towards a clearer quality monitoring of the work of the Probation Officer (as grinder). He advocates that the SPO role upholds the integrity of the probation agenda, and preserves a notion of collective responsibility. The SPO primary task remains essentially romantic with a clear understanding of practice issues and practitioner needs. Quality is served from a careful crafting of tasks and processes and reflective evaluation of outputs with careful adjustment of tasks and processes. Control emanates from within the self, accompanied by a respect for the professional authority of senior management – the expert power of the senior practitioner and the layers of management above that.

### 14.3.3    The hidden patterns of quality and control in chaos and complexity

In relation to issues of control and quality this ideology provides a more radical context than that of incrementalism within which the professional ideology can be played out. The mindset is one in which there is an understanding of the world both within the organisation and in the environment as 'highly complex and unpredictable. However it is possible that people's experience within a particular context can help them become sensitive to the complexity and uncertainty around them' (Johnson and Scholes, 1999: 26).

The core quality issue here that comes from this ideology is the development of members' abilities to understand the hidden patterns of behaviour and action, to develop an understanding of the latent consequences of action, getting beneath the symptoms. The core control issue is that at each layer of the organisation there are clear boundaries of authority such that members need to build 'appropriate levels of support before they embark on any new direction' (Stacey, 1996: 465) through the practices of 'extraordinary management' (Stacey, 1996). Parallel to the boundaries provided by hierarchy is the development of self-organising networks, both inward and outward facing, of organisational members. The management of quality is through crafting the interface between the visionary capability of senior management and the development of local knowledge at the periphery, with a high emphasis on cultural and personal control through identification with the core values of the profession and the organisation (Nonaka, 1991; McAuley et al., 1999).

One of the issues in exploring issues of quality for a professional such as those working in Probation is the need, from this perspective, to expand the network such that members co-ordinate with other stakeholders and escape from the confines of their own professional cluster. This might involve, for example, in this example from the USA, the development of 'creative and critical thinking' such as teaming 'local probation officers with local police officers' and getting 'probation officers to work with inner-city clergy' (Dilulio, 1997: 42). Broussine and Wakefield (1997) argue that the development in the Probation Service of uniform rational sets of expectations is profoundly flawed on the grounds that the constituencies served by different services are highly differentiated one from another. They cite the development, within Avon Probation Service, working with Bristol Business School, of a means of assessing user-defined quality of service as a complex but more telling means of developing understanding of quality.

### 14.3.4   *Culture, control and quality*

Some institutional theorists argue that this model invites a degree of managerial impotence in the development of strategies and quality. They argue that understandings of the world 'can be so taken for granted, so institutionalised, it is difficult for people to question or change them' (Johnson and Scholes, 1999: 27). It might be suggested, however, that the concept of the reflective manager is one who is not entrapped by the culture but rather works with it.

The concept of culture as the locus of quality and control would seem to be the most romantic of all the ideologies for they lie within the culture of the organisation and the self. Quality and control are emotional matters (Harrison, 1993). Understanding comes from self-critical self-understanding and empathy, the ability to take a detached view of the commitments to internal and external stakeholders. This ideology, in its gaze on quality, can be rigorous. The concept of 'tough love' expresses understanding of boundaries and places normative controls on members' behaviour and conduct. A key issue is to develop qualitative measures that capture the relational aspects of quality. In this light, Downing and Lynch (1997: 186) argue that professional development in probation would be 'enhanced by peer gatekeeping, team audit exercises and management monitoring. ... Quality would be related to the expressive good of fulfilling client needs, reducing harm to the individual and society and excellence in practice.' In their writing they stress ideas like the development of discourse and implicitly the creation of a clear relationship between the culture of probation and the development of a broader, social culture which promotes 'the potential of all individuals' (1997: 187). This aspiration may be seen within the Centro Three-Year Plan, where one of four key imperatives is seen to be the application of the findings of research. The service, it is asserted, 'must be seen to monitor and review the effectiveness of what it does itself. ... The professionalism to which the service aspires requires the rigorous application of research, and the disciplined use of knowledge.'

This ideology links with concepts such as the learning organisation. In this perspective there is emphasis on the development of personal mastery (with its emphasis on self-control) aligned with the development of the organisation (Senge, 1990) and with the concept of organizational tolerance. In this latter view 'increasing the mobilisation of available brain capacity' involves a synthesis of creating space in order to experiment and take risks, and control in relation to the observance of organisation purpose (de Geus, 1997: 153).

### 14.3.5   Quality as a feature of organisations driven hither and thither by the forces of the marketplace

From a theoretical perspective this ideology is one in which the organisation is dominated by its environment. It may be understood as a 'profoundly fatalistic' (Alford, this volume) model that suggests impotence because the badly placed organisation is so lodged in its culture that it cannot adapt to the environment (Johnson and Scholes, 1999: 27). There is, however, an alternative. It is to understand the organisation as essentially stakeholder driven and therefore entirely responsive to market forces. Whilst this position has its discomforts for members, management are assured that they are doing what is needed to facilitate the organisation's survival. This provides a basis for action in organisations (Alford, this volume). This view of organisations as poised between withering on the vine because they cannot adapt to new conditions or surviving because their driving passion becomes meeting the needs of the marketplace was deeply embedded in the neo-free market philosophies which underpinned the political agendas of the New Right in the 1990s. Public sector organisations required a market, competition and the 'presence of customers'. Within this philosophical milieu the 'criminal justice services were marginally and intermittently affected' (James and Raine, 1998: 33). In terms of quality, emphasis is, philosophically, placed on customer definitions of the service, which are translated into the organisation without local mediation; there is a high emphasis on administrative control.

In this ideology there is an appeal to the marketplace as control mechanism (Johnson and Scholes, 1999: 471). In the case of the Probation Service, for example, the argument would be that there are others in the market that are also in the same business in some respects, primarily the police and prison officers. The task of senior management in the Service, according to this view, is for Probation to recognise (a) the nature of its *true* business and then (b) gain clarity as to its unique added value within the business so that it gains competitive advantage, and then (c) ensure that staff within the Service understand the issues, and overcome their professional conservatism. As an example of this, the author worked as consultant to a probation service in the early 1990s. One aspect of the consultancy was to work with divisions in relation to issues of understanding the nature of the customers and the nature of the competition. For example, senior managers undertook activities such as Portfolio Analysis (e.g. Johnson and Scholes, 1999: 186) in order to develop shared understanding of the key activities and processes, and the quality criteria to be associated with them, they needed to undertake in order to maximise their share of the sun. They also undertook analysis of their competitors in order to more deeply understand ways in which they could, in terms of quality of output, outstrip them in relation to establishing marketplace dominance within overlapping arenas.

A different, more passive, example of this approach could well be that of the following analysis of social service departments and nature of social work since the 1980s in the UK. It is suggested the 'rhetoric of treatment and inclusion' traditionally associated with social work has been replaced, as a consequence of the emergence of a market society, 'by containment, rationing and surveillance'. The requirement placed on social workers is that they are able 'to follow instructions, to complete procedures and assessments on time ... and to work in such ways that will not expose the agency to public ridicule or exposure' (Jones, 1999: 47). Quality criteria which emanate from a centralised regime and which are associated with a 'standardisation of work processes or outputs' lead not only to uniformity of service and relative deskilling (Johnson and Scholes, 1999: 464) but also to passive repositioning of the service.

It could be argued, however, that the attention on markets is a transitional phenomenon based on a particular New Right political ideology. It may be that this has been replaced by agendas that are more interested in a mixed economy approach to criminal justice (James and Raine, 1998: 46), although interest in the assessments of quality evoked by the market approach may well persist.

### 14.4 Conclusions: Developing a shared model of quality to achieve best value

A model of quality that enables the achievement of best value is one that is crafted such that it reconciles the classical and the romantic and in which there is a judicious mix of strategic ideologies in order to create a normative balanced scorecard. Such a model would be one which, for example in Probation, would, as Kemshall suggests, synthe-sise the 'scientific', the 'humanistic' and 'the consumer' perspectives on quality (Raine, 1993) with the 'user, delivery and stakeholder voices involved in the service all included' (Kemshall, 1996: 8). This approach seems to be acknowledged in the underpinning philosophy of 'best value' as applied to local government and as implicit in the develop-ment of public sector organisations. Thus there is the romanticism of synthesis, holism, learning and partnership in the delivery of 'seamless service provision' and in pursuit of ' "quality of life" of customers' (e.g. Anonymous, 1999). There is also the classical discipline in the value placed on such matters as accountable, measurable performance information, clearly set local targets and performance which are seen to respect those set by the central stakeholder, and external auditing to confirm 'the integrity and comparability' of the service (Rose, 1997: 24).

Models of resource allocation through the strategic planning process (Johnson and Scholes, 1999: 466) provide a useful echo for the development of a balanced scoreboard approach to quality. Within the literature the concept of the balanced scorecard is taken to be quali-tative and quantitative measures in order to assess 'not only to short-term outputs but also to the way in which processes are managed' (Johnson and Scholes, 1999: 468). Using this concept as metaphor, it may be seen how judicious mixtures of the romantic and the classical can be used across the repertoire of models of strategy to create a bal-ance of modes of approach to quality issues that confront the organis-ation. This is illustrated in Exhibit 14.1

The key issue for the development of quality, as far as the senior echelons of management are concerned, is the way in which the claims of external stakeholders are understood, their claims for attention weighed up and acted upon in relation to organisational members' own sense of integrity. This accords with the philosophy of best value in which there is an invitation to address issues of quality assessment through both peer and stakeholder review (Freer, 1998).

Within the balanced scorecard the sense of negotiation pervades the organisation. In terms of the development of bottom-up planning, the ability to develop the criteria and boundaries of quality and respect local knowledge satisfies members' need for autonomy in task achievement and enables members to understand quality as facilita-tive, supporting and enabling rather than punitive. There is also a requirement for balanced assessments of risk and a judicious empha-sis on the financial and the quantitative aspects of quality. This is part of the negotiated arena. The culture facilitates openness of the nego-tiation and the development of a sense of confidence. This can be reflected in the ability to share understandings of quality and best practice within the framework. This sense of negotiation, mutual

*Exhibit 14.1   Classical and romantic elements of the five models of strategy*

| | Rational Planning | Crafting/Logical Incremental | Chaos/ Complexity | Culture | Market |
|---|---|---|---|---|---|
| **Classical elements** | Tight control through rational analysis. Alignment of quality control to accountability. Regulatory framework. Preference for quantitative data. | | Boundaries of legitimacy in relation to quality and control. | | Accountability to customers. Administrative quantitative approach to culture to ensure uniform delivery. Standardisation of processes at different levels. |
| **Romantic elements** | Identification with the vision. Members can influence the quality agendas. The elevation of the individual as leader, role model | Quality as lever for personal, professional development. Quality is crafted. Emphasis on consensus within high professional standards. Personal control. Preference for qualitative data. | Ability to understand hidden patterns in quality and control. Extraordinary management of quality issues. Constant negotiation between the centre and the periphery. Quality developed through autonomous networks. | Issues of quality and control embedded in the culture and in emotion. Qualitative measures which respect the quality. Link between quality and professional development through colleagueship. Quality and control as aspects of learning. | |

learning and empowerment needs to be part and parcel of reconciliation of the legitimate classical and romantic requirements and the repertoire of control processes available for development of quality and best value.

## References

Anonymous (1999) 'Effective performance management in a best value environment', *Management Accounting*, Apr.

Becker, H.S. (1970) 'The nature of a profession', in H.S. Becker (ed.), *Sociological Work: Method and Substance*, New York: Aldine Publishing Company.

Berger, P. and Luckmann, T. (1967) *The Social Construction of reality*, London: Allen Lane.

Boston, J. et al. (1991) *Reshaping the State: New Zealand's Bureaucratic Revolution*, Auckland: Oxford University Press.

Broussine, M. and Wakefield, R. (1997) 'Quality defined by public service users – the case of Avon Probation Service', *Public Money and Management*, Jan.–Mar., **17** (1), 27–34.

Collins, J.C. and Porras, J.I. (1996) *Built to Last: Successful habits of visionary companies*, London: Butterworth.

Dale, B.G., Cooper, G.L. and Wilkinson, A. (1997) *Managing Quality and Human Resources: A guide to continuous improvement*, Oxford: Blackwell Business.

Davenport, T.H. (1993) *Process Innovation: Reengineering work through Information Technology*, Harvard, MA: Harvard Business School Press.

de Geus, A. (1997) *The Living Company: Habits for survival in a turbulent business environment*, Harvard, MA: Harvard Business School Press.

Dilulio Jr., J.J. (1997) 'Reinventing parole and probation', *The Brookings Review*, **15** (2), 40–42.

Downing, K. and Lynch, R. (1997) 'Pre-sentence reports: does quality matter?', *Social Policy and Administration*, **31** (2), 173–190.

Freer, S. (1998) 'Making a success of best value', *Public Money and Management*, Oct.–Dec.

Gephart, R.P. (1996) 'Management, social issues and the postmodern period', in D.M. Boje, R.P. Gephart Jr. and T.J. Thatchenkery (eds), *Postmodern Management and Organization Theory*, Thousand Oaks, CA: Sage Publications.

Gibbons, M., Limoges, C., Nowotny, H., Schwartzman, S., Scott, P. and Trow, M. (1994) *The Production of Knowledge: The dynamics of science and research in contemporary societies*, London: Sage Publications.

Gioia, D.A. and Chittipeddi, K. (1991) 'Sensemaking and sensegiving in strategic change initiation', *Strategic Management Journal*, **12**, 433–88.

Goode, W.J. (1967) 'The protection of the inept', *American Sociological Review*, **32**, 5–19.

Harley, S. (1999) 'Academics divided: research selectivity and the commodification of academic labour'. Paper presented to the Sheffield University Management School Seminar Series.

Harrison, R. (1993) *Organization Culture and Quality of Service: A strat-*

*egy for releasing love in the workplace*, London: Association of Management Education and Development.

Hatch, M.J. (1997) *Organization Theory: Modern symbolic and postmodern perspectives*, Oxford: Oxford University Press.

Hicks, J. (1995) 'Quality, PSR's and Probation work in court'. Presentation to the Association of Chief Probation Officers.

Jaques, E. (1990) 'In praise of hierarchy', *Harvard Business Review*, Jan./Feb., 127–133.

James, A. and Raine, J. (1998) *The New Politics of Criminal Justice*, London: Longman.

Johnson. G. and Scholes, K. (1999) *Exploring Corporate Strategy*, 5th edn, London: Prentice Hall.

Jones, C. (1999) 'Social work: regulation and managerialism', in M. Exworthy and S. Halford (eds), *Professionals and the New Managerialism in the Public Sector*, Buckingham: Open University Press.

Kanter, R.M. (1983) *The Change Masters*, New York: Simon and Schuster.

Kemshall, H. (1996) 'Quality in Probation: getting it right first time?', *VISTA*, May, 2–14.

Larson, M.S. (1977) *The Rise of Professionalism: A sociological analysis*, London: University of California Press.

Lattimore, P.K., Baker, J.R. and Clayton, E.R. (1998) 'A non-linear multiple criteria model base for the problem of balancing caseload risk in probation departments', *Computers and Industrial Engineering*, **35** (4), 511–514.

Lave, J. and Wenger, E. (1991) *Situated Learning Legitimates Peripheral Participation*, Cambridge: Cambridge University Press.

Locke, R.R. (1997b) *The Collapse of the American Management Mystique*, Oxford: Oxford University Press.

McAuley, M.J. (1996) 'Ethical issues in the management of change', in K. Smith and P. Johnson (eds), *Business Ethics and Business Behaviour*, London: Thomson Business Press.

McAuley, J., Tietze, S., Cohen, L. and Duberley, J. (1999) 'Developing the interface between centre and periphery as an agent for organisational learning: issues of strategy and local knowledge', in M. Easterby-Smith, L. Araujo and J. Burgoyne (eds), *Organizational Learning 3rd International Conference (Vol. 2)*, Lancaster University, June.

McAuley, M.J., Cohen, L. and Duberley, J. (2000) 'The meaning professionals give to management and strategy', *Human Relations*, **53** (1), 87–116.

Macdonald, K.M. (1995) *The Sociology of the Professions*, London: Sage Publications.

MacIntyre, A. (1981) *After Virtue: A study in moral theory*, London: Duckworth.

Middlehurst, R. and Kennie, T. (1997) 'Leading professionals: towards new concepts of professionalism', in J. Broadbent, M. Dietrich and J.

Roberts (eds), *The End of the Professions? The restructuring of professional work*, London: Routledge.

Morgan, G. (1997) *Images of Organization*, 2nd edn, London: Sage Publications.

Nellis, M. (1999) 'Towards "the field of corrections": modernizing the probation service in the late 1990's', *Social Policy and Administration*, **33** (3), 302–333.

Nevis, E.C. (1987) *Organizational Consulting: A gestalt approach*, New York: Gardner Press.

Nonaka, I. (1991) 'The knowledge creating company', *Harvard Business Review*, Nov.–Dec., 96–104.

Oldfield, M. (1994) 'Talking quality, meaning control: McDonalds, the market and the probation service', *Probation Journal*, **41** (4), 186–192.

Pirsig, R. (1974) *Zen and the Art of Motorcycle Maintenance: An enquiry into values*, London: Bantam.

Pollitt, C. (1993) *Managerialism and the Public Services*, 2nd edn, Oxford: Blackwell Business.

Praill, T. and Baldwin, S. (1988) 'Beyond hero-innovation: real change in unreal systems', *Behavioural Psychotherapy*, **15** (1).

Prichard, C. and Willmott, H. (1997) 'Just how managed is the McUniversity?', *Organization Studies*, **18** (2), 287–316.

Raine, J. (1993) 'Perspectives on quality in the Magistrates' Court Service', *Justice of the Peace*, 6 Feb., 85–88 and 13 Feb., 101–105.

Raine, J.W. and Willson, M.J. (1997) 'Beyond managerialism in criminal justice', *The Howard Journal*, **36** (1), 80–95.

Rose, N. (1997) 'Lowest price rarely means best value', *The British Journal of Administrative Management*, July/Aug., 24–26.

Scholes, K. (1994) *Strategic Management in Professional Service Organizations*, Occasional Paper, Sheffield Business School.

Senge, P.M. (1990) *The Fifth Discipline: The art and practice of the learning organization*, London: Century Business.

Smith, G. (1997a) 'Senior practitioners vital to "what works"', *The Probation Manager*, **1**, 1–4.

Smith, G. (1997b) 'Senior practitioners vital to "what works" (Part II)', *The Probation Manager*, **2**, 1–4.

Stacey, R. (1996) *Strategic Management and Organisational Dynamics*, 2nd edn, London: Pitman Publishing.

Strauss, A. and Bucher, R. (1961) 'Professions in practice', in A. Strauss (ed.) (1991) *Creating Sociological Awareness: Collective images and symbolic representations*, New Brunswick, NJ: Transaction Publishers.

Travis, A. (1999) 'Straw's tough probation order', *Guardian*, 8 Dec.

Webster, A., Caddick, B. and Reed, M. (1998) 'Functional versus critical literacy in the rehabilitation of offenders: a survey of probation services in England and Wales', *International Journal of Lifelong Education*, **18** (1), 49–60.

Whittington, R. (1992) *What Is Strategy and Does It Matter?*, London: Routledge.

Williams, B. (1972) *Morality: An introduction to ethics*, Cambridge: Cambridge University Press.

## *Note*

1    This is a pseudonym.

# 15

# Business process re-engineering in the public sector: A case study of the Contributions Agency

### By Barbara Harrington, Kevin McLoughlin and Duncan Riddell

### Editor's introduction

An important theme throughout *Exploring Corporate Strategy* is the relationship between an organisation's performance (in terms of the value-for-money which it delivers in its services) and the extent to which the organisation is able to sustain organisational competences. These competences are concerned with both the management of the separate activities of the 'business' and also, crucially, the linkages between these separate activities (of the value chain) both within and outside the organisation. These concepts are introduced in Chapter 4 of *Exploring Corporate Strategy* and continued as an issue of strategy implementation in Chapter 10. In the 1990s this debate tended to occur under the umbrella of Business Process Re-engineering (BPR), where organisations seek to create dramatic improvement in performance through reconfiguring business activities and linkages.

Clearly these aspirations are relevant to both the public and private sector organisations. Given the timing of the BPR debate (early 1990s) it is not surprising that many public sector organisations seized BPR as a tool to pursue the 'new public sector agenda'. In particular, improved value-for-money, devolved structures and output-related performance measurement. The timing also made it inevitable, particularly in service organisations, that the application and exploitation of increasingly powerful and cheap information technology (IT) would take centre stage in BPR initiatives. So in many public sector organisations we have seen attempts to re-engineer activities to simultaneously improve efficiency, quality of service and job satisfaction.

Against this background of the potential benefits of 'IT-assisted BPR' this chapter by Harrington, McLoughlin and Riddell is a timely reminder that

BPR needs to be planned and executed as part of a wider change management strategy. The softer cultural and political issues also need to be understood and managed alongside the harder systems redesign issues of BPR. This is a message in tune with *Exploring Corporate Strategy*. Their case study is one where the 'opening conditions' for successful BPR were relatively favourable: a culture already used to change and an appreciation of the reasons for and the need to change. But even here BPR encountered some real problems and, at least in the early stages, resulted in outcomes which were far short of BPR's 'radical change' aspirations. They were much closer to an incremental shift of automating processes that had already existed. The re-engineering of linkages (often the step which really transforms performance) had taken a back seat – perhaps waiting a second phase of change.

## 15.1   Introduction

Since the 1980s public sector organisations have been encouraged to become more entrepreneurial and take on board business ideas. The emergence of 'New Public Management' in the 1980s emphasised the importance of bringing competition and efficiency to the public sector (Carter and Greer, 1993) and the application of management ideas and techniques (Hood, 1991). In the 1990s this was followed by the idea of 'reinventing government', of changing 'staid bureaucracies into innovative, flexible, responsive organisations' (Osborne and Gaebler, 1992, p. xxii). The public sector was opened out to competition through the creation of internal and external markets.

It is scarcely surprising that public sector organisations, eager to be seen as being more like the private sector, followed many other businesses in the 1990s in embracing Business Process Re-engineering (BPR) as a framework for change. Nor is it surprising that, like the private sector, there have been varying degrees of success.

Our case study provides an example of how a BPR approach has been used in a public sector organisation (the Contributions Agency) and identifies some of the problems of implementing BPR. We will argue that these problems stem to a large extent from the inherent contradictions which have been identified in the growing critical evaluation of BPR.

## 15.2   Growing critique of BPR

Since Hammer (1990) introduced the concept of Business Process Re-engineering (BPR), businesses were very attracted to BPR because of claims that such re-engineering would greatly increase competitiveness and profitability. Much of the literature on BPR concentrates on giving guidelines for successful implementation, rather than presenting a critique of BPR (Davenport, 1993; Keeble, 1995; Klein, 1995). This is certainly the case in the few studies which have looked at BPR in the public sector. Thus Jackson (1995) on the Post Office discusses the importance of starting with a 'blank sheet of paper' to develop process; carrying out a review of current process; understanding what is world class for the process; understanding customers' requirements in implementing BPR in a public sector organisation; and the problems of an organisation not being open to innovation and empowerment. Similarly Hutton (1995) cites the obstacles to change in the civil service. These obstacles include the traditional civil service culture with its emphasis on continuity, predictability and fairness; lack of senior management commitment; initiative fatigue; resistance to change; misunderstanding of the requirements of the business; unwillingness to take risks at senior management level; and communication with staff.

BPR has, however, been criticised because of concerns about the low level of financial gains by some companies. Oliver (1993) quotes Hammer's own estimate that '70% of organisations fail to achieve any results from their re-engineering efforts'. It has been estimated that 50–70 per cent of re-engineering efforts fail to achieve their goals (Grey and Mitev, 1995). In terms of our case study it is too early to know whether the Contributions Agency (CA) will have made significant gains from BPR. However, some of the other problems with BPR with have been identified in the literature are already causing concern at the CA.

There is now a growing literature which from a social science perspective seeks to critically assess the use of BPR in effecting radical change in organisations. Although Hammer has claimed that BPR is 'novel', BPR has been firmly identified with the traditions of Taylorism and 'the machine model of organisation' (Taylor, 1995). It has been described as 'an essentially mechanistic, almost seventeenth century view of how organisations function and can be changed . . .' (Grint and Willcocks, 1995). BPR's emphasis on process reorganisation, it is argued, leads to a 'shallow technicist appreciation of the human dimension of organisational change' and ignores the value of human 'creativity, empowerment and fulfilment' which makes people different to the other factors of production (Grey and Mitev, 1995). Problems arise because the changes which BPR sets in motion are affected by the prevailing culture and internal politics of an organisation (Grint and Willcocks, 1995; Taylor, 1995). In addition, the production of BPR can be seen as 'an essentially political intervention' (Grint and Willcocks, 1995) by management.

Another underlying problem of BPR concerns commitment. One of the consequences of BPR has been unemployment. At first this issue was not addressed by the proponents of BPR. It was assumed that people within organisations would embrace BPR because it would secure the long-term survival of an organisation and provide future employment for some staff. So a lack of commitment to BPR was seen as being due to an unwillingness to change. However, Grey and Mitev (1995) argue that a lack of commitment by some staff is not driven by a fear of change but is in fact a very rational response to the situation:

> *Given all of these circumstances resistance to change should be understood not as an irrational, psychological attachment to the 'old days' but a rational response to the brutal and ... futile managerialism of BPR.*

Grey and Mitev go on to say that such job losses are actually 'part of a deliberate decision on the part of an organisation, rather than being inevitable'. That is, that in choosing BPR an organisation is making a deliberate choice for job losses. Rejection of BPR by staff is then very understandable as a response to the fear of impending redundancies and loss of promotion prospects.

A further underlying problem of BPR concerns empowerment. Empowering staff is a central tenet of BPR, allowing managerial decisions to be taken at lower levels, and a flatter management structure. However, BPR relies on top-down leadership to carry out BPR, which is inconsistent with ideas of empowerment:

> *There is an apparent inconsistency in BPR between its advocacy of delayering, in which managers are transformed from 'bosses' into 'coaches', and the advocacy of methods for implementing re-engineering that are hierarchical and even dictatorial. (Willcocks, 1995)*

Although hierarchical layers of management may be removed, hierarchical principles are reinforced. In addition, empowerment under BPR can become little more than delegation: it pushes down authority and responsibility but staff do not really gain empowerment (Eccles, 1992). In addition to the growing academic critique of BPR, there has been a popular critical evaluation which has argued that downsizing has gone too far, and that efficiency gains may have been made at the expense of lasting productivity enhancement. BPR has been 'corrupted into a means for removing staff' but US companies who have reduced their labour forces in this way had been 'less financial successful' than other similar companies. There has been growing employee dissatisfaction and a noticeable fall in employees' loyalty to a company (Jackson, 1996; Mumford, 1996; Roach, 1996; Smith, 1996; Walker, 1996).

What BPR has created is a 'fetish of change' and the 'current fashion' for delayering or slimming down, without questioning the process or the effect this can have on some organisations (Grey and Mitev, 1995). We turn now to look at how these problems, particularly those concerning empowerment and commitment, affected the CA when it used BPR as a framework for change.

## 15.3   *The case study: The change programme at the Contributions Agency*

The CA was established in 1991 as a 'Next Steps' Agency of the Department of Social Security. The 'Next Steps' initiative aimed to stimulate managerial flexibility, responsiveness and customer orientation in the civil service. The CA collects and keeps records of National Insurance contributions in respect of pensions and other benefits. It has two main areas of operation, work carried out centrally in its Newcastle-upon-Tyne office and a network of Field Offices throughout the country to provide a local interface and service to the CA's customers.

Since its establishment the Agency has conducted several major change programmes, including the development of an Information Systems Strategy, the implementation of a new Pay and Grading Structure and a full programme of 'market testing'. The aim was to integrate these changes through an approach based on BPR.

The CA began a programme of change in 1992 with a Business Unit Analysis. This Analysis reviewed 'the fundamental elements of the business unit ... and realigned these to meet the Business Vision of the Agency more effectively'. The purpose of the Business Unit Analysis and subsequent implementation was the 're-engineering' of the CA's business processes. In order to do this, the CA sought to reassess operations; empower the workforce; remove duplication; error-proof processes; streamline and simplify processes; increase the quality of service to the customer; gauge current and future performance measures; and use new technology to support the changes. These changes were supported by detailed costings, and individual Business Unit Implementation strategies for all main operational areas. The CA uses the language and ideas of BPR and sets their organisational changes firmly within the context of BPR.

One of the major changes is the replacement of the old National Insurance Recording System (NIRS1) which maintains records of all National Insurance contributions for the UK. A new computing system, the National Insurance Recording System 2 (NIRS2), is replacing the old batch computing system (NIRS1) beginning in 1997. NIRS1 is slow, inflexible, provides no online access and has become increasingly fragile. The new IT system will provide online access and change facilities for staff, and is a 'flexible system that will enable the CA to deliver known and anticipated future legislative change'. At present staff use Early Office Infrastructure (EOI): a half-way office computing system between NIRS1 and NIRS2. EOI is intended to speed up certain operations, and also to give IT experience to staff, some of whom will never have used a computer before. EOI does not have online change facilities for staff, but there is online access to view accounts.

The case study began, in late 1994, with a review of official documentation and in-depth interviews with senior managers which identified the main problems and issues generated by the changes. This was followed by a study of three main operational areas. These areas provided us with in-depth information whilst giving us a wider picture of what was happening across the Agency. The case study used a variety of methods: individual interviews, focus group interviews and a questionnaire survey. Staff who took part in the focus groups and survey were drawn from middle management, and front-line administrative and clerical posts. The first set of focus groups and the survey took place in autumn 1995. Follow-up interviews took place six months and one year afterwards. This enabled us to look at changes over time.

## 15.4   *Problems of BPR at the CA*

This section focuses on some examples of the problems and contradictions with BPR which occurred in the CA during its change programme, particularly those concerned with empowerment and commitment. Before looking at these problems, it is important to understand that staff at the CA were not against change per se. That is, that the subsequent problems concerning commitment and empowerment did not derive from a disgruntled workforce unwilling to change.

In 1995 most employees were in favour of change. They were either very pro-change or at the very least viewed change as a necessity if the CA was to survive:

> *It was really when the Agencies were set up, for me after years of constraints, fighting for customer focus, staff focus, communication with community – this was liberation.*

> *If we don't have these sorts of structures in place where there are fewer tiers, greater delegation, we'll not survive because someone else will come in and do it for us.*

Changes in IT were regarded extremely positively. Staff saw this as an opportunity to have a more interesting job and as something which would provide them with new skills in the job market. It made them as individuals more attractive to other outside employers and also improved the Agency's image as an up-to-date organisation. The focus groups showed that staff were able to cope with IT and, moreover, welcomed IT. No one had found it particularly difficult to work with the new systems or to handle a computer. Staff liked the variety of doing a new job and learning new skills. Far from being reluctant about IT, staff thought they should have had IT years ago. Staff had adapted quickly to the new systems and thought they could have moved straight onto the more complex NIRS2 system.

Staff recognised that the concept of a civil service job as a 'job for life' had gone. However, most staff attributed this change to the world outside the civil service, and accepted this insecurity as a part of modern life:

> *That's the way of the world isn't it? I think they [job losses] are inevitable, you're investing vast sums of technology and you've got to pay for that.*

There were nevertheless worries about change and particularly the pace of change. Staff were aware such views could be construed as being opposed to all changes but they felt this was unfair. They felt they had shown, by their embracing of IT and other changes, that they were not unwilling to change, but they had important reservations about the recommended changes.

It might have been expected that the civil service culture at the CA would be a barrier to the successful implementation of BPR (Hutton, 1995). However, our case study showed that the CA had already moved away from a traditional civil service culture. The old pre-agency culture was characterised as hierarchical, rigid, paper based and obsessed with checking:

> A *classic paper-based bureaucracy where management spend a lot of their time checking the work of their subordinates.*

In 1994 managers felt that the culture had already changed. Further evidence of changes emerged from the focus group interviews in 1995 and 1996. Most staff felt the changes had been taking place since the Agency had come into being in 1991. The Agency had become leaner, fitter and more entrepreneurial. Changes were not linked to the current change programme. Rather, the changes had come about either because the organisation was now an Agency, or because of changes in the outside world.

> *Very much more commercially oriented. I have friends who are outside business operational managers and I don't see that there's a marked difference. I operate with a budget. I have people to manage. I have outputs. The outputs may vary, I might be producing National Insurance accounts instead of widgets but at the end of the day I have an output process to manage.*

Some operational areas had already devolved power to lower levels. For example, the Field had inspectors who were used to using their own initiative and organising their own workload. Field Officers, many of whom were very distant from Central Operations, were used to acting as autonomous units:

> *With the setting up of the Agency, I think we began to break the mould, particularly in the field, life from day one in that because of the management structure that we had which was much flatter ... it was impossible to deal with all staff, so by default partly a management style developed which was to a certain extent hands off but with quite strong monitoring arrangements in place.*

What did remain from the old culture was a strong sense of a public service tradition. Staff still regarded their culture as one where such things as being apolitical, incorruptible, public servants and guardians of confidential records were important.

Culture within the CA is not therefore acting as a complete barrier to BPR. There are some problems concerning the culture but these are concerned with complexities arising from concerns that the 'mechanistic approach' of BPR fails to address.

## 15.5  *The problem of empowerment*

The idea of empowering staff was one of the key components of the Agency's re-engineering strategy. The aim of empowering the workforce was to increase job satisfaction and develop staff to become 'multi-skilled case-workers with end-to-end responsibility for all their activities'. With responsibility being devolved downwards, empowerment would also enable a flatter management structure and consequent savings.

Although empowerment was a key part of the changes, some senior managers initially had some doubts as to whether staff would be able to cope with empowerment:

> *I think with the current structure, the way things work, empowerment has a limited force. I think there's always a risk with delegation that people who receive the extra authority have not acquired the experience necessary to do that, perhaps to the standard. ... Some people won't be able to cope with empowerment, they can only exist in the more protected environment.*

This unease about the proposed changes could reflect a lack of senior management commitment to the idea of empowerment, and could be therefore one of the barriers to successful BPR that Hutton (1995) identified. However, this view was not shared by all grades of staff or indeed by all senior managers. Non-management staff actually wanted to have more responsibility and to do more demanding work.

There were, however, other more fundamental problems concerning empowerment. Staff were asked at focus groups whether they thought their jobs had fundamentally changed or whether the way they were managed had changed since the introduction of EOI. In the middle of 1996 most front-line staff thought their job roles and way they were managed had not changed. Field Office staff did not feel any more empowered. Inspectors and area managers had felt they had a fair amount of autonomy anyway. Inspectors had been responsible for reaching targets and organising their own surveys. Area managers had run local offices with a large amount of autonomy and were responsible for budgets. Far from feeling more empowered, Field Staff felt less empowered because parts of their job had been centralised:

> *Yes, we did it from beginning to end and you knew, you had control of what you were doing. You knew if somebody contacted you, you would see it through and that person would get the answer from you. Now you've got no control over it.*

This was also contrary to the avowed intention in the business strategy to increase end-to-end casework. Staff acknowledged this as a contradiction.

These controls did not diminish over time. Another example was the additional survey Field Office Inspectors were required to carry out in July 1996. The inspectors felt aggrieved because of the timing of the survey, which had not taken into account their work schedule (they are often booked up to carry out inspections one month in advance), or the work schedules of the firm to be inspected (the survey took place during the peak holiday season and many people in the firms were away). There were grumbles from the Field, as well, about being expected to do more work for the same amount of money.

In addition, IT was not being used as a tool for empowerment. Commitment of the staff to the changes in IT was not a problem and there was no reluctance to embrace the more radical changes in IT intended by the NIRS2 system. However, what the interim system had provided staff with were incremental rather than radical changes to their way of working. Although IT was intended to help change processes, we found little evidence that jobs were being fundamentally changed through IT. Existing work processes were just being automated and speeded up:

> *I don't think the actual work has changed that much. I think it's just the turnaround, the amount of information we can receive recently has changed and what we can sort of get rid of basically. . . . IT gives a more professional look but the actual content of the work, other than the work content because of IT rolling out, there's been little change in it.*

Another aspect of the empowerment issue was that the interim IT systems had not yet resulted in fewer supervisory checks being carried out. Some of the checks had been automated, or lists of cases to be checked by supervisors were now produced by the IT system, rather than the supervisor choosing which cases should be checked.

Few staff were actually involved in the design of the new IT systems. When staff were asked about the new systems it was to gather information to reproduce on a computer system the type of work they were already doing on the paper-based system. This may improve when NIRS2 comes online but as yet IT does not seem to be used as a tool for re-engineering processes. The problem here does not appear to be one of lack of commitment by staff either to IT or to the notion of the Agency as a competitor in a business world. There may have been some apprehension by senior managers about how the staff would cope with the introduction of new technology, and perhaps as a consequence of that radical change to systems has not yet taken place. Nevertheless, IT is not being used yet as a 'critical enabler' of change. Despite the stress, in the CA's Business Unit Implementation strategies, on using IT for process re-engineering, at present the interim system appears to be automating the existing systems.

The interim system actually gave less scope to make individual comments or amendments. Staff were frustrated by set proformas, produced by the computing system, which did not give room for individual comments or explanations. This was an example of IT being used to take away decision making from staff and, as others have noted (Grey and Mitev, 1995), is indicative of the technological determinism of BPR. What is happening in the Agency supports the view that empowerment becomes little more than increased delegation, where people's initiative is restricted by the technology in place (Eccles, 1992).

Another example of control being imposed on staff was the Quality Control Sections which were set up on two of the operational areas we studied. These had been set up to take away the checking function of section supervisors and to ensure quality of work. Managers would then be free to manage rather than spend most of their time checking. However, what happened was that the checking function of the Agency had simply been removed to another part of the organisation. This is a problem if the aim is to empower staff. Staff disliked the Quality Control Sections. They were having to cope with huge workloads whilst learning a new job and how to use new computer systems. At the same time, the standard of their work was being criticised by the Quality Control Sections, which staff regarded as nit-picking and demoralising. It was particularly galling to staff as they had not been given a new set of written instructions for the new work. This is also an example of how surveillance is being maintained in the CA, and staff were worried that new IT systems would increase surveillance.

Another problem some managers had was the loss of technical expertise. 'Technical expertise' within the Agency is used to describe the ability to know what is required to process a record, which forms or letters to use and how to complete those forms; and the right steps to take during the process. This expertise used to reside in section leaders to whom staff would go with queries about process. Technical expertise had been seen as an important part of a manager's job. Part of the way managers had gained promotion was through their technical expertise. With the impetus now to make staff more self-reliant, it is expected that technical expertise will be taken on by all administrative grades. Managers will be left to manage sections rather than being a repository of technical knowledge and responsible for checking the work of their staff. Staff understood this and accepted it, although some were worried where they will find technical expertise. Some managers were worried about this change in role:

> *I had a reasonable amount of technical knowledge and it's getting less and less, particularly in the practices that you have now, but I think maybe that's my being uncomfortable with a total new management role ...*

This suggests there may still be some reluctance to hand over responsibility for quality to individuals or there may be a conflict within the Agency about how to include a checking or monitoring function within the business process. The problems of empowerment echo the concerns outlined earlier about how BPR can deliver empowerment whilst retaining and using hierarchical and centralist controls.

### 15.6　The problem of commitment

The Agency is facing large reductions in staff numbers. The Agency already reduced the numbers of staff from 12,000 to 8,000–8,400 between 1992 and 1996. More reductions are scheduled to reduce the workforce to approximately 6,000 by the year 2000. At present staff reductions are occurring through natural wastage or by offering staff generous exit packages. As yet there have been no compulsory redundancies. This may have mitigated some of the effects of the change in staff morale and commitment.

Commitment is not a simple issue in the CA. The problem of commitment was flagged up early on in interviews with senior managers:

> *How the hell do you give a business vision out to the Field where they've got to get down to 60 from 90 locations, they're going to lose fifty per cent of the management and somehow say, 'Isn't this a good thing?' Well, hell's teeth, the best manager in the world is going to be struggling to come out of that one with an upbeat end ... you've been told you've got to go willingly to the guillotine and you've really got to work hard.*

At first this did not appear to be a problem. Non-managerial staff viewed changes such as downsizing or the increased use of IT as part of a wider pattern, and thought that some of the changes would actually improve their prospects when going for other jobs. That is, although staff were understandably worried about the threat of job losses and how that might affect them personally, on a general level there was an acceptance that such downsizing would take place and that this was part of a wider economic pattern taking place in other businesses. There was an acceptance too that changes were needed if the Agency was going to survive in competition with more up-to-date companies.

However, by the end of 1996, middle managers in particular were beginning to query the changes as these began to affect them directly and to query their commitment. The new flatter management structure meant that managers (and those administrative staff with ambitions to become managers) would lose promotion opportunities, either because jobs would disappear or because there was now no obvious promotion ladder through grades.

Another example of the problem of commitment was what happened to the CA's programme of Culture Change. This was set up in 1995 and staff were to receive training in five Key Principles (via workshops and written information) which would inform staff about the dimensions of culture which were 'most crucial to the Agency's success'. The Culture Change programme represented a considerable investment by the CA in terms of time and resources.

Initially the response was mixed but by the middle of 1996 all the areas being studied had reservations about the programme. Partly, this was due to the wording of Key Principles 2 and 3 – 'Having Clear Goals' and 'Ensuring People are Valued'. 'Having Clear Goals' was meant to encourage staff to set their own work goals and to discuss the difficulties of having clear goals in a time of change. 'Ensuring People are Valued' was meant to help staff value themselves and customers. Unfortunately, there had been widespread misunderstanding. Staff expected 'Having Clear Goals' would be where the senior managers would explain the goals of the Agency. Similarly, 'Ensuring People are Valued' was expected to be an opportunity for the management to tell staff how much they were valued. This shows a lack of understanding behind the principles, but also, perhaps more importantly, showed that staff wanted to feel valued by the organisation and have a clear idea of where the Agency was going.

By the end of 1996 staff did not see the Key Principles as relevant to their work. The Key Principles were forgotten, regarded with cynicism or took second place to everyday workloads. The Culture Programme directorate was disbanded and individual managers were given responsibility for the rollout of the last two Key Principles.

As with other aspects of re-engineering, the picture about commitment in the CA is not clear-cut. Some of the changes have been accepted and welcomed but some have not. Partly this seems to depend on timing, and partly on which staff the changes affect, and how directly staff will be affected. As changes threaten particular individuals, such as middle management, problems of commitment arise. Again this reflects one of the inherent problems about BPR when staff begin to question their commitment as their own jobs are threatened.

## 15.7 Conclusion

The Agency is not an organisation totally opposed to radical change, although there are some problems in relation to BPR. The culture of the Agency has been changing over the last five years and most staff appear happy to be moving away from a rigid, hierarchical management structure to one where they have more freedom and can feel more empowered. The majority of staff recognise that there have been changes outside the Agency and no longer regard their employment as a 'job for life'. There is an acceptance that the world has moved on and that the Agency has to move on with it or cease to exist. The majority of staff have also welcomed the changes in IT and see this as an opportunity for the Agency to become up to date and part of the wider business world.

At the same time there have been a number of problems concerning control, empowerment, and commitment which reflect some of the problems other authors have identified in a BPR approach to change. These contradictions have not, as yet, been resolved or probably even acknowledged by the Agency. Some of these problems reflect how internal politics and relationships operate at a time of change, and also how BPR is adopted as if office politics will not exist in the new re-engineered organisation (Grint and Willcocks, 1995). In our case study, it is not unreasonable to think that some of the conflict between the Field and the Centre, where different areas have been acquiring control, has arisen from very human needs to justify one's role in the new organisation or individual managers' needs to maintain their power bases within the organisation. This accords with Taylor's view that 'the politics of "partisan mutual adjustment" would seem to be in the ascendant over the "root and branch" radical change agenda of BPR'. Taylor argues that major organisational changes encourage intensive political activity as members within the organisation seek new roles and domains of influence. The outcome is then more likely to be incremental rather than radical change (Taylor, 1995). It will be interesting to see whether these contradictions are resolved and the barriers overcome during the next phase of organisational transformation due to take place over the next five years.

## Acknowledgements

The research for this chapter was funded as a partnership by the University of Northumbria and the Contributions Agency.

# References

Carter, N. and Greer, P. (1993) 'Evaluating agencies: next steps and performance indicators', *Public Administration*, **71**, Autumn, 407–416.

Davenport, T.H. (1993) *Process Innovation: Reengineering Work through Information Technology*, Boston, MA: Harvard Business School Press.

Eccles, T. (1992) 'Brief case: de-layering myths and mezzanine management', *Long Range Planning*, **25** (4), 105–107.

Grey, C. and Mitev, N. (1995) 'Re-engineering organisations: a critical appraisal', *Personnel Review*, **24** (1), 6–17.

Grint, K. and Willcocks, L. (1995) 'Business process re-engineering in theory and practice: business paradise regained?', *New Technology, Work and Employment*, **10** (2), 99–109.

Hammer, M. (1990) 'Reengineering work: don't automate, obliterate', *Harvard Business Review*, July–August, 104–112.

Hood, C. (1991) 'A public management for all seasons', *Public Administration*, **69**, 3–19.

Hutton, G. (1995) 'BPR – overcoming impediments to change in the public sector', *New Technology, Work and Employment*, **10** (2), 147–150.

Jackson, S. (1995) 'Re-engineering the Post Office', *New Technology, Work and Employment*, **10** (2), 142–146.

Jackson, T. (1996) 'Now it's a case of dumbsizing', *Financial Times*, 20 May.

Keeble, P. (1995) 'A new methodology for Business Process Re-engineering', *Infor*, **33** (4), 234–246.

Klein, M.M. (1995) 'Requirements for successful re-engineering', *Infor*, **33** (4), 225–233.

Mumford, E. (1996) 'Restructuring: values, visions, viability', *Financial Times*, 19 April.

Oliver, J. (1993) 'Shocking to the core', *Management Today*, Aug., 18–23.

Osborne, D. and Gaebler, T. (1992) *Reinventing Government*, Addison-Wesley.

Roach, S. (1996) 'America's recipe for industrial extinction', *Financial Times*, 14 May.

Smith, D. (1996) 'The jobs are there for the taking', *Sunday Times*, 19 May.

Taylor, J.A. (1995) 'Don't obliterate, informate! BPR for the Information Age', *New Technology, Work and Employment*, **10** (2), 82–88.

Walker, M. (1996) 'Dumbsizers take the shift off your back', *The Observer*, 19 May.

Willmott, H. (1994) 'Business process re-engineering and human resource management', *Personnel Review*, **23** (3), 34–46.

Willmott, H. (1995) 'The odd couple? Re-engineering business process; managing human relations', *New Technology, Work and Employment*, **10** (2), 89–98.

# 16

# *Devolution and control within the UK public sector: National Health Service Trusts*

*By Tom Forbes*

### Editor's introduction

Chapter 14 by John McAuley looked at some theoretical frameworks of management control and positioned current management practice in the public services within this framework. This related to the general issues of management control raised in Chapter 10 of *Exploring Corporate Strategy*. This chapter by Tom Forbes is based on his own research into the issues of control surrounding new structural arrangements in the National Health Service (NHS) in the UK (Scotland in particular). These are important links with the issues of devolved structures discussed in Kevan Scholes' Chapter 13 in this book.

## 16.1  Introduction

The UK public sector in the 1990s saw the development of devolved management structures within the main public services. Within the National Health Service (NHS) this has been demonstrated by the emergence of NHS Hospital Trusts (Trusts). This chapter focuses on the NHS in Scotland, and is the result of a major research project[1] which examined the development of strategic behaviour within five Trusts, named A–E. The chapter will specifically explore and examine issues associated with *management control* and *devolution*, and although the evidence is from the NHS, these issues have relevance for the wider public sector in general.

### 16.1.1  Background

Trusts were created in 1991 following the 1989 Conservative Government White Paper, *Working for Patients* (WfP) (Department of Health, 1989). WfP heralded a number of changes within the UK NHS. These changes focused on the delivery of health services. Health

Authorities who in the past had been *both* purchasers and providers of health services were recast as *purchasers* and hospitals as *providers* of health services. An internal market was created which was intended to make hospitals more efficient in their use of resources and to improve their performance. The hospitals were to compete with one another for resources from Health Authorities and in so doing they would have to change the way they operated. Health Authorities were encouraged to 'shop around' for service from providers who could provide the best quality of care at the cheapest prices. Annual contracts for agreed levels of clinical work or activity were established between purchasers and providers within this internal market through a process of negotiation.

Not all hospitals became Trusts at once. There was a gradual transition, with an initial 57 Trusts created in 1991 in England, with Scotland seeing the first Trusts set up in 1992 (Bruce and Forbes, 2000). The remainder of NHS hospitals had become Trusts by 1996. Trusts were given a certain degree of operational freedom in areas including finance, personnel and management. In practice the financial and personnel freedoms were limited. The financial freedom to borrow money was restricted to borrowing on the best terms available, which ultimately meant from the government. This was compounded by an externally imposed financial limit on borrowing set each year by the UK Department of Health. On personnel matters, although Trusts were free to move away from national terms and conditions of service, very few Trusts made significant changes. This was due partly to the diverse nature of the NHS workforce, but also the degree of negotiation that this would entail. It was, though, in the *managerial freedoms and changes* that the Trusts were more involved. Within the context of the internal market, Trusts developed management arrangements to deal with the demands and complexities that the market introduced. Many Trust managers, who in the past had been very operational in focus, now had to think and act strategically for the first time, and additionally hospital doctors were drawn into management roles.

### 16.1.2   Trust management arrangements

The Trusts took their management arrangements from WfP and had a Chair, supported by five Executive Directors, and five Non-Executive Directors. The NHS in the UK was subsequently reorganised in 1999, and although not reflected in this chapter, the Non-Executive Directors have been renamed Trustees.

The Executive Directors and Non-Executive Directors formed a Trust Board. The Trust Board can have a strategic role (Ferlie et al., 1996), but within the five Trusts, this strategic role developed through the actions of the Executive Directors, with the Board mainly rubber-stamping their decisions (Forbes, 1999). The Executive Directors typically number five and include the Trust Chief Executive and the Directors of Finance, Human Resource Management, Nursing and a Medical Director. In two of the Trusts, A and C, their Chief Executives had recently arrived from management careers in the private sector, with the remaining Chief Executives having followed management careers within the NHS.

Within the Trusts are the clinical specialties. The clinical specialties are arranged in Clinical Directorates (Directorates). The Directorates are the operational and strategic business units (SBUs) of the Trusts and effectively carry out the work of the Trusts. Directorates vary in size and number depending on the size of the individual Trust. District General Hospitals outside the major cities can have around three to six Directorates, while large City Trusts, which have research and teaching responsibilities, can have as many as 15. The Directorates have their own management teams, typically consisting of a senior hospital consultant who takes on the role of a Clinical Director, supported by a Business Manager and/or a nurse or PAM[2] manager (Forbes and Prime, 1999). The Clinical Director, although the managerial head of the specialty, is not a full-time manager, and continues to carry out clinical duties. The Executive Directors and Clinical Directors make up the Trust Management Group. Directorates are allocated a budget on an annual basis to operate the Directorate. This budget is determined centrally by the Trust

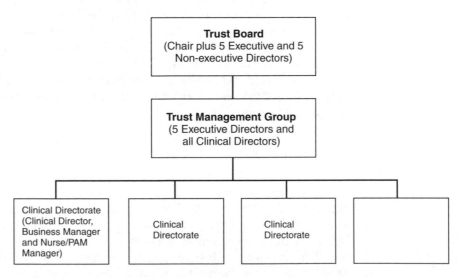

*Exhibit 16.1   The typical management structure of a Trust*

Management Group based on previous years' clinical activity and future projected levels. The Trust Management Group is also the forum where the Directorates are represented within their Trusts and where they attempt to influence the Executive Directors of their Trusts. Exhibit 16.1 illustrates the typical management arrangements of the Trusts.

## 16.2   Analytical framework

There were a number of related issues associated with devolution and control within the five Trusts. These issues have been combined into three themes, which will build upon Chapter 6 of *Exploring Corporate Strategy* and Kevan Scholes' chapter 'Strategy and structures in the public sector' in this book. These themes are:

- the role of the Trust Executive Directors as corporate parents;
- managerial and professional tensions/conflicts;
- creating synergy between Directorates.

## 16.3   The role of the Trust Executive Directors as corporate parents

All of the Trust senior managers agreed that the devolution of authority and responsibility for managing the Directorates was appropriate for their Trusts. The major advantages of Directorates included the creation of management arrangements capable of exercising *significant* delegated authority, and there would be the direct involvement of doctors in management at both operational and strategic levels. However, there was a degree of hesitancy in completely 'letting go' of control.

> *One of the difficulties, I think, is the potential for the blurring of accountability, because of the model of devolution within the NHS. Where on the one hand you could say, Clinical Director, here's your business and operational support, here's your budget, please go away and run a £15m business, I'll see you in March and see how you got on. If the Clinical Director makes a 1 per cent error on the Directorate budget, this could be £150,000 that the Trust has to find. (Chief Executive Trust A)*

Directorates were also seen as imbuing the organisation with local ownership of decision making, fostering creativity and innovation, and allowing decisions to be made nearer the patient, but this had to be mediated with the risks and difficulties associated with local control such as financial and corporate accountability. By devolving financial responsibility to the Directorates the Trust senior managers created value by allowing the Directorates to take the financial responsibility for the clinical services they provided. The Directorates had a considerable degree of freedom over how they spent their budgets, according to the Trust Chief Executives, but their freedoms were very much at the margins as their budgets tended not to be very different from one year to the next. All of the Directorates had to produce operational plans for each year and had accountability reviews each quarter, where their performance was measured against their operation plan. These operational plans were then pulled together into the Trust's strategic plan. So although there appeared to be a certain degree of freedom for the Directorates, there still was considerable control exercised by the Trusts' senior managers.

The parenting styles could also vary between Trusts. With Trust B, the Directorates were told what the parameters were within which the Trust was working. Strategy was very much based on a top-down approach. The senior managers were, in parenting terms, using a *strategic planning* style of management with well-prescribed detailed roles for their Directorates.

> *They [the Directorates] are told what the corporate policy is and they are told what the style is. They are then invited to work within it. (Chief Executive Trust B)*

The Chief Executive of Trust C was very supportive of the Clinical Directorate model. There were two main reasons for adopting Directorates at the Trust, which saw the senior managers using a much more relaxed parenting style using a combination of *financial and strategic control*.

- The NHS in the past did not have a very good understanding of its costs, and

> *One way of segmenting costs and looking at them in detail, and therefore in theory at least controlling them and spending the money where you see your priorities, is segmentation into business units of some sort, and that's one reason we have gone down the road of Directorates. (Chief Executive Trust C)*

- Having decisions made at the top of the organisation would mean

> *Things wouldn't happen very much, because there is only so much time in the day for that small group of decision makers. Further, some of the decisions aren't very good ones because that small group is so far removed from the information. (Chief Executive Trust C)*

The Chief Executive of Trust E was of the opinion that devolution of authority and responsibility needed to be continued to be pushed down to Directorate level so that there were fewer levels of control from Corporate to Directorate level. Directorates had provided a mechanism to allow such budget devolution to the clinical specialties. This

Trust's senior managers had added value by using a combination of strategic and financial control parenting styles. The degree of devolution had again been made quite explicit to the Directorates.

> *They have been given a certain degree of power to change things without it having to go higher, or just standing back and complaining that nothing ever happens. (Chief Executive Trust E)*

### 16.3.1 Conclusion

To conclude this section, we can see that there is an issue surrounding the accountability of the Directorates to their Trust senior managers. Given that the public sector is supported financially by the state, this has implications for the degree of devolution that will develop inside public sector organisations, in this case the NHS. It may therefore be difficult for complete devolution to occur within the public sector given the degree of accounting and auditing measures used by central and local government to 'police' public spending. There was very little actual freedom to 'manage' by the Directorates as SBUs, especially in relation to finance. The parenting style of senior managers varied between Trusts, although it can be said that more than one style was in operation at any time, a combination of strategic and financial control. This may indicate that it is also difficult to use one particular parenting style given the nature of devolution within the NHS and wider public sector. Many senior managers were still finding their feet in this 'new world' of devolution, which may have been one explanation for the degree of caution exercised by these Trust senior managers. The Chief Executives of Trusts A and C were more comfortable with the idea of devolution, which may have been related to their experiences gained whilst working in the private sector, where there were potentially fewer constraints.

## 16.4 Managerial and professional tensions/conflicts

There were a number of areas of tension that developed in the relationships between the Directorates and their senior managers.

### 16.4.1 Management time for the clinical directors

The majority of Clinical Directors were allocated one session per week for management duties, approximately 4 hours, but often did more while still undertaking their clinical work. If you were dealing with budgets of around £15m, the Clinical Directors argued, it was critical that medical input should be recognised and that resources were needed to allow the system to work. The Clinical Directors needed more time to allow them to manage their Directorates, and as one Clinical Director commented,

> *If you want clinicians to contribute usefully, and not just turn up and be seen to rubber-stamp decisions, then resources have to be properly allocated to allow this to happen. (Clinical Director, Obstetrics and Gynaecology, Trust A)*

### 16.4.2 The strategic involvement of the directorates

A Clinical Director at Trust B stated that the Trust Management Group was supposed to be where all the Clinical Directors met with the Trust Executive Directors to discuss strategy; however, in many instances he felt that the Trust Chief Executive had already made decisions beforehand, with the Clinical Directors simply rubber-stamping them. The Chief Executive of Trust B was described by this Clinical Director as 'all powerful ... akin to a one-man band with a group of helpers'. Although the Trust Management Group was supposed to make decisions, the Clinical Directors and their Directorates did not have very much input. The majority of the Clinical Directors within the five Trusts had made it clear to their Trust senior managers that there was a great deal of discontent about the way management decisions were taken. Instead of the Trust Management Group, which included the Clinical Directors, influencing the Trust Board, the impression of the Clinical Directors was that management decisions were simply fed back to them, rather than the Clinical Directors providing advice and support to the Trust Board. There needed to be more management devolution from the Trust senior managers, as one Business Manager commented,

> *With total devolved management there would be a much faster move towards Strategic Business Units, and the interest would then lie in the Strategic Business Unit, the Directorate, and not the Trust. (Business Manager, Obstetrics and Gynaecology, Trust B)*

All the Trusts had a business planning year which included two or three 'away-days' held off the hospital site with all the Trust Clinical Directors, their Directorate management teams and the Trust Executive Directors attending. At these away-days, as well as brainstorming sessions on the future development of the particular Trust, the Directorates presented their individual business plans and why they thought that service developments should be funded. The Trust Executive Directors then gave their view of the Trusts' environment and why some Directorates' service developments would be funded and others not. The strategy process was one of iteration and involved negotiation and bargaining to reach a solution which had elements of brokerage and investment building, as discussed in Chapter 6 of *Exploring Corporate Strategy*.

> *Then we go into the final contractual round [with the Trusts purchasers]. Having been through the first skirmishes, we come back and tell them [the Directorates] what we got. (Chief Executive Trust B)*

A recurring theme within all the Trusts was the perception by the senior managers that their Clinical Directors provided leadership, but not *management* leadership. They were expensive in terms of the actual management contribution they made to their Directorates and to the management of the particular Trust. Indeed some did not make any contribution to the management of their Trusts, but could not be forced to make a contribution. The view of the Trust senior managers was that Clinical Directors should have been providing vision, strategic direction, leadership, and contributing to their Trust's strategic plan. However, some Clinical Directors were managing down and not upwards and outwards, and while many Clinical Directors were embracing management at the Trusts, others had taken up the role to support their existing cultural paradigm, which gave them symbolic leadership and power, but were not prepared to take on board the management decisions that came with it. For example within Trust B,

> *Others [Clinical Directors] have taken to it [management] like a duck to water, and are making very difficult decisions because only they know where the money is being spent inappropriately, and people like me in ivory towers could never get to that level of change management. There are [also] a number of Clinical Directors who came into the Directorate structure because of the leadership it would confer on them, but who also do not like taking management decisions. These individuals have to be tolerated as a result of the Clinical Directorate model. (Chief Executive Trust B)*

### 16.4.3 Directorate involvement in the contracting arrangements with purchasers

All of the Trusts had a central contracting department which conducted contract negotiations on behalf of their Directorates with the Trusts' purchasers. The Directorates were not happy about being excluded from these negotiations as their absence could have an impact on their own strategic programme. One Business Manager indicated that this was when contract negotiations could become 'interesting'.

> *This is when the negotiations really get going, and it is when the*

*activity that has been agreed all along the way suddenly gets changed. As a Directorate, we would want to become involved at this level in the negotiation cycle. (Business Manager, Paediatric Surgical Directorate, Trust D)*

Many Clinical Directors felt that the Directorate system was essentially being blocked by the Trust central contracting process. There was no flexibility nor opportunity for the Directorates to have an impact within the contracting system. However, the Trust Chief Executives felt that it was better to negotiate on behalf of *all* their Directorates, especially where there could be as many as 12, rather than having them all negotiating separately with purchasers, which would be time consuming and lead to increased transaction costs. This illustrates Kevan Scholes' observation that devolution can cause problems in its own way by the introduction of complex management processes, such as contracting between purchasers and providers. In this case, the centre considered itself to be adding value to the Directorates as SBUs by *collectively* negotiating with purchasers, as a *middleman*, thus achieving more leverage and allowing the SBUs to concentrate on providing clinical services in particular areas.

Other Clinical Directors had misgivings concerning the financial aspects of the contracting process. The Directorates suffered financially if things went wrong, but when things were going well, they did not see as much of the money they generated because their Trust would take a slice of it for overheads and central services. However, the Trust Chief Executives indicated that they had done a number of things to get the Directorates and their management teams closer to the contracting and wider management processes:

- The *basis* of contracting was well worked through with the Clinical Directors and Business Managers, and there was a weekly meeting with the Trust Contracting team. Clinical Directors and Business Managers were also pulled into contracting for specific agenda issues.
- The Clinical Directors were invited to every contract meeting, so if they felt strongly about something they had the opportunity to attend and voice their concerns.
- The Clinical Directors worked 'opportunistically' with the Trust Chief Executives in attempting to influence and lobby them to allocate resources to their Directorate.
- And the Clinical Directors worked collectively or corporately as part of the Trust management group to 'pull' the Trust's strategic plan together.

### 16.4.4   *Managerial imperatives versus clinical autonomy*

The development of Directorates introduced management roles to hospital clinicians. This meant that the clinicians would have to interact more with senior hospital managers than they had done in the past. The relationships between the Trusts' senior managers and their clinicians was described by the Chief Executives as generally good, and as can be the case with most large organisations, there was a degree of 'robust' conflict which was seen as being healthy. Two areas of tension, though, had arisen which indicated a difference in *perceptions* between the senior managers and clinicians within the Trusts. These were generic to all the Trusts and concerned managerial and clinical differences. The Chief Executive of Trust C illustrated these two areas succinctly by stating,

> *One is where the imperatives of people like myself in terms of money and control of activity are not medical, and therefore they are not something that medics think about on a daily basis, and we sometimes miss a trick as a Trust because of that. So it is not a question of somebody playing a game and being awkward or whatever, its that the framework for thinking is very different for somebody whose main criteria in life is seeing and treating patients.*

The second area concerned clinical activity.

> *If activity is running over contract, then I would rather we stuck to the contract. The way to put pressure on purchasers is to work to contract numbers, therefore waiting lists rise, therefore purchasers are more likely to say, right here's more money, treat these additional patients. What a clinician wants to do is to treat patients who have been referred to him, and that makes it difficult for us to get money from purchasers because we are actually treating those patients, so purchasers think, well, you've got the money, so why should they give us any more?*

Over time the accumulative effect of this may have meant that the Trusts could face a significant gap in their income from purchasers which then could have an effect on strategic areas such as new service developments, or compromise the delivery of negotiated contracted levels of clinical activity. The Trusts were only paid for agreed contracted levels of clinical work.

### 16.4.5   Conclusion

To conclude this section, we can observe a number of points. Senior managers in the Trusts displayed varying approaches to devolution that were enacted with their Directorates as SBUs, the tight/loose agenda. The Directorates were taking this agenda on board together with the associated responsibility and accountability to the Trust as a whole, and not just to their Directorate as an SBU. It is apparent that the concept of involving doctors, and therefore highly skilled public sector professionals, in management has not been well thought through. There are particular issues that need to be resolved associated with the time that a Clinical Director can realistically spend on managerial and clinical duties. It could be the case that the combined roles are unworkable in their present form and more resources and support needs to be provided by the Trust senior managers. What would appear critical is the relationship between the Clinical Director and his/her Directorate Management Team. The Business Managers are full-time managers and as such can be seen as the 'workhorses' of their Directorates. It might be time to reconsider the role of the Business Manager as more than just providing support to the Clinical Director, perhaps as Directorate General Managers. It could also be argued that the involvement of highly trained doctors in management is detrimental to the operation of the Directorates given that although clinically very competent, clinicians, and wider public sector professionals, are not managers and have not been conditioned in their training to develop managerial capabilities. A bridge between clinicians and the Trust senior managers needs to be developed whereby the concept of Directorates as SBUs can be workable without the above problems surfacing. Directorate General Managers could provide this link and the degree of management control that is required over clinicians and other public sector professionals to allow devolution to work.

## 16.5    *Creating synergy between Directorates*

This was one area where all of the Trusts were actively involved to varying degrees. There was a general recognition in some cases that existing Directorate configurations had outlived their usefulness, or indeed were not achieving the objectives of devolved management.

### 16.5.1    *Directorate size and scope*

Directorates had been set up when the particular hospital became a Trust. This had led to 'off-the-shelf models' and configurations being adopted, which over time began to show inherent weaknesses. Examples included specialties grouped together that had no clear links, but had more to do with powerful hospital doctors who had specific clinical interests, or indeed Directorates emerging to deal with the diversity and complexities surrounding the provision of specialist clinical services. Directorates had also been set up that were too small to make any contribution, as a critical mass, to the Trust management process. Some of the Trusts saw a 'parenting' opportunity to alter their directorate configurations. Within Trust A, mergers had already occurred between Directorates, especially where there was commonality, (e.g.) Accident and Emergency and Orthopaedics. The Trust senior managers were creating value through a *strategic control* parenting style and were creating *synergy* by transferring and sharing skills between these specialisms.

The Chief Executives of Trusts B–D also indicated that there were plans to reduce the number of Directorates in the future as some of them had developed as far as they could, particularly because of their size. If a Trust had around 12 Directorates, this would be reduced to eight or nine, with mergers with larger Directorates which would add value through related competencies, services and purchasers. In other cases Clinical Directors had not been performing managerially, or were approaching the end of their tenure with no identifiable replacement available, so again a 'parenting' opportunity presented itself. One Chief Executive suggested that some Directorates were not worth supporting because:

> *You are taking all the decisions anyway, so therefore it would be better to link them in with a more forceful Clinical Director who is prepared to offer an opinion outside his or her own specialty. (Chief Executive Trust B)*

This Chief Executive continued to say that each Directorate produced its own service development plan consisting of services which it hoped purchasers would want to buy. If urology is taken as an example, once the Trust had provided a urology service to a purchaser, the issue would then turn to how the surgical facility could be used more *effectively*; again parenting opportunities were identified by the senior managers. In this case the senior managers of Trust B took the view that its *facilities management* (in this case of surgical facilities) needed to get away from them being dedicated to urology. Having a single, larger, Directorate with a powerful Clinical Director who would manage theatre time or clinic time across a range of specialties (such as urology, ophthalmology, ENT and general surgery) would be better than several smaller Directorates vying for these resources. By cutting across existing formal structures and combining Directorates the Trust senior managers, as corporate parents, would be adding value through creating synergy in resource management.

Many Directorate Business Managers indicated that the Directorate system at the Trusts did not follow the practice of the actual work that was carried out. A patient may come into hospital and undergo a variety of tests and treatments, but the Directorate system did not reflect this, and instead reflected clinical disciplines or functions. However, if the true *sense* of Directorates were added, for example in an area such as Surgery, and everything in this area belonged to a Surgical Directorate, then they would work better. All surgical procedures would then be carried out under one Directorate, rather than being fragmented depending on the surgical specialty, as had been the case in the past because of the historical development of many hospital services. These managers saw the opportunity to create synergy between Directorates focusing on the service provided, rather than the particular discipline.

### 16.5.2  Directorate realignment

Of the five Trusts used in the research, Trust E was the only Trust which was *actively* reorganising all of its Directorates. The Chief Executive felt that there were *too many* Directorates within the Trust with an imbalance between local identity and the difficulties of flexible working. Clinical Directors were also finding it increasingly difficult to carry out their management responsibilities with the existing arrangements. This had led to a conflict of interest between their clinical and managerial roles, and there was the added danger that this could cause further problems as pressure mounted to meet clinical aspirations, reduce costs and increase value for money. The Chief Executive stated that,

> *Directorates more jealously guard their own budgets and staffing and can be reluctant to share, even though this might be in the best interest of the Trust as a whole. (Chief Executive Trust E)*

The number of Directorates was reduced from nine to four. Value was created by this Trust's senior managers through a combined strategic and financial control parenting style. The Directorate Management Teams were also reorganised, with the Business Managers being renamed Directorate Managers and taking more *responsibility* for operational issues, which would leave their Clinical Directors to focus on strategic matters. Additional management training in contracting, finance and strategy was also provided to the new Directorate Management Teams. The smaller Trust Management Group now worked much closely with the Trust Board. The intention of this new structure was to bring the influence of the Clinical Directors much higher onto the agenda in terms of the Trust's strategic thinking. The new Directorate Management Teams also had the responsibility to generate income, and in a development which was unique among the five Trusts, were encouraged by the Trust senior managers to enter into direct contract negotiations with purchasers rather than central contracting. Directorate budgets would be based on a certain amount of business that the Trust was contracted to provide. If a Directorate under-provided this business, its budget would be reduced; if it over-provided business, and this resulted in additional income, its budget would be increased. Directorates would become true

SBUs with income generation potential and would have a significant input to the Trust's strategic direction. The centre was fostering innovation, risk mitigation and allowing competence building within the new Directorates by using a combination of strategic and financial control parenting styles.

### 16.5.3   Conclusion

To conclude this section, we can note that the key issues were Directorate size, scope and diversity. The Clinical Directorate model of devolved management developed as a response to the setting up of Trusts in the early 1990s. Over time the Trust senior managers were beginning to alter their Directorate configurations to the circumstances of each individual Trust where they saw parenting opportunities. The senior managers were acknowledging that each of their Directorates was facing similar and different change agendas that had emerged over time. They were also realising that new Directorate structures and configurations had to be developed in an attempt to resolve many of the issues covered in previous sections. Both the Trust senior managers and Clinical Directors were *learning* over time elements of good practice through trial and error, and clinicians could play an active part in this process if appropriate management structures were developed in which they had an active part. This process was being augmented with appropriate management training for clinicians involved or who could have future management involvement.

## 16.6   Conclusion

This chapter has illustrated some of the key issues of creating and managing devolved management structures within a particular part of the UK public sector, and associated problems arising from such devolution. There are lessons that can be learnt by other public sector organisations. There needs to be clearer guidance from government, ultimately the main 'corporate parent', on the degree of devolution that is going to be 'allowed' within the state sector. This is undoubtedly linked to the tight financial control often exercised by the state in providing often diverse and complex services. In a sense we have to ask ourselves if there can ever be complete devolution given these restrictions and this uncertainty. The Trust senior managers themselves perhaps did not understand the full ramifications of devolution, which was reflected in the examples given in this chapter. Although there appeared to be a gradual move to hospitals becoming Trusts over a five-year period, there was not the same consideration of the appropriate configurations of Directorates until some years after the individual Trust was set up. A model was chosen which could quite often bear no resemblance to the actual work carried out by the hospitals, and clinical groups merged together with no natural mix. Time then is important, as the Trusts were in the process of altering their Directorate configurations as a result of experience of what was working and what was not. However, very often decisions are made in the public sector because of political influence and not genuine managerial or operational considerations, which tend to be 'discovered' once such systems are up and running. The Clinical Directorate system is such an example, with the Trust senior managers perhaps not quite understanding the role of the Clinical Directorate and more significantly the Clinical Director. This led to a lack of integration between Directorates, which was resolving itself over time through organisational learning. More involvement of professionals earlier would have solved many of these problems, given that many professionals still want to practise what they were trained to do. Indeed clinical professionals, particularly hospital doctors, often make short journeys into the world of the manager, and return to their professional arena after a period of time (Fitzgerald, 1997). Commitment and understanding from senior managers has to be fostered to allow highly skilled professionals to develop appropriate management skills and so make a contribution to management within their organisations, perhaps with fewer professionals as managers, but with an identification of the suitability of candidates and their potential successors.

## References

Bruce, A. and Forbes, T. (2000) 'From competition to collaboration in the delivery of health care: implementing change in Scotland', *Scottish Affairs* (forthcoming).

Department of Health (1989) *Working for Patients*, Cm 555, London: HMSO.

Ferlie, E., Pettigrew, A., Ashburner, L. and Fitzgerald, L. (1996) *The New Public Management in Action*, Oxford: Oxford University Press.

Fitzgerald, L. (1997) 'Clinical management as boundary management: a comparative analysis of Canadian and UK healthcare institutions', *International Journal of Public Sector Management*, **10** (2), 5–20.

Forbes, T.M. (1999) *Strategic Management and NHS Hospital Trusts: Empirical Evidence from the West of Scotland*. Unpublished Ph.D. thesis, University of Glasgow.

Forbes, T. and Prime, N. (1999) 'Changing domains in the management process: radiographers as managers in the NHS', *Journal of Management in Medicine*, **13** (2), 105–113.

Johnson, G. and Scholes, K. (1999) *Exploring Corporate Strategy: Text and Cases*, 5th edn, London: Prentice Hall.

## *Notes*

1   Acknowledgement is given to the Economic and Social Research Council for funding this project via a post-graduate research studentship.
2   PAM, Profession Allied to Medicine, such as a radiographer or physiotherapist. Some Clinical Directorates provide clinical support services, rather than being ward-based, and are managed by a PAM, rather than a Business Manager.

# 17

# Mapping and re-mapping organisational culture: A local government example[1]

## By Gerry Johnson

## Editor's introduction

Running throughout *Exploring Corporate Strategy* is the argument that strategy has to be considered within the cultural and political context of organisations and, further, that it needs to be translated into day-to-day aspects of the organisation in order to ensure effective implementation. The concept of the cultural web was originally developed by Gerry Johnson in the late 1980s and is explained in Chapter 2 of *Exploring Corporate Strategy*. Chapters 2 and 5 of *Exploring Corporate Strategy* suggest that it can be used as a descriptive and analytical device to understand the relationship between strategy and organisational culture, and Chapter 11 shows how it can be used to consider the management of strategic change. In particular, Chapter 11 suggests that comparing an existing cultural web with a desired cultural web can both help flag up potential problems of implementing strategy and stimulate thinking about means of managing change. This chapter provides specific guidelines on how this re-webbing might be carried out, the role that a facilitator of such an exercise might play, and the sort of lessons that might be drawn from such an exercise. The discussion is related to a local government example in the UK.

## 17.1 Introduction

One of the main problems organisations face in managing strategic change is effecting changes in organisational culture. Chapter 2 in *Exploring Corporate Strategy* shows how there is a tendency for organisations' strategies to persist because they are configured within that which is taken for granted in the organisation – assumptions about the nature of the organisation, its environment and the way things are done in the organisation. Even when a strategy is formulated, perhaps based on sound rational argument, organisations often find that achieving significant change to current strategy is difficult.

This chapter builds on the idea of the cultural web[2] to show how mapping culture can provide an understanding of barriers to change; and how re-mapping on the basis of the culture needed to deliver the strategy can help identify means of managing strategic change. It uses a case example to illustrate this.

## 17.2   *The concept of culture and the cultural web*

Culture is often explained as that which is taken for granted in a society or organisation. At its most basic this might be assumptions about what the organisation is there to do, or the reasons for its success historically. Culture can also be thought of as the 'artefacts' of the organisation – such as organisational routines, systems and structures. Again these are likely to be taken for granted as the 'way we do things around here'. These are the components of the cultural web (see Exhibit 17.1).

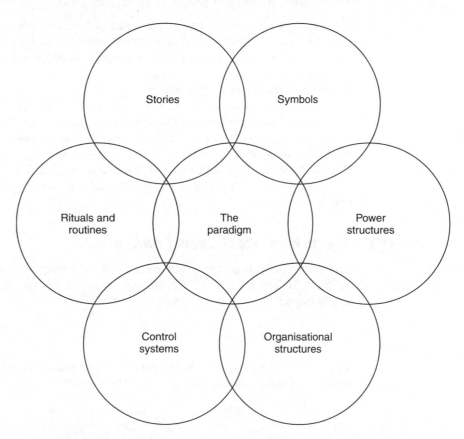

*Exhibit 17.1    The cultural web*

This 'taken for grantedness' tends to act as a 'filter' by which members of the organisation make sense of their world internally and externally. This can be very helpful for at least two reasons. First, it provides a 'shorthand' way of understanding often complex situations; second, it may be the basis of the organisation's success, providing competitive advantage because the culture itself is difficult to imitate. However, it can also be problematic for two reasons. First, because information, opinions and new ideas may be 'filtered out'; and second, because the culture is likely to be very difficult to change, particularly if the success of the organisation has been based upon it in the past. For a fuller explanation of the role of culture in strategy development readers should see Chapter 2 of *Exploring Corporate Strategy*.

## 17.3    The value of culture mapping

There are a number of purposes to mapping organisational culture:

- Surfacing that which is taken for granted can be a useful way of questioning what is normally rarely questioned. If no one ever questions what is taken for granted, then, inevitably, change will be difficult.
- By mapping aspects of organisational culture it may be possible to see where barriers to change exist.
- It may also be possible to see where there are linkages in the aspects of organisational culture which are especially resistant to change.
- A map of organisational culture can also provide a basis for examining what changes need to occur to deliver a new strategy.
- This in turn can be used to consider whether such changes can be managed. In this way practical ideas for implementing strategic change can be developed.

## 17.4    How to map organisational culture

The cultural web can be used as a device for mapping organisational culture. It has been used effectively in many strategic management workshops.[3] How this is done is now described.

### 17.4.1    The aim

The aim is to generate managers' own perceptions of the cultural aspects of their organisations using the cultural web as a tool.

### 17.4.2    The setting

The setting may vary; but the approach described here has been used most effectively in groups of 12–15 managers from the same organisation. They have usually been part of a workshop discussing strategy development for their organisation; or perhaps the problems of strategic change in their organisation. In any case the process is most effective when they have real understanding of the strategic issues faced by the organisation, and, ideally, some responsibility for implementing strategy. In the example used here, the workshop was for three departments of a UK local government authority; each department was represented by four or five managers.

### 17.4.3   *Originating a cultural web*

It is necessary for those taking part to understand the conceptual basis of the cultural web and its links to strategy development in the organisation. A review of the concepts and issues raised in Chapter 2 of *Exploring Corporate Strategy* is therefore useful. This explanation should reach the point where the importance of organisational culture, as described by the cultural web, is understood and, in particular, how organisational culture can constrain strategy development and impede strategic change.

In explaining the cultural web it is often helpful to use an example. There are, however, also dangers in this since, if the workshop is to be asked to produce their own web for their organisation, they may end up using elements of the example for convenience. This can be overcome as follows.

It is helpful to begin by explaining the elements of the cultural web as shown in Exhibit 17.2. As this is done, members of the workshop should be asked to note down examples of each of the aspects of the web as they see it for their own organisation. They should be asked to do this, noting those aspects that come to their mind readily.

Individuals can usually do this fairly easily for most aspects of the web, though there may be difficulties with routines, symbols and stories coming to mind as easily as other aspects. This is simply because they are so 'everyday'; they are the essence of that which is taken for granted in action. The other aspect of the web which is difficult for managers to conceptualise is the paradigm itself. This is hardly surprising since it is the assumptions that they live with every day. Most usually these are not regarded as problematic, and are hardly ever discussed; indeed, they are self-evident. It is the equivalent of you trying to conceptualise what you take for granted – not easy. This is probably better done in the group work that follows; and some guidance is given on this.

After the individuals have noted down their views individually, the workshop can be split into groups. Here, there were the groups from the three departments; and experience suggests that groups of four or five are effective. The managers are asked to compare their

- The *paradigm* is the set of assumptions about the organisation which is held in common and taken for granted in the organisation.
- The *routine* ways that members of the organisation behave towards each other, and that link different parts of the organisation. These are the 'way we do things around here', which at their best lubricate the working of the organisation, and may provide a distinctive and beneficial organisational competency. However, they can also represent a taken-for-grantedness about how things should happen which is extremely difficult to change and highly protective of core assumptions in the paradigm.
- The *rituals* of organisational life, such as training programmes, promotion and assessment, point to what is important in the organisation, reinforce 'the way we do things around here' and signal what is especially valued.
- The *stories* told by members of the organisation to each other, to outsiders, to new recruits, and so on, embed the present in its organisational history and flag up important events and personalities, as well as mavericks who 'deviate from the norm'.
- Other *symbolic aspects* of organisations such as logos, offices, cars and titles; or the type of language and terminology commonly used: these symbols become a shorthand representation of the nature of the organisation.
- The formalised *control systems*, measurements and reward systems that monitor and therefore emphasise what is important in the organisation, and focus attention and activity.
- *Power structures* are also likely to be associated with the key constructs of the paradigm. The most powerful managerial groupings in the organisation are likely to be the ones most associated with core assumptions and beliefs about what is important.
- In turn, the formal *organisational structure*, or the more informal ways in which the organisations work, are likely to reflect power structures and, again, delineate important relationships and emphasise what is important in the organisation.

*Exhibit 17.2    Elements of the cultural web*

individual views and discuss the extent to which they are similar or different. Sometimes there will be considerable similarity. Sometimes there will be differences which might reflect the fact the managers have different experience or have been with the organisation for different lengths of time. In any case it cannot be expected that there will be total consensus. The aim is to find the common aspect of organisational culture rather than to expect that everyone will see everything the same. So the task is for the managers to discuss that which is most held in common.

It is worth noting the following:

- Identification of the paradigm is usually the most difficult task. The reasons are explained above. Managers may try to over-intellectualise this and slip into substituting the notion of strategy for paradigm. They start discussing what the organisation *should* take for granted or what it should do rather than what it *does* take for granted.
- Remember that which is taken for granted may be very simple and apparently straightforward. Nurses, for example, tend to take for granted the importance of professional healthcare; professors in universities take for granted the importance of research; police take for granted the importance of social order. None of these are surprising and should not be. The point is that they are likely to be very embedded and changing them, if change is required, is extremely difficult. So

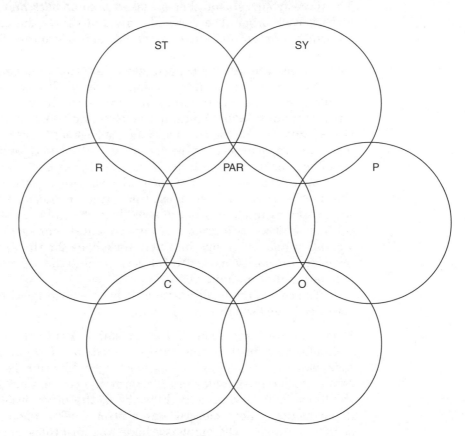

*Exhibit 17.3    The cultural web of an organisation*

the managers should be advised to look for that which is so obvious they would rarely debate or discuss it.

- The managers may also seek for a whole catalogue of constructs to do with the paradigm. This may not be very helpful. It may be that there are very few constructs taken for granted and held in common.
- The elements of the cultural web in the outer circles might give clues as to the nature of the paradigm. The managers might, therefore, find it useful to begin with these outer circles and end by considering how they would characterise the paradigm.

The managers should be asked to note down their views on a blank web like the one shown in Exhibit 17.3. This might be given to them in the form of an acetate so that it can be presented back in plenary session by each of the groups.

### 17.5    *Discussing the cultural webs*

The three groups should then be asked to come back and present their webs to each other. The views of individuals have therefore been discussed in groups and then compared across groups. These presentations can be made by asking someone from each group to talk through the web. At this point it is useful if the managers are encouraged to take a lead in interpreting the web. The session facilitator should avoid the temptation to over-interpret the web as a whole or parts of it since he or she cannot be expected to know as much about the organisation as the managers themselves; and very likely the managers will raise aspects of the organisation that may be meaningful to them but not to the facilitator.

Exhibit 17.4 shows the cultural web drawn up by managers in the Technical Services of a local government authority and will be used as an example in what follows. In fact similar webs were drawn up by the other two groups of departmental managers at the same workshop and by groups in other workshops for the same local government authority as a way of considering the issues of strategic change for that organisation.

The role of the facilitator should be to encourage the managers to consider issues such as the following:

- What the web says about the organisational culture as a whole; for example, how much is the culture linked to the organisation's heritage; how uniform is it; how long has it been like this; is it a culture of challenge and questioning or constraint and convention? In the case of the Technical Services and the webs of the other local government departments, what emerged was a strong belief about high-quality service. However, the emphasis here was on professional standards, with service being defined in these terms rather than necessarily as

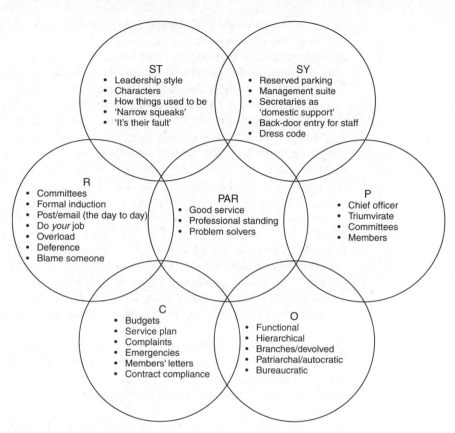

*Exhibit 17.4    Technical Services – current*

satisfying users of the service. The danger was, then, of a self-referential legitimacy. In turn this professional legitimacy was linked to the departmental structure. Departments tended to be organisational siloes within which services were delivered and the conventions of service preserved. These departments were headed by chief officers who tended to control access to and influence by elected members of local government and, inevitably, filter or translate elements of overall strategy to determine departmental response. The organisation was also characterised, both within Technical Services, but also in other departments, by an hierarchical and mechanistic approach to management with a strong emphasis on structuring, budgeting and bureaucracy. Of course in some respects this should be of no surprise in a large and complex organisation, inevitably governed by statute to a great extent.

In the Technical Services department there was also an emphasis on being reactive rather than proactive. Managers saw themselves as problem solvers – indeed overloaded problem solvers –

reacting to the wishes of elected members, or to complaints; attempting to avoid mistakes and often only doing so narrowly. The way of dealing with this was to 'get your head down and get on with the job'; and if anything did go wrong, try to blame someone else.

- Is the culture compatible with the strategy being followed by the organisation and with the strategy being advocated for the organisation? For example, it might be that the managers see that the strategy and the culture are closely aligned. Indeed in some organisations they might come to see that the strategy is, in effect, a product of the culture; that the culture is 'managing' the strategy rather than the managers. In this local government authority, the chief executive was very keen to develop a strategy focusing on major local issues which crossed department responsibilities and therefore required co-operation across departments. The problem with the sort of culture described above was that it was not only inherently departmental and functional, but that functionalism was preserved and legitimated by a professional ethos, protected by powerful departmental heads. These departmental heads might take part in discussions on overall local government strategy; they might agree to the logic of such a strategy; but back in their departments their focus was on preserving service standards strongly influenced by professional norms and established procedures. The danger was a local government strategy on paper only but a continuation of departmental strategies driven by the long-established culture and powerful individuals dedicated to its preservation.

- It is interesting to get managers to consider why organisational cultures are so difficult to change; why they contribute to the continuity and momentum of strategies. Some generalised explanations which have emerged as managers have discussed cultural webs in such workshops are these:

  - There exist linkages throughout the web. For example, powerful individuals or groups are closely associated with organisational structures that preserve power bases, with dominant routines which tend to persist; with symbols of hierarchy or authority and with stories about their power or the origins of their power. In the Technical Services department the dominant influence of the chief officer was preserved in an essentially hierarchical structure, formal committees for decision making, and control over budgets (in formal terms); but more informally this took form in symbols of hierarchy such as privileges for senior managers (e.g. parking, offices and secretarial services). On the other hand, more junior staff entered offices through a different door and from their early induction understood the importance of deferring to senior personnel and focusing on *their* responsibilities.

- In some organisations there may be informal linkages throughout the system which are at least as strong as formal systems. For example, there might exist networks of long-standing organisational members with, again, informal rituals of memberships such as social gatherings and symbols and stories embedding their influence. Such linkages may be strongly linked to the paradigm. They both embed that paradigm and take authority or influence from the widely held assumptions within it. In the case of local government departments such networking not only exists within departments, but in many cases exists at a professional level across departments or functions between different local government authorities. So Technical Services would identify with Technical Services from other local government authorities; social workers would network with other social workers; and it would be the same for teachers, library staff, and so on. The point is that the professional functionalism is preserved not only within the culture of the department, but by the institutionalised nature of the professions.
- These linkages mean that it is not always helpful to think of the cultural web as discrete elements. The linkages bind the elements together; and this makes the task of changing the culture the more difficult.
- Elements within the web may compensate one for another. For example, if there are external threats or internal attempts at strategic change giving rise to political conflict or tension, there could be heightened symbolic activity such as story telling of the past which refers organisational members back to core assumptions and defuses the threats. For example, in situations where there might be perceived threats to departmental service standards, the subject might be turned quickly to stories focusing more on the importance of a highly professional service or on 'characters' of the past or how things used to be; stories which had within them central elements of the paradigm.
- The result is that the organisation as a cultural system can often readily absorb or cope with threats and shocks. It is a coping mechanism which means that existing ways of doing things tend to persist.

- The cultural web is also a useful way of getting executives to think about the importance of the everyday in relation to strategy. Senior executives, in particular, often conceive of strategy to do with decisions made at the top and the management of strategy in their control. What the cultural web often highlights is that it is the more mundane aspects of the organisation that are delivering the strategy; the routines of the organisation, for example. In a workshop with National Health Service (NHS) managers this was put graphically. They used analogies of organisation concluding that top executives tended to conceive of organisations as pyramids when, in fact, the organisation of the NHS was more like a 'termite's nest' in which everyday routines, mutual adjustments and deference ensured things happened. They went on to observe that many of the more formalised controls and structures which had been introduced in the NHS had been imposed by management on the assumption that they would effect changes; but that this assumed a structure of order which was essentially pyramidal. Within the 'termite's nest' there was a capacity to adjust to such intrusions whilst carrying on with the routines – the reality – of organisational life. Whether executives use such imagery or not, it is common to find that the webs prompt discussion and insight about the nature of the organisation as everyday reality and a clearer understanding that changing that everyday reality becomes crucially important in changing strategy. For the Technical Services, for example, people's day-to-day routines of their work were a good deal more 'real' than concepts of strategy in the organisation. They were overloaded; they were responding to issues that came up on a day-to-day basis; they were coping with this by getting on with their jobs and blaming someone else if something went wrong. Clearly this set of coping routines was a long way away from what was envisaged in a strategy of proactively focusing on local needs in co-operation with other departments.

Discussion of these sorts of issues, whilst at a rather generalised level, can help sensitise managers to the need to recognise the importance of cultural aspects of organisations. However, leading on from this, the cultural web can be used in more organisationally specific ways to think about the problems and means of managing change.

## 17.6    *Identifying blockages to change*

The cultural web can be used to identify more specific blockages to change. For example, the managers who drew up the cultural web for the Technical Services department knew about the espoused strategy for the organisation and, at least intellectually, largely agreed with it. However, they could also see that the sort of culture described in Exhibit 17.4 was unlikely to deliver this strategy. Moreover, they could identify some quite specific blockages as to why this would be so. The view was that there existed a series of interrelated blockages: the preservation of standards within organisation siloes by the chief officers but also by institutionalised professional norms; this in turn was reinforced by the structure of the organisation and the deferential attitude of staff. In turn this was embodied in the formality, not only of committees and plans, but also, for example, in dress code. Moreover,

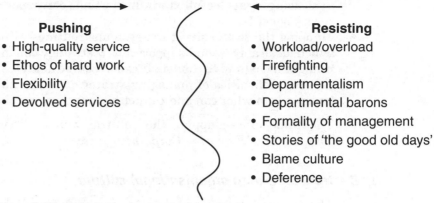

| Pushing | Resisting |
| --- | --- |
| • High-quality service | • Workload/overload |
| • Ethos of hard work | • Firefighting |
| • Flexibility | • Departmentalism |
| • Devolved services | • Departmental barons |
| | • Formality of management |
| | • Stories of 'the good old days' |
| | • Blame culture |
| | • Deference |

*Exhibit 17.5    Forcefield analysis*

individuals focused on getting on with their own jobs; and if something went wrong there was always a way of finding someone else to blame. This was not a culture of co-operation.

It might be, of course, that aspects of the culture might also facilitate change. Here the managers saw the dedication to good service, the ethos of hard work and the flexibility in service delivery that had developed as potentially positive, if only some of the blockages could be overcome. Moreover, the devolved nature of some services (to local offices) might be harnessed positively in a different culture. Both barriers and opportunities for change may be identified by using the culture web; and a forcefield analysis such as that described in Section 11.3.2 and Figure 11.4 of *Exploring Corporate Strategy* can be a helpful way of clarifying this. In the workshop described here, such a forcefield analysis was used and is shown as Exhibit 17.5.

### 17.7   The value of re-mapping organisational culture

Conceiving of what the culture would need to look like if a different strategy were being followed is useful and important for the following reasons:

- Conceptually it gives an idea of the extent to which the present culture is an impediment and the extent to which change is required.
- Traditional notions of managing strategic change suggest that organisations will change if people can be persuaded to change their views about what makes for success in the organisation. In effect, if they can be persuaded to change their taken-for-granted assumptions – the paradigm. This is a worthy aim, perhaps, but difficult to achieve. An alternative or complementary approach is to develop a work environment and ways of doing things in line with the desired strategy; and

in so doing create a context in which people can experience change and see its benefits.

- Mapping the sort of structure, systems, routines, rituals and symbols which, desirably, would support a new strategy can give clues to what it might be helpful to change. It can of course also give further insights into the difficulties of managing strategic change and therefore give insights into what can and cannot be managed in culture change.

The value of re-mapping the cultural web is discussed further in Chapter 11 of *Exploring Corporate Strategy*.

## 17.8   *How to re-map organisational culture*

The approach to re-mapping using the cultural web is much the same as already described.

### The aim

The aim is to re-map the web but this time to represent how culture would be if the strategy which has been developed was working successfully.

### The setting

The setting may be the same sort of event as described above; indeed it might be the same group of managers following on from the previous exercise.

### The approach

The approach is also similar to that described above. The workshop itself may have developed its own strategy for the organisation; or it may be that they or others have done so previously. But the starting point should be a clear statement of the desired strategy for the organisation.

The next step is to ask the managers to repeat the exercise but this time for how the organisation would be if the strategy was working effectively. Again, this should be done individually, then in groups and then by the groups reporting back to each other. Exhibit 17.6 shows what this looked like when Technical Services did it.

It is likely that the following will be observed:

- The managers may find it relatively easy to describe the desirable paradigm that would be in place given the new strategy. It is likely to be a reflection of the intended strategy. For example, Technical Services recognised there would be a need for a greater focus on what they

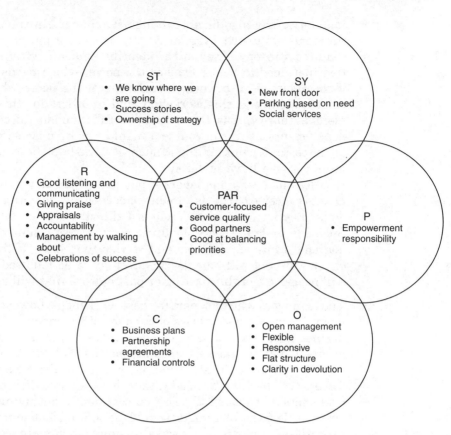

*Exhibit 17.6 Technical Services – future*

called 'the customer' rather than just a professional definition of good service; and much more emphasis on being partners across departments.

• Especially where senior managers are concerned, they are also likely to find it easy to spell out the sorts of structural and systemic aspects of the organisation. Senior managers in particular often see strategy implementation in these terms; change the structure, the measurements and control systems and how people are rewarded and people will behave differently. To some extent this is just what had been happening at the most senior levels in this local government authority; having drawn up a strategic plan the initial debates had mainly been about organisational structure, more effective control systems and, to some extent, changes in personnel. These are important aspects of managing change, but they could well be insufficient because they may not address the day-to-day realities of those responsible for 'delivering' the strategy; and may not overcome many of the more day-to-day blockages of change.

- Managers may also be able to identify changes in the political structure and influence systems in the organisation in line with the required strategy. They might identify elements within the organisation that need to be removed or the power which needs to be reduced if the strategy is to work. Clearly one of the issues that was raised most evidently in this workshop, and in others for this local government authority, was the very powerful influence of chief officers of departments. It was of course a highly sensitive issue; but this raises an important point. Without such a workshop the centrality of this issue may not have surfaced.

- It is less usual for managers – particularly senior managers – to be able to conceive of the day-to-day aspects of organisational culture and what they would need to be like if the strategy were to be effective. Such day-to-day aspects of culture are more represented by the organisational routines, symbols and stories that exist. If these aspects of culture are not in line with the strategy to be followed, very likely it will be aspects of the existing or past culture that will be drawn upon.

The managers who took part in these workshops, however, were able to identify several possibilities of changes of a symbolic, ritual or routine nature. There should be a good deal more emphasis on project or task groups which would be transient; more social events which brought together different levels of managers; more direct exposure to 'customers'; car parking by need rather than by rank; direct feedback from customers, not just in the form of complaints but by more systematic surveys. Letters of thanks should be shared and circulated. Senior executives, in particular, needed to have much more exposure to staff and be prepared to listen to them in informal gatherings. The chief executive in particular needed to come across as more friendly, outgoing and in touch with the day-to-day concerns and problems of staff. There needed to be much more giving of praise, rather than blame, and willingness to talk about successes rather than near failures. It ought to be normal to question and challenge ways of doing things.

### 17.9  *Managing strategic change*

The re-webbing exercise can be especially useful in getting managers to think what can be managed in effecting change in the culture of the organisation. The managers have two maps. One represents the organisation as it is; the other the organisation as they would wish it to be. Useful questions are:

- What is the extent of change required? It could be relatively small scale or very considerable. It is likely that the greater the change, the more there is a need for comprehensive change in aspects of the web. The more fundamental, or transformational, the change, the more it is likely that it needs to be managed by making multiple changes throughout the different aspects of culture described in the web. The local government example here makes an important point. It is quite likely that, technically, the services provided by, for example, the Technical Services department would change very little. However, culturally the change would be fundamental if the new strategy was to work.

- Which aspects of change are relatively straightforward to manage and which are difficult? For example, managers may conclude that the ones which are most likely to be straightforward are those to do with structure and systems and the more difficult are the symbolic and routine aspects of the organisation which are embedded in years of organisational history.

- Are there any changes which would have particularly high impact? This might be because they especially symbolise significant change or some aspect of the strategy to be followed. Or it could be that such a change would have a 'knock on' effect. For example, the removal of powerful blockages to change could itself become a story and a symbol of change. The difficulty in the local government example was that one of the major blockages was the power of a number of senior individuals whose expertise was undeniable. However, as was pointed out by one of the workshop groups, the 'conversion' of one or two of these individuals to commitment and role modelling of the new strategy would certainly have a major effect. It was a point not lost on the chief executive.

The management of strategic change through the various aspects of organisational culture and systems are described more fully in Chapters 9, 10 and 11 of *Exploring Corporate Strategy*.

## 17.10   Summary

'Culture' is often seen as a barrier to change, the more so because it is difficult to be clear about what is meant by it or if anything can be done to change it. The cultural web has proved to be a useful device for achieving some clarity on what constitutes the culture of an organisation, why this is significant in strategy development and the ways it might be possible to manage change. In particular, it highlights the importance of that which is taken for granted in an organisation in influencing the persistence of existing strategies, acting to prevent change but, potentially, giving clues as to important levers and mechanisms of achieving change.

### Notes and references

1   The illustrative example used in this chapter, whilst based on actual events, is anonymised and disguised. An earlier version of this chap-

ter appeared in *Exploring Techniques for Analysis and Evaluation in Strategic Management* by Véronique Ambrosini, with Gerry Johnson and Kevan Scholes, Harlow: Prentice Hall, 1998.

2   The original development of the cultural web can be found in Gerry Johnson, *Strategic Change and the Management Process*, Oxford: Blackwell, 1987.

3   'Managing strategic change: strategy, culture and action' by Gerry Johnson in *Long Range Planning*, **25** (1), 1992, pp. 28–36 discusses the links between organisational strategy and culture using the cultural web as a basis of explanation and drawing on a number of organisational examples from such workshops.

# Index